Stories from the Country of

LOST BORDERS

Stories from the Country of
LOST BORDERS

MARY AUSTIN

Edited and with an Introduction by

MARJORIE PRYSE

RUTGERS UNIVERSITY PRESS

New Brunswick, New Jersey

Second paperback printing, 1995

Library of Congress Cataloging-in-Publication Data

Austin, Mary Hunter, 1868–1934.
Stories from the Country of Lost Borders

(American women writers series)
Bibliography: p.
  1. Indians of North America—Fiction.   2. California—
Description and travel—1869–1950.   3. Natural History—
California.   I. Pryse, Marjorie, 1948–
II. Austin, Mary Hunter, 1868–1934. Lost borders. 1987.
III. Title.   IV. Series.
PS3501.U8A6   1987   917.94'045   86-26091
ISBN 0-8135-1217-4
ISBN 0-8135-1218-2 (pbk.)

British Cataloguing-in-Publication Information Available

CONTENTS

I do not know how nearly it is the case with others, but of this I am certain, that the pattern was set for me, the main lines of it clearly indicated, the important evidences of it cleared, before I had lived the first third of my life. . . . Long before that time it was clear that I would write imaginatively, not only of people, but of the scene, the totality which is called Nature, and that I would give myself intransigently to the quality of experience called Folk, and to the frame of behavior known as Mystical.

(Earth Horizon: An Autobiography)

Mary Hunter Austin writes that she discovered at the age of four a second and significant inner self whom she named "I-Mary" and whom she associated with the pages of books and the act of reading. She found in I-Mary a source of comfort and, later, her impulse to write. As a child she needed such comfort: she knew herself to be unwanted and unmothered for reasons she could never understand. She describes an early memory in which she tried to press against her mother's knee while her mother sat rocking baby Jennie and allowing older brother Jim to lean against her shoulder. She felt her mother "subtly withdrawing" her knee, excluding only her from the intimate circle. She remembers that "I-Mary suffered no need of being taken up and comforted; to be I-Mary was more solid and satisfying than to be Mary-by-herself." Then, at the age of five, "God happened to Mary under the walnut tree."[1] Walking through the orchard near her home in Carlinville, Illinois, she became aware of a Presence and a Voice, which she associated with the tree, and which she would look for again and again in the California desert and in the mountains and cañons of the Southwest. The Presence she felt as a child would reappear in her work as a mystical source of creative power that enabled I-Mary to exist.

Austin was born September 9, 1868, upon the "stroke of midnight" to Susanna Savilla Graham and George Hunter of Carlinville. Her father had emigrated from England as a young man. He told his children stories about his entry into the American West, and Austin loved to hear him use words "that weren't to be said in front of Mothers" (5). He became "more or less involved" in the Underground Railway at Carlinville and enlisted in the Civil War on the Union side. A self-styled American intellectual, he owned a library that included Melville, Hawthorne, Poe, Longfellow, and Emerson, as well as Keats, Shelley, and Elizabeth Browning, and he encouraged the "forthright and wide-angled" atmosphere that prevailed in the Middle West at that time. Austin writes that, as a child growing up in such an atmosphere, she was aware of the temperance movement, woman suffrage, and the Indian defeat in the Black Hawk War, and that she grew up in a household "where race prejudice did not exist" (82).

Her mother, Susanna, was the daughter and granddaughter of pioneer women whose strengths derived from their discovery of the "predominance of happenings of the hearth, as against what happens on the battle-field and in the market-place, as the determinant of success." Her great-grandmother demonstrated the capacity of women of her day "to cause a culture to eventuate out of their own wit and the work of their hands," and thereby to create a context that would bring to fruition the "hope of American democracy" (15). But her grandmother died young and Susanna, raised by a stepmother, would be trained not in the pioneer tradition but rather in "all the household arts that were proper to young ladies" (22).

Young Mary began her formal education at five and a half, before she was legally entitled to go to school, because "her mother did not know . . . what on earth to do with her" (58). Once enrolled, she was promoted beyond her years on the basis of her reading achievement. Always ahead of her age level in reading, she remained deficient in other skills—

penmanship, spelling, and arithmetic. The two years' difference between Austin and her school peers contributed to the loneliness she experienced and to her tendencies toward willfulness and nonconformity. She earned acceptance from her schoolmates, however, by telling stories, and by the age of ten had begun to write poetry and a verse play. That same year her father died, perhaps of complications resulting from fevers he had suffered during the Civil War, and two months later, sister Jennie followed, a victim of diphtheria. In her autobiography Austin would write: "In time I recovered from my father's death. . . . But with Jennie it is not so. She is not changed or gone. . . . The loss of her is never cold in me, tears start freshly at the mere mention of her name. And I would not have it otherwise. She was the only one who ever unselfishly loved me. She is the only one who stays" (87).

After the death of her husband, Susanna Hunter moved her children from the orchard and farm of Mary's early vision into the town of Carlinville, where she began to support herself by nursing. Mary had to take on domestic responsibilities in her mother's absence—caring for her brother George after school, cooking and cleaning, and packing lunches for herself and older brother Jim. At the same time she "suffered through her mother the strange indignities" of widowhood, and discovered that in the eyes of society a woman possessed status only as wife and mother, never as a result of her individual value. She writes in *Earth Horizon* that during this period her mother continued to feel "reluctant" toward Mary, and it was only when "they entered upon the thin edge of being women together" that they were able to develop a more satisfactory relationship. Yet that relationship was one-sided, entirely dependent on Mary's ability to empathize with her mother. She offers no evidence that her mother empathized with or emotionally supported her.

On the contrary, Susanna consistently undermined Mary's development, and Austin describes the way she learned to keep her favorite objects and her inner thoughts "out of sight." Of the house her mother built with the proceeds from the sale of the farm, Austin writes: "We lived there about seven years, and Mary was never at home in it at all. At that time nobody ever thought of inquiring what Mary thought of anything, so nobody found out" (107). But harder than living in her mother's house was the lack of recognition of her own point of view: "Mary's case was rendered more desolate by her not being able to refuse the conviction that was pressed upon her from every side, that any dissatisfaction she might have felt was inherently of herself, that she was queer and ungrateful and insensitive to the finer aspects of existence" (108). She gives her mother chief responsibility for having "repressed and misguessed" her, but her brother Jim shared and supported his mother's position.

For, although Mary had been forced to take on the drudgery of domestic life as a consequence of her father's death, Jim gained in status within the family as Susanna began to accord him the same privilege that her husband had enjoyed. Austin recalls an incident that "served to fix the pattern of family reaction" to her own difference: she asked to have a five-minute instead of a four-minute boiled egg. For her mother and for Jim, this simple request became an issue that threatened her brother's status as new head of the family; it became "a constantly annoying snag in the perfect family gesture of subservience to the Head," which all of Susanna's life had gone to create. "And perhaps there was latent in Susie's mind, in spite of her avowed liberality toward the woman movement, something of the deep-seated conviction . . . that drove many girls of Mary's generation from the domestic life, that a different sort of boiled egg was more than a female had a right to claim on her own behalf." Recalling her brother's judgment that "'somehow you never seem to have any feeling for what a HOME should be,'" Austin writes of continuing to feel her own oddity as itself an anomaly, "not in the least realizing that there was growing up in the mind of thousands of young American women at that moment, the notion that [home], at least, *shouldn't* be the place of the apotheosis of its male members" (129).

Austin never received from her mother any encouragement in her literary aspirations. Susanna discouraged her reading, gave away the first book she bought for herself (Hugh Miller's *The Old Red Sandstone*, an early [1841] study of geology), and seems to have had an uncanny ability to discourage Austin's development. She took great pains to impress upon her daughter "the childish character of her interest in nature and the inexpedience of talking about it. Especially you must not talk appreciatively about landscapes and flowers and the habits of little animals and birds to boys; they didn't like it" (112). According to her mother's thinking on the subject, "the gentleman would tell the lady what to think" (113). Later, after Austin presented her mother with her first published story in the *Overland Monthly,* Susanna's only comment was, "I think you could have made more of it" (240). Throughout her life Mary would return to her mother, "being in great need of her, and yet somehow always failing to make a vital connection" (254).

Austin experienced a great deal of stress in the process of acquiring a college education. First she left Blackburn College due to illness; then "it was decided" for her that she should prepare for teaching at the State Normal School at Bloomington. In the middle of her second semester there she suffered a nervous breakdown and had to be sent home. Austin writes that "she had broken down under the five months' rasping insistence on a regime that violated all the natural motions of her own mind." The doctor who examined her upon her return suspected that her illness "might have something to do with the natural incapacity of the female mind for intellectual achievement" (152). When she became well, she reenrolled in Blackburn College, choosing to major in science instead of English, believing that she felt an intuitive connection between science and the kind of writing she wanted to do, and arguing that anyway the teachers of writing had never written any books. She completed her degree at the age of nineteen and then, when brother Jim abruptly went west to homestead public lands, moved to California with her mother and younger brother just a week or two after college graduation.

Like most of the pioneer women whom Annette Kolodny describes in *The Land before Her,* Austin had not been consulted about the move west. And after she and her family arrived at their destination, she succumbed to malnutrition and nervous collapse within months. Jim had filed claims to land without irrigation in the California desert about thirty miles south of Bakersfield and they arrived in a year of drought. Even so, Austin's first impressions of the desert led her to write "for the first time directly, in her own character" (189), as she would in *The Land of Little Rain,* and she published an essay in the Blackburn College journal under the title "One Hundred Miles on Horseback." She writes in *Earth Horizon* about being taken with the land, as a naturist is, about discovering her intention to give a true report of the desert, about finding the wild grapes that cured her malnutrition, and about the moment, in the spring of 1889, when she went walking through a hollow and experienced again "the warm pervasive sweetness of ultimate reality" (198) as she once had under the walnut tree back in Illinois. The ability to find I-Mary had returned; and for the duration of her stay with her mother and brothers, she spent her time observing the desert and collecting stories of animals and local heroes. She traces the sources of "The Last Antelope" and "The Walking Woman," both from *Lost Borders,* to this period in her life.

Faced with the necessity of making a living, Austin took a teaching job in the Kern County schools about ten miles from Bakersfield, and she arranged to lodge with a family there. Unfortunately, her ability to keep the teaching position depended on passing an examination. When she failed the exam she lost her job. Now she found herself in a difficult financial situation. While tutoring to earn money, she tried to convince her mother and brother that she was entitled to part of the proceeds from the sale of the Carlinville property, as it had constituted her father's estate. When they did not recognize her inheritance, she resigned herself to marriage, although she had not previously been very successful in attracting suitors, and when a neighbor began to show an interest in her, she encouraged his attentions. After trying a second time to pass the teaching examination and failing again, she accepted novice vineyardist Stanford Wallace Austin's proposal and they were married May 18, 1891.

Marrying Wallace Austin temporarily gave Mary time to write. In *Earth Horizon,* she recalls that "it was as I-Mary walking a log over the creek, that Mary-by-herself couldn't have managed, that I wrote two slender little sketches . . ." (231). When the Austins' vineyard failed and Wallace decided to join his brother in San Francisco, Mary was delighted with the decision. Shortly after her arrival, she introduced herself to Ina Coolbrith. Coolbrith had been associated with Bret Harte in the early years of the *Overland Monthly,* and was the only western woman poet, according to Austin, "whose verse found welcome in the Eastern magazines" (231). Coolbrith gave Austin professional advice on how to prepare her manuscripts for submission and directed her to the current editor of the *Overland Monthly.* In this way Austin published her first story, "The Mother of Felipe," in November 1892.

During the decade between this story and her first significant publication, *The Land of Little Rain* (1903), Austin faced several major disappointments. Just two months after the move to San Francisco, Wallace became involved in an irrigation project in the Owens Valley, a region even more desolate than the one the Hunters had originally settled, and the Austins moved again, this time to the town of Lone Pine in Inyo County. Inyo lies between the Sierra Nevadas on the west, within view of Mt. McKinley, and Death Valley on the east. Cut off from coastal civilization by both mountains and desert, Austin became even more self-sustaining as she began to face the reality of her situation. Later, in an uncollected story, "Frustrate," she would write, "I know that I am a disappointed woman and that nobody cares at all about it . . ." ("Frustrate" 467). The story, and the novel she would publish in the same year, *A Woman of Genius* (1912), in part document her marriage. Wallace was a financial and an emotional failure.

Then, adding to her distress, the year after their arrival in Lone Pine, Austin gave birth to a mentally retarded daughter, possibly a genetic inheritance from her husband's family, possibly the result of a protracted delivery and poor obstetrical care at her mother's house in Bakersfield, where she had delivered the baby. Her husband and her mother both gave the child, Ruth, totally into Austin's care, and in order to make time to write she was forced to restrain Ruth physically for hours each day. During one of the many separations from Wallace that would eventually result in divorce, Austin took a teaching job in Bishop, sixty miles north of Lone Pine, and while she was working left three-year-old Ruth alone in a room with food and water. This treatment, and her decision to place Ruth in an institution at the age of twelve (never to see her daughter again), may seem harsh, but Austin's experience reflects the extreme pressures to which a woman writer is subject when she is also a mother.

Susanna Hunter died during the summer of 1896, when Austin was 27. In *Earth Horizon,* she wrote, "There is an element of incalculable ravening in the loss of your mother; deep under the shock of broken habit and the ache of present grief, there is the psychic wound, the severed root of being . . ." (273). Then, abruptly deciding to leave Lone Pine, Wallace Austin took the job of registrar of the Desert Land Office at Independence, about fifteen miles north of Lone Pine, on the slope of Kearsarge mountain. It was in this town in which Mary's married adventure came to an end. Wallace's attitude, which Austin draws upon in creating some of her male characters in *Lost Borders,* was based on a dream of the nebulous "promise of the land," and an indefinite expectation that "*something* was due to happen soon." And it was in the house in Independence, within view of the Sierras, that Austin began to write her first book. Reminiscence and a sense of loss gave her the necessary detachment from her material: "For though I was there in the midst of it, I began to write of the land of little rain as of something very much loved, now removed."[2]

Austin devotes almost all of her autobiography to the influences in her early life which made her a writer and led to *The Land of Little Rain*. In summarizing her life here, I have followed her lead in emphasizing the significance of her inner and early development. She left the California desert for the first time in 1899 and permanently in 1906, and nothing she experienced in her life after she left California appears to have made as deep an impression on her work. She built a house in Carmel, where she wrote *Lost Borders* and associated with a bohemian group that included George Sterling and Jack London; she traveled to Italy and England, where she walked in suffragist parades; she lived in New York for twelve years, during which time she became friends with Mabel Dodge and had a disappointing love affair with Lincoln Steffens; she spent time in Taos, New Mexico, visiting Dodge. In 1924, she sold her house in Carmel and moved to Santa Fe, where she built Casa Querido, the "beloved house," and spent the last years of her life working to support the Indian Arts Fund, founded to preserve and encourage the arts of the Pueblo Indians in New Mexico. There she wrote *Earth Horizon,* opened her house to Willa Cather for the completion of *Death Comes to the Archbishop,* cultivated a relationship with her niece and namesake, and fought a series of debilitating illnesses. After struggling with nervous and physical exhaustion throughout her entire life, she survived a diagnosed case of breast cancer during the summer of 1907, a gall bladder operation shortly after her move to Santa Fe, a heart attack in 1932 followed by subsequent attacks, and finally died in her sleep August 13, 1934. Her ashes are encased in cement amid boulders near the summit of Mt. Picacho, on the edge of the Sangre de Cristo Mountains, within view of Casa Querido.

AUSTIN'S WRITING PLACES HER in a tradition of other American nature writers, especially Henry David Thoreau and John Muir. Like Thoreau in *Walden,* she creates analogies between nature and human life and yet remains faithful to literal accuracy in her natural description. She herself refers to John Muir, in "Nurslings of the Sky" from *The Land of Little Rain,* as a writer of California landscape who is also devout. The nature writer perceives the universe, as she describes weather in "Nurslings of the Sky," as the "visible manifestation of the Spirit moving itself in the void."

The themes and short sketch forms she chose for much of her fiction and nature writing even more specifically place Mary Austin among a group of late nineteenth-century women writers who worked in the genre of literary regionalism. Harriet Beecher Stowe, Rose Terry Cooke, Mary Wilkins Freeman, and Sarah Orne Jewett, to name just a few predecessors, also wrote fiction that emerged from their own and their characters' intimate connection to region. For these writers, the concept of region often includes features of landscape, but more often derives from their characters' common heritage, from the pervasive effects of Calvinism on New England life, and from their sense of community. In Mary Austin's work, the land solely determines the nature of the region. The land is the only link among Indians, miners, and the people she calls the borderers: instead of having a place in a theological universe, Austin's characters, whether human or animal, learn the meaning of isolation; instead of ministers, Austin presents Indian women as spiritual guides; and instead of assuming a shared community, Austin offers community as a goal for her region in the final sketch in *The Land of Little Rain.* Like her New England predecessors, however, Austin created characters who could not have existed outside of their region. In "Shoshone Land," from *The Land of Little Rain,* she might have been defining the regional writer's general intention when she writes, "the manner of the country makes the usage of life there, and the land will not be lived in except in its own fashion." And like the earlier regionalists, Austin also explores the meaning of women's lives in her writing. The feminism that informs *Lost Borders* (as well as several of her novels) links Austin to a tradition that allows women to speak for themselves.

Austin reports on her early reading in *Earth Horizon,* and among her influences she mentions Stowe and Jewett. There is further evidence in *The Land of Little Rain* that she may have been deeply influenced by Jewett's *The Country of the Pointed Firs* (1896) during the decade in which she was gathering material for *The Land of Little Rain.* She describes her desert land alternatively as "the country of lost borders," "the country of the painted hills," and "the country of the silver firs." And she must have admired Jewett's Mrs. Todd, an older woman who teaches the younger female narrator about nature and the healing powers of herbs, and who offers connections to mystical and visionary experience. For Austin herself possessed the mystical and visionary qualities Jewett attributes to Mrs. Todd, and in other work, as well as in *The Land of Little Rain,* Austin creates shamanistic characters as artist figures, and even as self-portraits.

Also like her regionalist predecessors, Austin wrote at her best when she wrote of her adopted region, the California desert. Among her twenty-seven books, including a dozen novels or collections of short stories, *The Land of Little Rain* and *Lost Borders,* both reprinted here, are superior to her other work. Three other regional books reflect some of the same qualities that make *The Land of Little Rain* and *Lost Borders* so compelling. *The Flock* (1906) is a series of sketches about sheep, sheepherders, and what Austin calls the "flock-mind" that continues, like *The Land of Little Rain,* to focus on the intimate connection among animals, nature, and people. In *The Basket Woman* (1904), a collection for children, and *The Arrow Maker* (1911), a play produced at the New Theatre in New York, Austin shows how the "manner of the country makes the usage of life" for American Indians.

Austin's work recalls Lydia Maria Child's *Hobomok* (1824) and Catharine Sedgwick's *Hope Leslie* (1827) in the potential she recognizes for alliance and sympathy between white women and Indian women, and in her lifelong recognition of the value of Indian culture. Austin knew what it meant to be excluded in childhood, to be viewed as "other," to be scorned and mistreated by the men she cared about, and to look within herself for a source of vision and mystical connection. Perhaps this knowledge made her more receptive to women like Seyavi, the basket maker (who also appears in *The Land of Little Rain*) or Chisera, the arrow maker, whose visions evolved out of their experiences as women as well as their Indian heritage. *The Arrow Maker* locates the ultimate source of human power in a woman, links female experience to the growth of shamanistic magic, and shows Chisera, the visionary, choosing to transcend her sense of her own personal injustice in order to serve and save her tribe and community.[3] Later in her career Austin published several explanatory books and essays about Indian art, including *The American Rhythm,* a collection of transcribed Indian poetry prefaced by a long introduction in which she traces one source of Imagist and modernist poetry to Amerindian development of the "landscape line," by which Indian poets and dancers weave the pattern of rhythms of the human organism and of the natural universe into their art.

Austin also developed and shaped her understanding of women's concerns by direct participation in the women's movements of her day. Through her mother she had met Frances Willard, the temperance pioneer, and one of her earliest mentors, Charles Lummis—who edited the magazine *Land of Sunshine* and whose Los Angeles house was a center for aspiring writers, artists, and intellectuals—introduced her to Charlotte Perkins Gilman. Later, in New York, Austin met Emma Goldman and became involved in both the suffrage and labor movements. She knew Margaret Sanger, birth control advocate, journalist Ida Tarbell, and labor leader Elizabeth Gurley Flynn, and gave some speeches on woman suffrage, although she writes in her autobiography, "I did not talk a great deal; talking on Suffrage bored me" (327). She did write about feminist women, and *A Woman of Genius* (1912) is the most successful of her novels. In this book, in which Austin draws heavily on her own biography, Olivia Lattimore struggles through a difficult childhood in which she was an unwanted child, a marriage that closely resembles Mary Hunter's to Wallace Austin, the death of a baby, and a passionate and difficult love affair and finally establishes herself as an artist and an actress with her own theater in New York. *A Woman of Genius* ranks with Elizabeth Stuart Phelps' novel *The Story of Avis* (1877), Jewett's *The Country of the Pointed Firs,* and Willa Cather's *The Song of the Lark* (1915) in its portrait of the development of the American woman as artist.

Mary Austin was a maverick in the literary world of the early twentieth century, and she formed no major enduring literary or professional connections. She knew many of the literary notables of her day, but she appears to have figured only on the periphery of their spheres of influence. During the Carmel years she was known for her eccentricity and although she found comradeship in the bohemian colony there, her major biographer focuses on the "atmosphere of intellectual ferment and social festivity" she discovered, rather than on the development of lasting friendship (Fink 130). Lincoln Steffens wrote an admiring piece about *The Land of Little Rain* ("Mary Austin"), and Austin may have fictionalized Steffens as Helmeth Garrett in *A Woman of Genius*. But when Steffens abruptly ended their relationship, Austin's behavior became the subject of ridicule. Justin Kaplan in his biography of Lincoln Steffens mocks Austin's eccentricities and in his tone expresses the attitudes that the men Austin thought of as her friends and literary associates might actually have held toward her:

> Trouble came in the ample form of Mary Austin, author of *The Land of Little Rain,* novelist, playwright, and mystic of the deserts and Indians of the Southwest. They had met in California, first at Carmel. There she wore long priestess robes and was given to meditating in a tree house. On occasion she took down her knee-length hair and spoke throbbingly about her need for a grand passion; she was one of the features as well as one of the terrors of the Carmel community. . . . Without reckoning the consequences, Steffens, who had a taste for large women, had turned the light of his personality upon her . . .(207).

But not for long. And after Steffens "skipped away across the continent," Kaplan writes that Austin "was generally in pursuit of Steffens and hoping to penetrate a protective cordon of his friends" (207–208). D. H. Lawrence, who met Austin in Taos in 1923, also mocked her in an unfinished play, "Altitude," which showed her "intoning *Om* like a hindu holy man as she faces the sun . . ." (Zolla 187).

Although Austin succeeded in finding publishers for her work, she struggled throughout her career to support herself by her writing, and she regretted her lack of public acclaim. Many of her books went out of print in her lifetime. Sherwood Anderson once wrote her, after reading her books about the California desert: "They have been such a relief to me after all the other books of the western country I have read. What Twain and Harte missed you have found and set down with such fine understanding" (Pearce, *Literary America* 177). Her few critics have generally tempered their enthusiasm for her work, however. *The Land of Little Rain* appears in critical commentary as a "minor classic," an echo of the ambivalent approbation often accorded Austin's regionalist predecessors.[4]

In one of her own critical essays entitled "Regionalism in American Fiction," Austin offers a twentieth-century interpretation of regionalism which retrospectively illuminates her nineteenth-century predecessors. At the same time the essay provides a clear basis for evaluating Austin's work

Introduction

on her own terms. She considers art "as the expression of any people as a whole," as the "response they make in various mediums to the impact that the totality of their experience makes upon them, and there is no sort of experience that works so constantly and subtly upon man as his regional environment." The influence of regional environment creates a "pattern of response common to a group of people who have lived together" long enough, and the best American fiction, for Austin, is the story that has "come up through the land, shaped by the author's own adjustments to it." She distinguishes between local-color and regional fiction, suggesting that local color might use region as scenic backdrop, but that the "first of the indispensable conditions" of regionalism "is that the region must enter constructively into the story, as another character, as the instigator of plot." The second condition is that the story must reflect "in some fashion the essential qualities of the land." Regionalism offers the "proverbial bird's-eye view of the American scene"; anything less intensely rendered creates instead "what you might call an automobile eye view, something slithered and blurred . . ." And regionalism prepares the reader to understand in human terms "the meaning of that country in which the action of the story takes place." Austin was one of the first twentieth-century writers and critics to vehemently insist that an American literature that did not develop an understanding of regionalism and racial patterns would remain impoverished and unfulfilled.

Her own regional writing, especially in *The Land of Little Rain* and *Lost Borders,* conveys the intensity of connection between natural landscape and human life. She believed that the writer's consciousness is influenced by that connection, and that the form of the literary work reflects the pattern of human response. In *The American Rhythm* she used the term glyphic to describe the immediate, whole, and visual form Indian poets used to provide a key to "the inner song, the meaning not expressed" (Ruppert 254). Long before her essay on Indian poetry she developed her own glyphic form in *The Land of Little Rain.* And why was she so interested in the desert? What did she find there? Her description of the way the primitive first arrives at writing and begins to evolve the glyph suggests that, in writing about the desert, Austin went in search of her own inner response. In *The American Rhythm* she imagines a "hypothetical aboriginal translator," an "Americanly educated Indian" who would both be able to experience the natural world in a glyphic, visual way and also be able to "translate" his poetry into English:

> [S]uch a translator's first care . . . would be to state the experience itself, usually by stating its most important reaction on himself. To this he would add no more than he found absolutely necessary by way of descriptive an associative phrases, to define the path of the experience through his own consciousness (51).

"To define the path of the experience through [her] own consciousness": in this way Austin characterizes her own "first care" as well. And in *The Land of Little Rain*, as in *Lost Borders*, the single line or visual image, an extension of its pattern throughout a sketch, and the development of pattern through a collection of sketches all allow Austin to find her way, both literally and literarily, as she attempts to map her own consciousness and ours.

AUSTIN'S "COUNTRY OF LOST BORDERS" does appear on actual maps, and a casual glance at an atlas or even a road map for the state of California will enable the reader to locate the Panamint and Amargosa mountain ranges of Death Valley, the towns of Lone Pine ("the little town of the grape vines"), Independence, and Mojave, the sand dunes and salt flats, Shoshone, Cerro Gordo and the Funeral Mountains, and Tonopah in Nevada. Many other places—names of ranches or mines, or Indian names for mountains and other locations—exist only in the imaginative geography and topography that emerge from the sketches and stories. Austin writes as if she were a thirsty traveler whose survival—and ability to orient her prose—depends on her ability to learn the ways of water. Austin "defines the path" of human emotional and spiritual experience by focusing on geological, biological, and botanical details of the desert. In both *The Land of Little Rain* and *Lost Borders,* she discovers patterns that animals and human beings make in their search for water, and ends with examples of the highest forms the discovery of water can take—in "The Little Town of the Grape Vines" (*The Land of Little Rain*) and in "The Walking Woman" (*Lost Borders*). In *Lost Borders,* she further associates thirst with women's emotional deprivation and betrayal. Trying to satisfy that "thirst," her desert women ironically offer themselves to men as water trails, hoping—mistakenly—that by giving themselves they will find themselves.

In the opening title essay from *The Land of Little Rain,* Austin at first deliberately disorients her readers and gets us lost. Instead of introducing us to characters or events, she begins to describe a "Country of Lost Borders." The cues that help us find our way in conventional narrative appear to be missing. The narrator's consciousness seems as unbounded as her prose; often she disappears from a long descriptive passage only to reemerge in the next paragraph as a mystic. She writes of her chosen region that "not the law, but the land sets the limit," and in her own lawlessness she makes room in her writing for the unruly, the untamed, and the experimental. Although many of the people who appear in *The Land of Little Rain* are men, Austin's mode of narration defines the book as a woman's text. What matters to her is the land, not the defeat of the land; relationships between human beings—including Indians and Spanish-speaking people—not their victories over each other; and the insights that lead to vision, rather than the organization of a tightly woven plot.

In creating a literary map of this borderless region, Austin looks for patterns that contain within themselves an apparent form. She organizes "The Land of Little Rain" as a series of glyphs or visual images that convey her sense of the desert's "inner song, the meaning not expressed." She focuses on various features of the desert which seem connected only in their patterns. The wind creates the "sculpture of the hills," for example; in this "land of lost rivers," desert floras adapt to seasonal limitations; in a drought, the "dwarfing effect" produces "species in miniature." What each of these descriptive features has in common is that the land "determines the plant." The plant—or the shape of a hill, or the behavior of an animal, or the character of a human being—may vary, but it has a basic "limit"—set by the land not the law—which remains the same. The limits provide an index or expression for the "voiceless land," and land "forces new habits on its dwellers," whether animal or human.

Yet in its limits the desert offers limitless understanding. Austin writes, "Go as far as you dare in the heart of a lonely land, you can not go so far that life and death are not before you." Humans express their own sense of limits by fencing in cattle ranges, or by penciling lines on pine head-boards to mark desert graves, or by trying to contain the desert's mystery in making up legends of lost mines. But even here,the land sets the limit; it is just that the "limit" can open a window into infinity. In its dealings with human beings, the land offers the experience of boundlessness as its ultimate "hold on the affections." The sketch ends with an insight:

> For all the toll the desert takes of a man it gives compensations, deep breaths, deep sleep, and the communion of the stars. . . . It is hard to escape the sense of mastery as the stars move in the wide clear heavens to risings and settings unobscured. They look large and near and palpitant; as if they moved on some stately service not needful to declare. Wheeling to their stations in the sky, they make the poor world-fret of no account. Of no account you who lie out there watching, nor the lean coyote that stands off in the scrub from you and howls and howls.

Lying "out there watching," the "no account" being first learns about human limitations. And then—having taught us this basic lesson—the desert enhances and expands our vision. It gives us the "communion of the stars." Such are the compensations of getting lost in a reading of *The Land of Little Rain*.

In "Water Trails of the Ceriso," Austin describes the way various small hill and desert animals "take the trail." Later, in *The Trail Book* (1918), she would write: "All the main traveled roads in the United States began as animal or Indian trails. There is no map that shows these roads as they originally were, but the changes are not so many as you might think. Railways have tunneled under passes where the buffalo went over, hills have been cut away and swamps filled in, but the general direction and in many places the actual grades covered by the great continental highways remain the same" (287). Although she makes very few references in these essays to human beings, the patterns she traces have relevance to human perception. Her own exploration of animal behavior gives her a trail marker to follow in her own writing, an expression of an inner voice—I-Mary?—guiding and directing her. In offering advice to one who might "venture to look for some seldom-touched water-hole," for example, she suggests paying close attention to the patterns of the converging trails: "No matter what the maps say, or your memory, trust them; they *know*." And "Water Trails of the Ceriso" ends with two glyphic or hieroglyphic figures,

Indian water signs on rocks "scored over with strange pictures and symbols that have no meaning to the Indians of the present day." They still hold meaning for Mary Austin. She trusts the instinct that tells her that, by tracing the sources of water in her arid country, she will also make contact with the springs of her own imagination.

In "The Scavengers" the buzzards, ravens, and coyotes also follow the trails of the living creatures who search for water, and especially of those who do not find it. Just as the number of desert plants depends on the amount of rain in a year, so does the number of scavengers increase "in proportion to the things they feed upon: the more carrion the more buzzards." To Austin's eye, the dying cattle become "basket-ribbed," suggesting even in their dying the forms and patterns of nature's design. Direct in her treatment of the scavengers' business, Austin withholds judgment until the end of the sketch. In the pattern or "economy" of nature, creatures eat other creatures, and are in turn eaten by scavengers at their own deaths, "but with it all there is not sufficient account taken of the works of man." Only the "ordinary camper" misses seeing that the woods are full of life: "Man is a great blunderer going about in the woods, and there is no other except the bear makes so much noise." The habits of men seem to verify her view, early in "Water Trails of the Ceriso," that "man-height is the least fortunate of all heights from which to study trails," for the man-creature violates nature's economy: "There is no scavenger that eats tin cans, and no wild thing leaves a like disfigurement on the forest floor."

From the land, to the plants, to the animals, to man—this is the trail she creates for her readers, in arriving at the story "The Pocket Hunter." The human inhabitant of the desert has adapted to its ways "as if he had that faculty of small hunted things of taking on the protective color of his surroundings." The reader may wonder what her pattern is here. Has she moved up some hierarchy of biological significance, or do her preceding discussions of plants and animals now serve to suggest that the Pocket Hunter is a parallel form of life, with no greater, no lesser significance? And what kind of human being is this, who "had gotten to that point where he knew no bad weather, and all places were equally happy so long as they were out of doors"? The man does take account of the elements; "the weather instinct does not sleep," and the Pocket Hunter, lost in a snowstorm, finds himself amid the "heavy breathing" of a flock of sheep.[5] Human beings and nature are interdependent in the land of little rain. In Austin's fascination with the Pocket Hunter she creates the first of several self-portraits, for all of the creatures and humans who try to locate trails or find "pockets" of gold in the desert remind her of her own attempts. "Of course with so much seeking" the Pocket Hunter "came occasionally upon pockets of more or less value . . . but he had as much luck in missing great ledges as in finding small ones." Still, when he does strike it rich and tries to live in London, the desert pulls him back. Austin writes: "Therefore it was with a pricking sense of the familiar that I followed a twilight trail of smoke, a year or two later," and came upon the Pocket Hunter again. The Pocket Hunter is himself one of many "pockets" of desert tales Austin has also hunted; and in her perseverance in following "a twilight trail of smoke," this particular pocket "of more or less value" turns into one of her own "big strikes." She has a story that expresses the pull of the desert, and she can conclude, as if speaking of herself as much as the Pocket Hunter: "No man can be stronger than his destiny."

It seems that in the Country of Lost Borders, individuals find their own shapes and forms—their destinies—from which they do not deviate, if they manage to survive. "Shoshone Land" is the story of Winnenap̓, a Shoshone medicine man who has lived his life among the Paiutes, but whose idea of heaven is Shoshone Land. The story holds several clues to Austin's own "trail" through *The Land of Little Rain*. "Once a Shoshone always a Shoshone," Winnenap̓ is also a creature of pattern, and he has been formed by the land of his childhood. Perhaps Austin modeled Winnenap̓ on Tinnemaha, a Paiute medicine man with whom she studied for several weeks shortly after her mother's death. Tinnemaha introduced her to the Friend-of-the-Soul-of-Man and ways to contact her creative power. In "Shoshone Land," the narrator remembers Winnenap̓'s power as a storyteller: "It is true I have been in Shoshone Land, but before that, long before, I had seen it through the eyes of Winnenap̓ . . ." Winnenap̓ resembles the Pocket Hunter of the previous sketch in that he, too, has learned that "the land will not be lived in except in its own fashion." But for Austin, much as she is intrigued by the adaptability of the white Pocket Hunter, following the "trail" of Winnenap̓ leads her back much further to the source, the spring, the "water-hole" of human creative energy. One of the trails Austin follows in this book and throughout her life led her back again and again to Indian ritual, art, and culture; there she found the shape of original—aboriginal—patterns of human being which, for her, offered the promise of revitalizing twentieth-century civilization.

In "Jimville" Austin moves closer to pursuing the storyteller's trail; she opens with a reference to Bret Harte which helps a reader understand what she is trying to accomplish in her own writing:

> When Mr. Harte found himself with a fresh palette and his particular local color fading from the West, he did what he considered the only safe thing, and carried his young impression away to be worked out untroubled by any newer fact. He should have gone to Jimville. There he would have found cast up on the ore-ribbed hills the bleached timbers of more tales, and better ones.

In this opening statement she distinguishes between Harte's local color and her own regionalism. Unlike the Pocket Hunter of her own sketch, Harte did not stay long enough in the West, Austin suggests, to make his "big strike," which might have helped him write "more tales, and better ones." He avoided troubling himself by "any newer fact" and based his stories about the West on "his young impression" instead of on an immersion in the land and its people. And Harte was not alone. "Western writers have not sensed it yet"—have not, before Austin herself, discovered the way the "hunch" works for westerners. And Jimville "prefers a 'hunch.' That is an intimation from the gods that if you go over a brown back of the hills, by a dripping spring, up Coso way, you will find what is worth while." Jimville is a town comprised of three hundred inhabitants, many of whom seem to be named Jim, and four bars, which serve the town as the water hole serves the small animals in "Water Trails of the Ceriso": between the ore dumps and small cabins "run foot-paths drawing down to the Silver Dollar saloon." She describes the inhabitants as if she were cataloguing desert creatures—they are "fierce, shy, profane, sun-dried derelicts of the windy hills." "Bret Harte would have given you a tale. You see in me a mere recorder, for I know what is best for you . . ." She offers "Jimville" as one more in a series of "hunches." Read this story, and those to come, she seems to be saying, and you too will experience the "intimation from the gods," will find a "sense of personal relation to the supernatural." Austin prefers the hunch to the tale, and the form the hunch takes. A collection of hunches like *The Land of Little Rain* may not initially seem to get us anywhere at first, if we are looking for conventional plot; but, as she says of the water trails that appear to deviate from memory, from what the maps say,—or from what the critics define as stories—, "trust them; they *know.*"

The first six sketches establish Austin as capable of following a hunch, and she continues her pattern in "My Neighbor's Field." Knowing the real estate history is one way of tracing the trail of a particular piece of land, and she sees the traces left by the Indians and the sheep, its previous owners. She watches the retaking of the field by wild plants, and observes: "It is not easy always to be attentive to the maturing of wild fruit." Without calling attention to the implications of her statement, she seems here to be sympathizing with her own reader. The individual sketches in *The Land of Little Rain* may seem, the first time through, like "wild" material; the reader may have initial difficulty in following the author's hunches as she gathers her insights together toward the end of the collection. Yet like the field she describes, her own book contains "a little touch of humanness, a footpath trodden out by moccasins." The meaning of *The Land of Little Rain* "matures" for the reader as we follow Austin's own trail.

In "The Mesa Trail" she chooses her particular path to Seyavi's camp because mesa trails "were meant to be traveled on horseback," and "a foot-pace carries one too slowly past the units in a decorative scheme that is on a scale with the country round for bigness." She is also "speeding up" the accumulation of insight, working toward a larger and a more grandiose pattern. "The Mesa Trail" brings back many of the creatures she studied in the opening sketches in the collection; here she moves more quickly past them to arrive at the "beginning of other things that are at the end of the mesa trail."

Seyavi, "The Basket Maker," lives at the end of the trail and the beginning of a spiritual and artistic journey that Mary Austin would make to the end of her life as a writer. Once again she insists on the patterned relationship between Seyavi's life and the land she has lived in, and Seyavi's genius is that she manages to capture this same pattern, "nearly the same personal note," in her baskets. Seyavi, more than any other person or animal in *The Land of Little Rain,* serves as Austin's model and mirror. She writes: "Every Indian woman is an artist,—sees, feels, creates, but does not philosophize about her processes." And yet she makes an appeal in "the sense that warns us of humanness in the way the design spreads into the flare of the bowl." Seyavi teaches her "things to be learned of life not set down in any books." Like the basket maker, Austin herself, in becoming immersed in the land and in creating a book that reflects her regionalism, knows to nourish "her spirit against the time of the spirit's need."

"The Basket Woman" is the most important single sketch in *The Land of Little Rain*. Almost as if the portrait of Seyavi breaks the drought of a deprived land, the four sketches that follow step back from the intensity of Austin's feeling for Seyavi and begin to suggest that a personal vision can become a communal one. In "The Streets of the Mountains," trails have become streets and all "lead to the citadel." The mountains here have a sense of pageantry; the business of the streets of the mountains "is tremendous, world-formative." In "Water Borders," she traces mountain streams to their origin and finds them nourishing the firs. Among trees, the fir represents the artist. It waits fifty years to bear fruit, "loves a water border, loves a long wind in a draughty cañon, loves to spend itself secretly on the inner finishings of its burnished, shapely cones." And in "Other Water Borders" despite the "proper destiny of every considerable stream" to become an irrigation ditch, Austin delights in observing the "avoidance of cultivated tracts by certain plants." Even though there is little rain in this land, there are some waters that refuse to meet their "proper destiny"; these form "overflow waters," and in "Other Water Borders," she traces the overflow to its ending—in alkali-collecting pools, and in the marshy places overgrown with reeds and known as "tulares." Yet once she traces the waters to their source, and to their endings, she in effect begins all over again, in "Nurslings of the Sky." "Choose a hill country for storms," she writes, and like the water once it reaches earth, water in the sky has also "habits to be learned, appointed paths, seasons, and warnings."

The final sketch in the collection, "The Little Town of the Grape Vines," lacks the intensity of "The Basket Maker" but it serves as a resting place. In her description of the town, Austin creates a pastoral haven whose location she claims she will never reveal. Like the young female protagonist in Jewett's story "A White Heron," who refuses to betray the heron's nest to the older male ornithologist who wants to kill and stuff the bird, Austin suggests that Las Uvas exists, but leaves it to the reader to find: "rather would I show you the heron's nest in the tulares." Las Uvas contrasts markedly with Jimville. In Las Uvas there is no mining boom, no saloon called the Silver Dollar. There is only a Spanish-speaking community, which keeps up "all the good customs brought out of Old Mexico," where the young quail seem to have walked off the designs on Seyavi's basket, and the "simple folk" spend much of their time in church. In this sketch Austin leaves her reader with a utopian vision of a community in which "every house is a piece of earth." In *Earth Horizon*, Austin will describe the malnutrition she suffered when she and her mother first arrived in the Tejon. One day she discovered some wild grapes; eating them cured her illness and marked the beginning of her psychological recovery as well. The inhabitants of Las Uvas do not achieve the primitive communion of Seyavi and the old women at the campoodie. And yet Austin's intention to reach toward heaven in her description of Las Uvas is clear. Perhaps she is recalling the personal significance of grapes in creating El Pueblo de Las Uvas. In her own imagination she finds an oasis in a land of little rain; she discovers grapes in a world of brackish water.

Although *The Land of Little Rain* possesses more unity as a collection than *Lost Borders*, the later volume also contains some of Austin's most powerful pieces of writing, and its final sketch comes closer than "The Little Town of the Grape Vines" to expressing the culmination of Austin's vision of the desert. The sketch that opens the volume, "The Land," builds upon the title sketch in *The Land of Little Rain* and it also moves beyond the earlier collection in its descriptions of the natural world. In "The Land" Austin continues to be fascinated by the way "every story of that country is colored by the fashion of the life there," but she shifts her focus to the strange stories of human beings who live in the desert rather than relating the habits and patterns of animal and plant behavior. In *The Land of Little Rain*, some of the people resemble desert creatures, and Austin views both humans and animals as if they were part of a larger landscape generally lacking in human qualities. In *Lost Borders*, Austin tries to understand the desert's mysteries in human terms, so much so that the desert "herself" takes on human form. At the end of "The Land," Austin writes:

Introduction

> If the desert were a woman, I know well what like she would
> be: deep-breasted, broad in the hips, tawny, with tawny hair, great
> masses of it lying smooth along her perfect curves, full lipped like a
> sphinx, but not heavy-lidded like one, eyes sane and steady as the
> polished jewel of her skies, such a countenance as should make men
> serve without desiring her, such a largeness to her mind as should
> make their sins of no account, passionate, but not necessitous, pa-
> tient—and you could not move her, no, not if you had all the earth
> to give, so much as one tawny hair's-breadth beyond her own desires.

"Tawny" is the word Austin uses frequently in *Earth Horizon* to describe her
own coloring, and she uses the word in *The Land of Little Rain* as well to
describe the desert. In reading her description of the deep-breasted, full-
lipped, sphinx-like woman who possesses "great masses" of tawny hair, I
am struck by the similarities between this image and Mary Austin's own
personal appearance. The desert becomes a mirror in which Austin explores "her own desires."

In her portraits and tales of the "lost" borderers, Austin has fully
assimilated her knowledge of the land into an expanding understanding of
human passion, and in exploring what motivates that passion, she chooses
the short-story form more often than the sketch. In *The Land of Little Rain*,
Austin became a pocket hunter, hoping to find herself in pursuit of a story
(as if fiction were her "gold"). In *Lost Borders*, she discovers that "you can
get anybody to believe any sort of a tale that has gold in it. "This is because
gold, not water, fascinates the men who live on the desert and, in their
passion for gold, they neglect their women. She writes in "The Land," by
way of introducing the tales that follow: "I have seen things happen that I
do not believe myself." Has she once again stumbled upon her tales, or has
she made them up? Perhaps Austin's attempt to tell a story of the desert
"that should be its final word" is her way of easing the emotional "thirst"
of the women on the desert. By telling their stories, her collection becomes
a true water hole, not another mirage.

Lost Borders portrays many betrayed and deprived women; yet in
Turwhasé, Mrs. Wills, the Woman at the Eighteen-Mile, and the Walking
Woman, Austin also displays the largeness of mind and unmoving patience

and passion of women who know that relationships to the land and to work or to other human beings will nurture them beyond their inheritance of deprivation, betrayal, and abandonment. Among all the characters in *Lost Borders,* the Walking Woman best epitomizes the desert's spirit in human flesh. But the desert, and the reflection of herself and her own strengths that Mary Austin saw in the desert, remains the most powerful image of vision and desire in either *The Land of Little Rain* or *Lost Borders.* Many of Austin's human characters come close to providing her with a model, to serving as her guide in her artistic and visionary quest, but her relationship to the land remains primary. In "Regionalism in American Fiction" she would write that region must enter the fiction "as another character, as the instigator of plot." The desert "herself" enters every story in *Lost Borders* as a character and serves to unify and motivate each one.

Many stories in *Lost Borders* trace the sources and effects of men's betrayal of women, of the land, of nature, and of their own best selves. In "The Hoodoo of the Minnietta," Jake Hogan acquires the Minnietta mine by cheating an acquaintance, and so sets in motion a kind of hoodoo that leads him and other men after him into ruin. In this story, the desert seems to work the hoodoo; she has one of the mine's superintendent's "cat-like, between her paws." And there is a woman in the story: Mrs. McKenna, who is forced to live at the mine, who loses a child, and then, to ease what Austin describes as the "emptiness" in her life, runs off with her husband's assistant.

In "A Case of Conscience," Saunders, an Englishman with a lung complaint, goes to the desert for his health and falls in love with an Indian woman named Turwhasé. They have a child, and for awhile Saunders's conscience "allowed him to do a great many things that by the code and the commandments" are wrong—until the year the doctor in Los Angeles tells him that he has cured his lung disease. "Oh, I *said* he had a man's conscience," Austin writes; for Saunders makes plans to leave Turwhasé, to return to England—and to take Turwhasé's child away from her.

Tiawa, of "The Ploughed Lands," also falls in love with a white man, who accepts her help when he is too ill to help himself. When he recovers and wants to return to "the ploughed lands" of southern California, Tiawa offers to be his guide in crossing the desert. But Gavin is in the power of the "tawny-throated one," and when Tiawa offers herself to him he rejects her.

Only when they come within view of civilization does Gavin begin to respond to Tiawa the way a "sophisticated male" knows how to do. And, in the way of the "sophisticated male," in the end Gavin "went back to his own kind."

Mrs. Wills, in "The Return of Mr. Wills," one of Austin's best stories, almost escapes the life of deprivation and subordination to which her husband has subjected her. In this story Austin writes a moving account of a woman who pulls herself out of the "drugging despair common among women of the camps" and makes the "remarkable discovery" that she can support herself and her children and still have "a little over" at the end of the month. In the next phase of her progress toward "independence and power," she begins to realize that "she not only did not need Mr. Wills, but got on better without him." When Mr. Wills unexpectedly returns, she experiences the "stroke of desolation." The ironic twist in this story is Mrs. Wills's discovery that, as forlorn and neglected as she might have felt in her husband's absence, in his return she discovers the depth and extent of her deprivation.

"The Last Antelope," another very strong story, extends the theme of betrayal to the natural world. Little Pete is "near akin to the wild things," humanizes his sheep, and develops a relationship based on friendliness and trust with a solitary antelope who learns that during the months when Pete is pasturing his flocks in the Ceriso, he will have help fighting off the packs of coyotes. As it does for the women who sacrifice for men in *Lost Borders,* the "friendliness of the antelope for Little Pete betrayed him," for he forgets his wild mistrust of mankind and becomes game for the white homesteader who takes up residence at the "remotest edge of settlement."

"Agua Dulce" presents another relationship between a white man and an Indian woman, but in this story the woman sacrifices herself to keep the man she loves alive. The simplicity of this story—it is told by the stage driver on the Mojave road—contrasts with the complexity of "The Woman at the Eighteen-Mile." Austin seeks the latter story out, after hearing bits and pieces of it at a fireside, then again between waking and sleep on another stagecoach on another desert road. Austin's own reader will have just as much trouble deciphering what actually happened as the narrator does. We get as close as Austin did to understanding that "there was a mine in it, a murder and a mystery, great sacrifice, Shoshones, dark and incredibly discreet, and the magnetic will of a man making manifest through all these. . . . And at the last it appeared there was a woman in it." For the story Austin wants to tell is about the Woman at the Eighteen-Mile, not the men whose behavior initially led her on the trail of the story.

What fascinates the narrator about the Woman at the Eighteen-Mile is the "certain effect she had of being warmed and nourished from within," her ability "to keep a soul alive and glowing in the wilderness," even though it turns out that she does so by keeping to herself the details that might have given Austin a different story. But unlike "Agua Dulce," "The Woman at the Eighteen-Mile" is not a story about love and sacrifice. The woman, who began her life in the desert with "great power and possibilities of passion," has once in her life caught a glimpse of what it means to work side by side with a man, "running neck and neck," watching her companion's spirit enlarge as a result: "The two must have had great moments at the heart of that tremendous coil of circumstance." This is the feeling that Austin describes as her own "pay dirt," and it is what the woman knows of passion. At the end of the story, Austin writes, "If it were not the biggest story of the desert ever written, I had no wish to write it." And she has written a story different from the one she set out to find—the story of a woman making a life out of a spark of sustenance: "One must needs be faithful to one's experiences when there are so few of them."

"The Fakir" and "The Pocket-Hunter's Story" pick up again the theme of betrayal. The Fakir abandons Netta Saybrick, whom he appears to have seduced, and in the process manages to turn Austin herself into a fakir, as she conspires to keep Netta's secret and permit the woman to fool even herself. But here, as at the end of "The Woman at the Eighteen-Mile," Austin as storyteller behaves very much like the desert whom she has cast in her own image; "you could not move her . . . so much as one tawny hair's-breadth beyond her own desires." For despite her promises both to Netta Saybrick and to the Woman at the Eighteen-Mile to keep silent, she ends by telling in *Lost Borders* what has been confided to her.

In "The Pocket-Hunter's Story," either the desert, or some other supernatural force, manages an even more unsettling transformation than Austin's narrator undergoes in "The Fakir." Is Tom, Tom? or is he Mac? Are we to believe that Mac, managing to travel just to that point in the desert where Tom has collapsed and died, gains enough power from his hatred for Creelman, the man he intends to kill, to leave his own body behind and move forward down the trail in Tom's body? As the Pocket Hunter hints to Austin's narrator before he tells the story, the mind can sometimes take "another body" in place of its own. The "mutual distrust" that links Mac and Creelman manages to transform Tom. Is this a supernatural event? Or has the partnership between Tom and Shorty gone the way of other relationships in the camps, in which "mutual distrust . . . grew out of an earlier friendliness"? Austin's narrator and the Pocket Hunter share the opinion that it is very difficult not to get "lost" in the desert.

"The Readjustment" and "Bitterness of Women" explore the tenuous grounds on which communication between men and women becomes possible. In order to put his wandering wife's ghost to rest, Sim Jeffries must find out what it is Emma still wants from him. In the process of talking out his own inadequacies, "the advertisement of his incompetence," he expresses a cramped love for his wife. He is a "little soul knowing itself and not good to see." The neighbor who listens and who also senses Emma Jeffries' presence in the house speaks to the ghost. If you think the fact of your death will change your husband, or break the silence between you, she says to the ghost, you would be making a mistake, " 'and in a little while, if you stay, it will be as bad as it always was. . . . Men are like that. . . . You'd better go now while there's understanding between you.'" Emma Jeffries, like Mrs. Wills, has paid a high price for the form of having been loved. Marguerita Dupré, in "Bitterness of Women," pays an even higher price. She has the satisfaction of knowing that her injured and scarred husband cannot leave her; but she faces the knowledge as well that he will refuse to love her. Louis Chabot is one of the "scavengers" in *Lost Borders.*

In the final two stories Austin offers communication between women and mutual understanding as the healing counterpart to the betrayal most of the women borderers experience. Despite her conventionality, Mrs. Henby in "The House of Offence" is moved by Hard Mag's situation; her "humanness got the better of her." She may not be able to fully empathize with the mother; but she can mother the mother's daughter. And Austin ends her collection with one of her most brilliant portraits in "The Walking Woman." In making contact with the Walking Woman, Austin's narrator writes the quintessential story of the desert, the one that nearly does serve as "its final word."

Unlike men who go into the desert, the Walking Woman has felt driven to the open not in search of a lost mine but to become "sobered and healed at last by the large soundness of nature." Austin sees herself mirrored in the desert; but what draws her to the Walking Woman is also an image of herself. For the Walking Woman has passed beyond the need for guides; although some question her sanity, "in her talk there was both wisdom and information, and the word she brought about trails and waterholes was as reliable as an Indian's." The Walking Woman has become as much of a shaman as any white woman on the desert, with the possible exception of Austin herself. And she has negotiated the world of men as successfully as she has learned the ways of the land; in spite of going about alone "in a country where the number of women is as one in fifteen," the Walking Woman has passed through the world of men in the desert "unarmed and unoffended." She serves as an imaginative and self-reflective water hole for the narrator, for in a land of deprivation for women, she has managed to "walk off" society-made values and, "knowing the best when the best came to her, was able to take it."

The narrator does not follow the Walking Woman's track in the sand, but she eases her own emotional aridity by making her portrait. Not mad, but sane; not twisted, but filled with feeling; not lame but even footed: the Walking Woman creates her own "water trail" for Mary Austin to follow, instead, in her storytelling. When women settle for permanency in lieu of passion or conventional life at the expense of vision, *Lost Borders* implies, they create their own Death Valley. Yet they do not need to look any farther outside themselves than the natural world for their "agua dulce." "If the desert were a woman, I know well what like she would be," Austin writes in "The Land." If the desert were a woman, she would be like the Walking Woman, which is to say, like Austin herself: the pattern tracer, the basket maker, the Chisera, the tawny storyteller.

Yet even the Walking Woman, like the Woman at the Eighteen-Mile, locates her source of vision in the months she spent loving and working with a man. In a memoir published just three weeks after Austin's death, her friend Elizabeth Shepley Sergeant wrote that "her work continued to the very end the central, basic joy, interest, and high adventure of her essentially lonely life. . . . And to the end, although women loved her, although in theory she was a feminist, believing that women more than men carry the creative fire, she actually preferred the society of men, and depended on men for her deepest companionship." *Lost Borders* stops short of allowing Austin's narrator full communion with the land through friendship with the Walking Woman, and in this way the collection moves away from her concerns in *The Land of Little Rain*, where Seyavi, the basket maker, becomes Austin's visionary and creative double. Seyavi has learned "how much more easily one can do without a man than might at first be supposed"; the Walking Woman, for all of her independence from men, still suggests that work, "love, man love," and a child are the three things that women desire.

Finally Austin reserves for herself the image of the tawny desert sphinx; she allows the desert to "get" her characters, but she stands apart, in her artist's power rivaling the power of the desert. Like the land she portrays in *The Land of Little Rain* and the women she writes about in *Lost Borders*, Mary Austin was thirsty throughout her life. She knew the meaning of aridity; and yet, she wrote as if storytelling were the one water trail, the single path to an oasis of emotional and spiritual nourishment, the great love that, more than any human relationship, more even than the land itself, might open out for her the "earth horizon."

1. My discussion of Mary Austin's life draws on the following sources: Mary Austin, *Earth Horizon: An Autobiography;* Augusta Fink, *I-Mary;* and T. M. Pearce, *Mary Hunter Austin.* All biographical quotations, unless otherwise indicated, are from *Earth Horizon;* quotations here are from pages 47, 51.

2. "How I Learned to Read and Write," in *My Maiden Effort,* ed. Gelett Burgess for the Authors' League of America, 1921; rpt. in *My First Publication,* ed. James D. Hart, The Book Club of California, 1961. Quoted in Fink 106–107.

3. Elémire Zolla praises *The Land of Little Rain* but scorns *The Arrow Maker.* He writes that when Austin turned to novels or plays, her explicit support for feminist issues made her a victim of ideology, that "her obsession as a protesting feminist—not merely sentimental but often petulant—had a distorting effect" (189–190). To this reader, the explicit feminism of *The Arrow Maker* is a particularly interesting aspect of Austin's work, for she convincingly demonstrates that feminism is a concern for Indian as well as white women.

4. There is some evidence that Austin may be undergoing a critical revival. In the best essay on her own work as a critic and a scholar of Indian poetry and tales, James Ruppert suggests that she "may be a pivotal figure in understanding the relation between American Indian literature and modern American literature" and that she "was commonly regarded as an expert on all things Indian" (251). And in a recent essay, Blanche Gelfant considers similarities between Austin's life and the lives of Willa Cather and Katherine Anne Porter, suggesting that all three refused as women to make accommodations that might have brought social approval, adopting instead, as writers, "resistant feminist" positions (244).

Notes to Introduction

5. The intensity of Austin's descriptions of sheep on the Mojave, clear here, in "The Mesa Trail," and again in "The Woman at the Eighteen-Mile" and in "The Walking Woman" in *Lost Borders,* will give the reader a glimpse of the power of her descriptions of sheep, shepherds, and their habits in *The Flock.*

SELECTED BIBLIOGRAPHY

WORKS BY MARY AUSTIN

The American Rhythm. New York: Harcourt, Brace, 1923; Boston and New York: Houghton, 1930.

The Arrow Maker. New York: Duffield, 1911; rev. ed. Boston: Houghton, 1915.

The Basket Woman. Boston and New York: Houghton, 1904.

Cactus Thorn. With foreword and afterword by Melody Graulich. Reno and Las Vegas: U of Nevada P, 1988.

Earth Horizon: An Autobiography. Boston and New York: Houghton, 1932.

The Flock. Boston and New York: Houghton, 1906.

"Frustrate." *The Century Illustrated Monthly Magazine* 83. 3 (Jan. 1912): 467–471.

Isidro. Boston and New York: Houghton, 1905.

The Land of Journey's Ending. New York and London: Century, 1924.

The Land of Little Rain. Boston and New York: Houghton, 1903.

Lost Borders. New York and London: Harper and Brothers, 1909.

One Hundred Miles on Horseback. Rpt. Los Angeles: Dawson's Book Shop, 1963.

One-Smoke Stories. Boston and New York: Houghton, 1934.

"Regionalism in American Fiction." *English Journal* 21 (Feb. 1932): 97–107.

Taos Pueblo. Photographed by Ansel Adams and described by Mary Austin. San Francisco: Grabhorn, 1930.

Notes to Introduction

The Trail Book. Boston and New York: Houghton, 1918.

A Woman of Genius. New York: Doubleday, Page, 1912; Boston and New York: Houghton, 1917; Old Westbury, N.Y.: Feminist, 1985.

OTHER SOURCES

Fink, Augusta. *I-Mary.* Tucson: U of Arizona, 1983.

Gelfant, Blanche H. "'Lives' of Women Writers: Cather, Austin, Porter / and Willa, Mary, Katherine Anne." *Women Writing in America.* Hanover, N.H.: UP of New England, 1984. 225–248.

Kaplan, Justin. *Lincoln Steffens: A Biography.* New York: Simon, 1974.

Kolodny, Annette. *The Land before Her.* Chapel Hill: U of North Carolina P, 1984.

Pearce, Thomas Matthews. *Mary Hunter Austin.* New York: Twayne, 1965.

———, ed. *Literary America, 1903–1934: The Mary Austin Letters.* Westport, Conn.: Greenwood, 1979.

Porter, Nancy. Afterword. *A Woman of Genius* by Mary Austin. Old Westbury, N.Y.: Feminist, 1985. 295–321.

Ruppert, James. "Discovering America: Mary Austin and Imagism." *Studies in American Indian Literature.* Ed. Paula Gunn Allen. New York: MLA, 1983. 243–258.

Sergeant, Elizabeth Shepley. "Mary Austin: A Portrait." *Saturday Review of Literature* 11. 8 (8 Sept. 1934): 96.

Steffens, Lincoln. "Mary Austin." *The American Magazine* 72. 2 (June 1911). 178–181.

Stineman, Esther Lanigan. *Mary Austin: Song of a Maverick.* New Haven: Yale UP, 1989.

Work, James C. "The Moral in Austin's *The Land of Little Rain.*" *Women and Western American Literature.* Ed. Helen Winter Stauffer and Susan J. Rosowski. Troy, N.Y.: Whitston, 1982. 297–309.

Wynn, Dudley. *A Critical Study of the Writings of Mary Austin.* Graduate School of Arts and Science of NYU, 1941.

Zolla, Elémire. *The Writer and the Shaman: A Morphology of the American Indian.* New York: Harcourt, 1969.

Throughout her life Mary Austin remained a poor and erratic speller, and throughout *The Land of Little Rain* and *Lost Borders,* she frequently uses secondary spellings of common words. She is also inconsistent, so that some words may have variant spellings, such as Panamint (sometimes Panimint) or Amargosa (sometimes Amorgosa). With the exception of misspellings that clearly result from typographical errors, which I have corrected, this edition retains Austin's original spelling and punctuation. The texts of both volumes reprinted here are from the first edition. Several individual sketches and stories, from both collections, appeared for the first time in the *Atlantic Monthly.*

*Stories from the
Country of Lost Borders*

THE LAND
OF
LITTLE RAIN

BY MARY AUSTIN

ILLUSTRATED BY E. BOYD SMITH

I confess to a great liking for the Indian fashion of name-giving: every man known by that phrase which best expresses him to whoso names him. Thus he may be Mighty-Hunter, or Man-Afraid-of-a-Bear, according as he is called by friend or enemy, and Scar-Face to those who knew him by the eye's grasp only. No other fashion, I think, sets so well with the various natures that inhabit in us, and if you agree with me you will understand why so few names are written here as they appear in the geography. For if I love a lake known by the name of the man who discovered it, which endears itself by reason of the close-locked pines it nourishes about its borders, you may look in my account to find it so described. But if the Indians have been there before me, you shall have their name, which is always beautifully fit and does not originate in the poor human desire for perpetuity.

Nevertheless there are certain peaks, cañons, and clear meadow spaces which are above all compassing of words, and have a certain fame as of the nobly great to whom we give no familiar names. Guided by these you may reach my country and find or not find, according as it lieth in you, much that is set down here. And more. The earth is no wanton to give up all her best to every comer, but keeps a sweet, separate intimacy for each. But if you do not find it all as I write, think me not less dependable nor yourself less clever. There is a sort of pretense allowed in matters of the heart, as one should say by way of illustration, "I know a man who . . . ," and so give up his dearest experience without betrayal. And I am in no mind to direct you to delectable places toward which you will hold yourself less tenderly than I. So by this fashion of naming I keep faith with the land and annex to my own estate a very great territory to which none has a surer title.

The country where you may have sight and touch of that which is written lies between the high Sierras south from Yosemite—east and south over a very great assemblage of broken ranges beyond Death Valley, and on illimitably into the Mojave Desert. You may come into the borders of it from the south by a stage journey that has the effect of involving a great lapse of time, or from the north by rail, dropping out of the overland route at Reno. The best of all ways is over the Sierra passes by pack and trail, seeing and believing. But the real heart and core of the country are not to be come at in a month's vacation. One must summer and winter with the land and wait its occasions. Pine woods that take two and three seasons to the ripening of cones, roots that lie by in the sand seven years awaiting a growing rain, firs that grow fifty years before flowering,—these do not scrape acquaintance. But if ever you come beyond the borders as far as the town that lies in a hill dimple at the foot of Kearsarge, never leave it until you have knocked at the door of the brown house under the willow-tree at the end of the village street, and there you shall have such news of the land, of its trails and what is astir in them, as one lover of it can give to another.

NOTE ON THE ILLUSTRATIONS
(FROM FIRST EDITION)

THE PUBLISHERS FEEL that they have been peculiarly fortunate in securing Mr. E. Boyd Smith as the illustrator and interpreter of Mrs. Austin's charming sketches of THE LAND OF LITTLE RAIN. His familiarity with the region and his rare artistic skill have enabled him to give the very atmosphere of the desert, and graphically to portray its life, animal and human.

CONTENTS

THE LAND OF LITTLE RAIN

THE LAND OF LITTLE RAIN

EAST AWAY FROM the Sierras, south from Panamint and Amargosa, east and south many an uncounted mile, is the Country of Lost Borders.

Ute, Paiute, Mojave, and Shoshone inhabit its frontiers, and as far into the heart of it as a man dare go. Not the law, but the land sets the limit. Desert is the name it wears upon the maps, but the Indian's is the better word. Desert is a loose term to indicate land that supports no man; whether the land can be bitted and broken to that purpose is not proven. Void of life it never is, however dry the air and villainous the soil.

This is the nature of that country. There are hills, rounded, blunt, burned, squeezed up out of chaos, chrome and vermilion painted, aspiring to the snowline. Between the hills lie high level-looking plains full of intolerable sun glare, or narrow valleys drowned in a blue haze. The hill surface is streaked with ash drift and black, unweathered lava flows. After rains water accumulates in the hollows of small closed valleys, and, evaporating, leaves hard dry levels of pure desertness that get the local name of dry lakes. Where the mountains are steep and the rains heavy, the pool is never quite dry, but dark and bitter, rimmed about with the efflorescence of alkaline deposits. A thin crust of it lies along the marsh over the vegetating area, which has neither beauty nor freshness. In the broad wastes open to the wind the sand drifts in hummocks about the stubby shrubs, and between them the soil shows saline traces. The sculpture of the hills here is more wind than water work, though the quick storms do

sometimes scar them past many a year's redeeming. In all the Western desert edges there are essays in miniature at the famed, terrible Grand Cañon, to which, if you keep on long enough in this country, you will come at last.

Since this is a hill country one expects to find springs, but not to depend upon them; for when found they are often brackish and unwholesome, or maddening, slow dribbles in a thirsty soil. Here you find the hot sink of Death Valley, or high rolling districts where the air has always a tang of frost. Here are the long heavy winds and breathless calms on the tilted mesas where dust devils dance, whirling up into a wide, pale sky. Here you have no rain when all the earth cries for it, or quick downpours called cloud-bursts for violence. A land of lost rivers, with little in it to love; yet a land that once visited must be come back to inevitably. If it were not so there would be little told of it.

This is the country of three seasons. From June on to November it lies hot, still, and unbearable, sick with violent unrelieving storms; then on until April, chill, quiescent, drinking its scant rain and scanter snows; from April to the hot season again, blossoming, radiant, and seductive. These months are only approximate; later or earlier the rain-laden wind may drift up the water gate of the Colorado from the Gulf, and the land sets its seasons by the rain.

The desert floras shame us with their cheerful adaptations to the seasonal limitations. Their whole duty is to flower and fruit, and they do it hardly, or with tropical luxuriance, as the rain admits. It is recorded in the report of the Death Valley expedition that after a year of abundant rains, on the Colorado desert was found a specimen of Amaranthus ten feet high. A year later the same species in the same place matured in the drought at four inches. One hopes the land may breed like qualities in her human offspring, not tritely to "try," but to do. Seldom does the desert herb attain the full stature of the type. Extreme aridity and extreme altitude have the same dwarfing effect, so that we find in the high Sierras and in Death Valley related species in miniature that reach a comely growth in mean temperatures. Very fertile are the desert plants in expedients to prevent evaporation, turning their foliage edgewise toward the sun, growing silky hairs, exuding viscid gum. The wind, which has a long sweep, harries and helps them. It rolls up dunes about the stocky stems, encompassing and protective, and above the dunes, which may be, as with the mesquite, three times as high as a man, the blossoming twigs flourish and bear fruit.

There are many areas in the desert where drinkable water lies within a few feet of the surface, indicated by the mesquite and the bunch grass (Sporobolus airoides). It is this nearness of unimagined help that makes the tragedy of desert deaths. It is related that the final breakdown of that hapless party that gave Death Valley its forbidding name occurred in a locality where shallow wells would have saved them. But how were they to know that? Properly equipped it is possible to go safely across that ghastly sink, yet every year it takes its toll of death, and yet men find there sun-dried mummies, of whom no trace or recollection is preserved. To underestimate one's thirst, to pass a given landmark to the right or left, to find a dry spring where one looked for running water—there is no help for any of these things.

Along springs and sunken watercourses one is surprised to find such water-loving plants as grow widely in moist ground, but the true desert breeds its own kind, each in its particular habitat. The angle of the slope, the frontage of a hill, the structure of the soil determines the plant. South-looking hills are nearly bare, and the lower tree-line higher here by a thousand feet. Cañons running east and west will have one wall naked and one clothed. Around dry lakes and marshes the herbage preserves a set and orderly arrangement. Most species have well-defined areas of growth, the best index the voiceless land can give the traveler of his whereabouts.

If you have any doubt about it, know that the desert begins with the creosote. This immortal shrub spreads down into Death Valley and up to the lower timber-line, odorous and medicinal as you might guess from the name, wandlike, with shining fretted foliage. Its vivid green is grateful to the eye in a wilderness of gray and greenish white shrubs. In the spring it exudes a resinous gum which the Indians of those parts know how to use with pulverized rock for cementing arrow points to shafts. Trust Indians not to miss any virtues of the plant world!

Nothing the desert produces expresses it better than the unhappy growth of the tree yuccas. Tormented, thin forests of it stalk drearily in the high mesas, particularly in that triangular slip that fans out eastward from the meeting of the Sierras and coastwise hills where the first swings across the southern end of the San Joaquin Valley. The yucca bristles with

bayonet-pointed leaves, dull green, growing shaggy with age, tipped with panicles of fetid, greenish bloom. After death, which is slow, the ghostly hollow network of its woody skeleton,with hardly power to rot, makes the moonlight fearful. Before the yucca has come to flower, while yet its bloom is a creamy cone-shaped bud of the size of a small cabbage, full of sugary sap, the Indians twist it deftly out of its fence of daggers and roast it for their own delectation. So it is that in those parts where man inhabits one sees young plants of *Yucca arborensis* infrequently. Other yuccas, cacti, low herbs, a thousand sorts, one find journeying east from the coastwise hills. There is neither poverty of soil nor species to account for the sparseness of desert growth, but simply that each plant requires more room. So much earth must be preëmpted to extract so much moisture. The real struggle for existence, the real brain of the plant, is underground; above there is room for a rounded perfect growth. In Death Valley, reputed the very core of desolation, are nearly two hundred identified species.

Above the lower tree-line, which is also the snow-line, mapped out abruptly by the sun, one finds spreading growth of piñon, juniper, branched nearly to the ground, lilac and sage, and scattering white pines.

There is no special preponderance of self-fertilized or wind-fertilized plants, but everywhere the demand for and evidence of insect life. Now where there are seeds and insects there will be birds and small mammals and where these are, will come the slinking, sharp-toothed kind that prey on them. Go as far as you dare in the heart of a lonely land, you cannot go so far that life and death are not before you. Painted lizards slip in and out of rock crevices, and pant on the white hot sands. Birds, hummingbirds even, nest in the cactus scrub; woodpeckers befriend the demoniac yuccas; out of the stark, treeless waste rings the music of the night-singing mockingbird. If it be summer and the sun well down, there will be a burrowing owl to call. Strange, furry, tricksy things dart across the open places, or sit motionless in the conning towers of the creosote. The poet may have "named all the birds without a gun," * but not the fairy-footed, ground-inhabiting, furtive, small folk of the rainless regions. They are too many and too swift; how many you would not believe without seeing the footprint tracings in the sand. They are nearly all night workers, finding

---

* Austin is referring to the first line of Emerson's 1842 poem, "Forbearance."

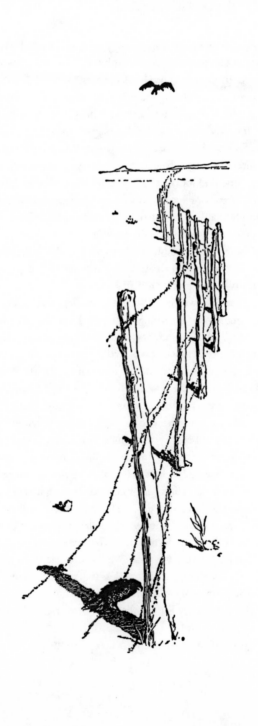

the days too hot and white. In mid-desert where there are no cattle, there are no birds of carrion, but if you go far in that direction the chances are that you will find yourself shadowed by their tilted wings. Nothing so large as a man can move unspied upon in that country, and they know well how the land deals with strangers. There are hints to be had here of the way in which a land forces new habits on its dwellers. The quick increase of suns at the end of spring sometimes overtakes birds in their nesting and effects a reversal of the ordinary manner of incubation. It becomes necessary to keep eggs cool rather than warm. One hot, stifling spring in the Little Antelope I had occasion to pass and repass frequently the nest of a pair of meadowlarks, located unhappily in the shelter of a very slender weed. I never caught them sitting except near night, but at midday they stood, or drooped above it, half fainting with pitifully parted bills, between their treasure and the sun. Sometimes both of them together with wings spread and half lifted continued a spot of shade in a temperature that constrained me at last in a fellow feeling to spare them a bit of canvas for permanent shelter. There was a fence in that country shutting in a cattle range, and along its fifteen miles of posts one could be sure of finding a bird or two in every strip of shadow; sometime the sparrow and the hawk, with wings trailed and beaks parted, drooping in the white truce of noon.

If one is inclined to wonder at first how so many dwellers came to be in the loneliest land that ever came out of God's hands, what they do there and why stay, one does not wonder so much after having lived there. None other than this long brown land lays such a hold on the affections. The rainbow hills, the tender bluish mists, the luminous radiance of the spring, have the lotus charm. They trick the sense of time, so that once inhabiting there you always mean to go away without quite realizing that you have not done it. Men who have lived there, miners and cattle-men, will tell you this, not so fluently, but emphatically, cursing the land and going back to it. For one thing there is the divinest, cleanest air to be breathed anywhere in God's world. Some day the world will understand that, and the little oases on the windy tops of hills will harbor for healing its ailing, house-weary broods. There is promise there of great wealth in ores and earths, which is no wealth by reason of being so far removed from water and workable conditions, but men are bewitched by it and tempted to try the impossible.

You should hear Salty Williams tell how he used to drive eighteen and twenty-mule teams from the borax marsh to Mojave, ninety miles, with the trail wagon full of water barrels. Hot days the mules would go so mad for drink that the clank of the water bucket set them into an uproar of hideous, maimed noises, and a tangle of harness chains, while Salty would sit on the high seat with the sun glare heavy in his eyes, dealing out curses of pacification in a level, uninterested voice until the clamor fell off from sheer exhaustion. There was a line of shallow graves along that road; they used to count on dropping a man or two of every new gang of coolies brought out in the hot season. But when he lost his swamper, smitten without warning at the noon halt, Salty quit his job; he said it was "too durn hot." The swamper he buried by the way with stones upon him to keep the coyotes from digging him up, and seven years later I read the penciled lines on the pine headboard, still bright and unweathered.

But before that, driving up on the Mojave stage, I met Salty again crossing Indian Wells, his face from the high seat, tanned and ruddy as a harvest moon, looming through the golden dust above his eighteen mules. The land had called him.

The palpable sense of mystery in the desert air breeds fables, chiefly of lost treasure. Somewhere within its stark borders, if one believes report, is a hill strewn with nuggets; one seamed with virgin silver; an old clayey water-bed where Indians scooped up earth to make cooking pots and shaped them reeking with grains of pure gold. Old miners drifting about the desert edges, weathered into the semblance of the tawny hills, will tell you tales like these convincingly. After a little sojourn in that land you will believe them on their own account. It is a question whether it is not better to be bitten by the little horned snake of the desert that goes sidewise and strikes without coiling, than by the tradition of a lost mine.

And yet—and yet—is it not perhaps to satisfy expectation that one falls into the tragic key in writing of desertness? The more you wish of it the more you get, and in the mean time lose much of pleasantness. In that country which begins at the foot of the east slope of the Sierras and spreads out by less and less lofty hill ranges toward the Great Basin, it is possible to live with great zest, to have red blood and delicate joys, to pass and repass about one's daily performance an area that would make an Atlantic sea-board State, and that with no peril, and, according to our way of thought, no particular difficulty. At any rate, it was not people who went into the desert merely to write it up who invented the fabled Hassaympa, of whose waters, if any drink, they can no more see fact as naked fact, but all radiant with the color of romance. I, who must have drunk of it in my twice seven years' wanderings, am assured that it is worth while.

For all the toll the desert takes of a man it gives compensations, deep breaths, deep sleep, and the communion of the stars. It comes upon one with new force in the pauses of the night that the Chaldeans were a desert-bred people. It is hard to escape the sense of mastery as the stars move in the wide clear heavens to risings and settings unobscured. They look large and near and palpitant; as if they moved on some stately service not needful to declare. Wheeling to their stations in the sky, they make the poor world-fret of no account. Of no account you who lie out there watching, nor the lean coyote that stands off in the scrub from you and howls and howls.

WATER TRAILS OF THE CERISO

BY THE END of the dry season the water trails of the Ceriso are worn to a white ribbon in the leaning grass, spread out faint and fanwise toward the homes of gopher and ground rat and squirrel. But however faint to man-sight, they are sufficiently plain to the furred and feathered folk who travel them. Getting down to the eye level of rat and squirrel kind, one perceives what might easily be wide and winding roads to us if they occurred in thick plantations of trees three times the height of a man. It needs but a slender thread of barrenness to make a mouse trail in the forest of the sod. To the little people the water trails are as country roads, with scents as sign-boards.

It seems that man-height is the least fortunate of all heights from which to study trails. It is better to go up the front of some tall hill, say the spur of Black Mountain, looking back and down across the hollow of the Ceriso. Strange how long the soil keeps the impression of any continuous treading, even after grass has overgrown it. Twenty years since, a brief heyday of mining at Black Mountain made a stage road across the Ceriso, yet the parallel lines that are the wheel traces show from the height dark and well defined. Afoot in the Ceriso one looks in vain for any sign of it. So all the paths that wild creatures use going down to the Lone Tree Spring are mapped out whitely from this level, which is also the level of the hawks.

There is little water in the Ceriso at the best of times, and that little brackish and smelling vilely, but by a lone juniper where the rim of the Ceriso breaks away to the lower country, there is a perpetual rill of fresh sweet drink in the midst of lush grass and watercress. In the dry season there is no water else for a man's long journey of a day. East to the foot of Black Mountain, and north and south without counting, are the burrows of small rodents, rat and squirrel kind. Under the sage are the shallow forms of the jackrabbits, and in the dry banks of washes, and among the strewn fragments of black rock, lairs of bobcat, fox, and coyote.

The coyote is your true water-witch, one who snuffs and paws, snuffs and paws again at the smallest spot of moisture-scented earth until he has freed the blind water from the soil. Many water-holes are no more than this detected by the lean hobo of the hills in localities where not even an Indian would look for it.

It is the opinion of many wise and busy people that the hill-folk pass the ten-month interval between the end and renewal of winter rains, with no drink; but your true idler, with days and nights to spend beside the water trails, will not subscribe to it. The trails begin, as I said, very far back in the Ceriso, faintly, and converge in one span broad, white, hard-trodden way in the gully of the spring. And why trails if there are no travelers in that direction?

I have yet to find the land not scarred by the thin, far roadways of rabbits and what not of furry folks that run in them. Venture to look for some seldom-touched water-hole, and so long as the trails run with your general direction make sure you are right, but if they begin to cross yours at never so slight an angle, to converge toward a point left or right of your objective, no matter what the maps say, or your memory, trust them; they *know*.

It is very still in the Ceriso by day, so that were it not for the evidence of those white beaten ways, it might be the desert it looks. The sun is hot in the dry season, and the days are filled with the glare of it. Now and again some unseen coyote signals his pack in a long-drawn, dolorous whine that comes from no determinate point, but nothing stirs much before mid-afternoon. It is a sign when there begin to be hawks skimming above the sage that the little people are going about their business.

Water Trails of the Ceriso

We have fallen on a very careless usage, speaking of wild creatures as if they were bound by some such limitation as hampers clockwork. When we say of one and another, they are night prowlers, it is perhaps true only as the things they feed upon are more easily come by in the dark, and they know well how to adjust themselves to conditions wherein food is more plentiful by day. And their accustomed performance is very much a matter of keen eye, keener scent, quick ear, and a better memory of sights and sounds than man dares boast. Watch a coyote come out of his lair and cast about in his mind where he will go for his daily killing. You cannot very well tell what decides him, but very easily that he has decided. He trots or breaks into short gallops, with very perceptible pauses to look up and about at landmarks, alters his tack a little, looking forward and back to steer his proper course. I am persuaded that the coyotes in my valley, which is narrow and beset with steep, sharp hills, in long passages steer by the pinnacles of the sky-line, going with head cocked to one side to keep to the left or right of such and such a promontory.

I have trailed a coyote often, going across country, perhaps to where some slant-winged scavenger hanging in the air signaled prospect of a dinner, and found his track such as a man, a very intelligent man accustomed to a hill country, and a little cautious, would make to the same point. Here a detour to avoid a stretch of too little cover, there a pause on the rim of a gully to pick the better way,—and it is usually the best way,— and making his point with the greatest economy of effort. Since the time of Seyavi the deer have shifted their feeding ground across the valley at the beginning of deep snows, by way of the Black Rock, fording the river at Charley's Butte, and making straight for the mouth of the cañon that is the easiest going to the winter pastures on Waban. So they still cross, though whatever trail they had has been long broken by ploughed ground; but from the mouth of Tinpah Creek, where the deer come out of the Sierras, it is easily seen that the creek, the point of Black Rock, and Charley's Butte are in line with the wide bulk of shade that is the foot of Waban Pass. And along with this the deer have learned that Charley's Butte is almost the only possible ford, and all the shortest crossing of the valley. It seems that the wild creatures have learned all that is important to their way of life except the changes of the moon. I have seen some prowling fox or coyote,

surprised by its sudden rising from behind the mountain wall, slink in its increasing glow, watch it furtively from the cover of near-by brush, un-prepared and half uncertain of its identity until it rode clear of the peaks, and finally make off with all the air of one caught napping by an ancient joke. The moon in its wanderings must be a sort of exasperation to cunning beasts, likely to spoil by untimely risings some fore-planned mischief.

But to take the trail again; the coyotes that are astir in the Ceriso of late afternoons, harrying the rabbits from their shallow forms, and the hawks that sweep and swing above them, are not there from any mechani-cal promptings of instinct, but because they know of old experience that the small fry are about to take to seed gathering and the water trails. The rabbits begin it, taking the trail with long, light leaps, one eye and ear

cocked to the hills from whence a coyote might descend upon them at any moment. Rabbits are a foolish people. They do not fight except with their own kind, nor use their paws except for feet, and appear to have no reason for existence but to furnish meals for meat-eaters. In flight they seem to rebound from the earth of their own elasticity, but keep a sober pace going to the spring. It is the young watercress that tempts them and the pleasures of society, for they seldom drink. Even in localities where there are flowing streams they seem to prefer the moisture that collects on herbage, and after rains may be seen rising on their haunches to drink delicately the clear drops caught in the tops of the young sage. But drink they must, as I have often seen them mornings and evenings at the rill that goes by my door. Wait long enough at the Lone Tree Spring and sooner or later they will all come in. But here their matings are accomplished, and though they are fearful of so little as a cloud shadow or blown leaf, they contrive to have some playful hours. At the spring the bobcat drops down upon them from the black rock, and the red fox picks them up returning in the dark. By day the hawk and eagle overshadow them, and the coyote has all times and seasons for his own.

Cattle, when there are any in the Ceriso, drink morning and evening, spending the night on the warm last lighted slopes of neighboring hills, stirring with the peep o'day. In these half wild spotted steers the habits of an earlier lineage persist. It must be long since they have made beds for themselves, but before lying down they turn themselves round and round as dogs do. They choose bare and stony ground, exposed fronts of westward facing hills, and lie down in companies. Usually by the end of the summer the cattle have been driven or gone of their own choosing to the mountain meadows. One year a maverick yearling, strayed or overlooked by the vaqueros, kept on until the season's end, and so betrayed another visitor to the spring that else I might have missed. On a certain morning the half-eaten carcass lay at the foot of the black rock, and in moist earth by the rill of the spring, the foot-pads of a cougar, puma, mountain lion, or whatever the beast is rightly called. The kill must have been made early in the evening, for it appeared that the cougar had been twice to the spring; and since the meat-eater drinks little until he has eaten, he must have fed and drunk, and after an interval of lying up in the black rock, had eaten and drunk again. There was no knowing how far he had come, but if he came

again the second night he found that the coyotes had left him very little of
his kill.

Nobody ventures to say how infrequently and at what hour the small
fry visit the spring. There are such numbers of them that if each of them
came once between the last of spring and the first of winter rains, there
would still be water trails. I have seen badgers drinking about the hour
when the light takes on the yellow tinge it has from coming slantwise
through the hills. They find out shallow places, and are loath to wet their
feet. Rats and chipmunks have been observed visiting the spring as late as
nine o'clock mornings. The larger spermophiles that live near the spring
and keep awake to work all day, come and go at no particular hour,
drinking sparingly. At long intervals on half-lighted days, meadow and field
mice steal delicately along the trail. These visitors are all too small to be
watched carefully at night, but for evidence of their frequent coming there
are the trails that may be traced miles out among the crisping grasses. On
rare nights, in the places where no grass grows between the shrubs, and the
sand silvers whitely to the moon, one sees them whisking to and fro on
innumerable errands of seed gathering, but the chief witnesses of their
presence near the spring are the elf owls. Those burrow-haunting,
speckled fluffs of greediness begin a twilight flitting toward the spring,
feeding as they go on grasshoppers, lizards, and small, swift creatures,
diving into burrows to catch field mice asleep, battling with chipmunks
at their own doors, and getting down in great numbers toward the lone
juniper. Now owls do not love water greatly on its own account. Not to
my knowledge have I caught one drinking or bathing, though on night

wanderings across the mesa they flit up from under the horse's feet along stream borders. Their presence near the spring in great numbers would indicate the presence of the things they feed upon. All night the rustle and soft hooting keeps on in the neighborhood of the spring, with seldom small shrieks of mortal agony. It is clear day before they have all gotten back to their particular hummocks, and if one follows cautiously, not to frighten them into some near-by burrow, it is possible to trail them far up the slope.

The crested quail that troop in the Ceriso are the happiest frequenters of the water trails. There is no furtiveness about their morning drink. About the time the burrowers and all that feed upon them are addressing themselves to sleep, great flocks pour down the trails with that peculiar melting motion of moving quail, twittering, shoving, and shouldering. They splatter into the shallows, drink daintily, shake out small showers over their perfect coats, and melt away again into the scrub, preening and pranking, with soft contented noises.

After the quail, sparrows and ground-inhabiting birds bathe with the utmost frankness and a great deal of splutter; and here in the heart of noon hawks resort, sitting panting, with wings aslant, and a truce to all hostilities because of the heat. One summer there came a road-runner up from the lower valley, peeking and prying, and he had never any patience with the water baths of the sparrows. His own ablutions were performed in the clean, hopeful dust of the chaparral; and whenever he happened on their morning splatterings, he would depress his glossy crest, slant his shining tail to the level of his body, until he looked most like some bright venomous snake, daunting them with shrill abuse and feint of battle. Then suddenly he would go tilting and balancing down the gully in fine disdain, only to return in a day or two to make sure the foolish bodies were still at it.

Out on the Ceriso about five miles, and wholly out of sight of it, near where the immemorial foot trail goes up from Sabine Flat toward Black Mountain, is a water sign worth turning out of the trail to see. It is a laid circle of stones large enough not to be disturbed by any ordinary hap, with an opening flanked by two parallel rows of similar stones, between which were an arrow placed, touching the opposite rim of the circle, thus (Fig. 1), it would point as the crow flies to the spring. It is the old, indubitable water mark of the Shoshones. One still finds it in the desert ranges in Salt Wells and Mesquite valleys, and along the slopes of Waban. On the other side of Ceriso, where the black rock begins, about a mile from the spring, is the work of an older, forgotten people. The rock hereabout is all volcanic, fracturing with a crystalline whitish surface, but weathered outside to furnace blackness. Around the spring, where must have been a gathering

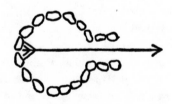

FIG. 1.

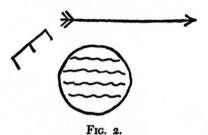

FIG. 2.

place of the tribes, it is scored over with strange pictures and symbols that have no meaning to the Indians of the present day; but out where the rock begins, there is carved into the white heart of it a pointing arrow over the symbol for distance and a circle full of wavy lines (Fig. 2) reading thus: "In this direction three [units of measurement unknown] is a spring of sweet water; look for it."

THE SCAVENGERS

THE SCAVENGERS

FIFTY-SEVEN BUZZARDS, one on each of fifty-seven fence posts at the rancho El Tejon, on a mirage-breeding September morning, sat solemnly while the white tilted travelers' vans lumbered down the Cañada de los Uvas. After three hours they had only clapped their wings, or exchanged posts. The season's end in the vast dim valley of the San Joaquin is palpitatingly hot, and the air breathes like cotton wool. Through it all the buzzards sit on the fences and low hummocks, with wings spread fanwise for air. There is no end to them, and they smell to heaven. Their heads droop, and all their communication is a rare, horrid croak.

The increase of wild creatures is in proportion to the things they feed upon: the more carrion the more buzzards. The end of the third successive dry year bred them beyond belief. The first year quail mated sparingly; the second year the wild oats matured no seed; the third, cattle died in their tracks with their heads towards the stopped watercourses. And that year the scavengers were black as the plague all across the mesa and up the treeless, tumbled hills. On clear days they betook themselves to the upper air, where they hung motionless for hours. That year there were vultures among them, distinguished by the white patches under the wings. All their offensiveness notwithstanding, they have a stately flight. They must also have what pass for good qualities among themselves, for they are social, not to say clannish.

The Scavengers

It is a very squalid tragedy,—that of the dying brutes and the scavenger birds. Death by starvation is slow. The heavy-headed, rack-boned cattle totter in the fruitless trails; they stand for long, patient intervals; they lie down and do not rise. There is fear in their eyes when they are first stricken, but afterward only intolerable weariness. I suppose the dumb creatures know nearly as much of death as do their betters, who have only the more imagination. Their even-breathing submission after the first agony is their tribute to its inevitableness. It needs a nice discrimination to say which of the basket-ribbed cattle is likest to afford the next meal, but the scavengers make few mistakes. One stoops to the quarry and the flock follows.

Cattle once down may be days in dying. They stretch out their necks along the ground, and roll up their slow eyes at longer intervals. The buzzards have all the time, and no beak is dropped or talon struck until the breath is wholly passed. It is doubtless the economy of nature to have the scavengers by to clean up the carrion, but a wolf at the throat would be a shorter agony than the long stalking and sometime perchings of these loathsome watchers. Suppose now it were a man in this long-drawn, hungrily spied upon distress! When Timmie O'Shea was lost on Armogosa Flats for three days without water, Long Tom Basset found him, not by any trail, but by making straight away for the points where he saw buzzards stooping. He could hear the beat of their wings, Tom said, and trod on their shadows, but O'Shea was past recalling what he thought about things after the second day. My friend Ewan told me, among other things, when he came back from San Juan Hill, that not all the carnage of battle turned his bowels as the sight of slant black wings rising flockwise before the burial squad.

There are three kinds of noises buzzards make,—it is impossible to call them notes,—raucous and elemental. There is a short croak of alarm, and the same syllable in a modified tone to serve all the purposes of ordinary conversation. The old birds make a kind of throaty chuckling to their young, but if they have any love song I have not heard it. The young yawp in the nest a little, with more breath than noise. It is seldom one finds a buzzard's nest, seldom that grown-ups find a nest of any sort; it is only children to whom these things happen by right. But by making a business of it one may come upon them in wide, quiet cañons, or on the lookouts of

35

lonely, table-topped mountains, three or four together, in the tops of stubby trees or on rotten cliffs well open to the sky.

It is probable that the buzzard is gregarious, but it seems unlikely from the small number of young noted at any time that every female incubates each year. The young birds are easily distinguished by their size when feeding, and high up in air by the worn primaries of the older birds. It is when the young go out of the nest on their first foraging that the parents, full of crass and simple pride, make their indescribable chucklings of gobbling, gluttonous delight. The little ones would be amusing as they tug and tussle, if one could forget what it is they feed upon.

One never comes any nearer to the vulture's nest or nestlings than hearsay. They keep to the southerly Sierras, and are bold enough, it seems, to do killing on their own account when no carrion is at hand. They dog the shepherd from camp to camp, the hunter home from the hill, and will even carry away offal from under his hand.

The vulture merits respect for his bigness and for his bandit airs, but he is a sombre bird, with none of the buzzard's frank satisfaction in his offensiveness.

The least objectionable of the inland scavengers is the raven, frequenter of the desert ranges, the same called locally "carrion crow." He is handsomer and has such an air. He is nice in his habits and is said to have likable traits. A tame one in a Shoshone camp was the butt of much sport and enjoyed it. He could all but talk and was another with the children, but an arrant thief. The raven will eat most things that come his way,—eggs and young of ground-nesting birds, seeds even, lizards and grasshoppers, which he catches cleverly; and whatever he is about, let a coyote trot never so softly by, the raven flaps up and after; for whatever the coyote can pull down or nose out is meat also for the carrion crow.

And never a coyote comes out of his lair for killing, in the country of the carrion crows, but looks up first to see where they may be gathering. It is a sufficient occupation for a windy morning, on the lineless, level mesa, to watch the pair of them eying each other furtively, with a tolerable assumption of unconcern, but no doubt with a certain amount of good understanding about it. Once at Red Rock, in a year of green pasture, which is a bad time for the scavengers, we saw two buzzards, five ravens, and a coyote feeding on the same carrion, and only the coyote seemed ashamed of the company.

Probably we never fully credit the interdependence of wild creatures, and their cognizance of the affairs of their own kind. When the five coyotes that range the Tejon from Pasteria to Tunawai planned a relay race to bring down an antelope strayed from the band, beside myself to watch, an eagle swung down from Mt. Pinos, buzzards materialized out of invisible ether, and hawks came trooping like small boys to a street fight. Rabbits sat up in the chaparral and cocked their ears, feeling themselves quite safe for the once as the hunt swung near them. Nothing happens in the deep wood that the blue jays are not all agog to tell. The hawk follows

the badger, the coyote the carrion crow, and from their aerial stations the buzzards watch each other. What would be worth knowing is how much of their neighbor's affairs the new generations learn for themselves, and how much they are taught of their elders.

So wide is the range of the scavengers that it is never safe to say, eyewitness to the contrary, that there are few or many in such a place. Where the carrion is, there will the buzzards be gathered together, and in three days' journey you will not sight another one. The way up from Mojave to Red Butte is all desertness, affording no pasture and scarcely a rill of water. In a year of little rain in the south, flocks and herds were driven to the number of thousands along this road to the perennial pastures of the high ranges. It is a long, slow trail, ankle deep in bitter dust that gets up in the slow wind and moves along the backs of the crawling cattle. In the worst of times one in three will pine and fall out by the way. In the defiles of Red Rock, the sheep piled up a stinking lane; it was the sun smiting by day. To these shambles came buzzards, vultures, and coyotes from all the country round, so that on the Tejon, the Ceriso, and the Little Antelope there were not scavengers enough to keep the country clean. All that summer the dead mummified in the open or dropped slowly back to earth in the quagmires of the bitter springs. Meanwhile from Red Rock to Coyote Holes, and from Coyote Holes to Haiwai the scavengers gorged and gorged.

The coyote is not a scavenger by choice, preferring his own kill, but being on the whole a lazy dog, is apt to fall into carrion eating because it is easier. The red fox and bobcat, a little pressed by hunger, will eat of any other animals' kill, but will not ordinarily touch what dies of itself, and are exceedingly shy of food that has been man-handled.

Very clean and handsome, quite belying his relationship in appearance, is Clark's crow, that scavenger and plunderer of mountain camps. It is permissible to call him by his common name, "Camp Robber:" he has earned it. Not content with refuse, he pecks open meal sacks, filches whole potatoes, is a gormand for bacon, drills holes in packing cases, and is daunted by nothing short of tin. All the while he does not neglect to vituperate the chipmunks and sparrows that whisk off crumbs of comfort from under the camper's feet. The Camp Robber's gray coat, black and

white barred wings, and slender bill, with certain tricks of perching, accuse him of attempts to pass himself off among woodpeckers; but his behavior is all crow. He frequents the higher pine belts, and has a noisy strident call like a jay's, and how clean he and the frisk-tailed chipmunks keep the camp! No crumb or paring or bit of eggshell goes amiss.

High as the camp may be, so it is not above timberline, it is not too high for the coyote, the bobcat, or the wolf. It is the complaint of the ordinary camper that the woods are too still, depleted of wild life. But what dead body of wild thing, or neglected game untouched by its kind, do you find? And put out offal away from camp over night, and look next day at the foot tracks where it lay.

Man is a great blunderer going about in the woods, and there is no other except the bear makes so much noise. Being so well warned beforehand, it is a very stupid animal, or a very bold one, that cannot keep safely hid. The cunningest hunter is hunted in turn, and what he leaves of his kill is meat for some other. That is the economy of nature, but with it all there is not sufficient account taken of the works of man. There is no scavenger that eats tin cans, and no wild thing leaves a like disfigurement on the forest floor.

THE POCKET HUNTER

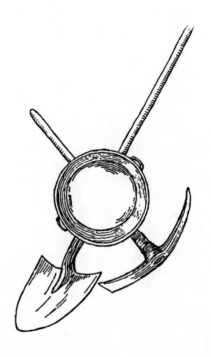

THE POCKET HUNTER

I REMEMBER VERY WELL when I first met him. Walking in the evening glow to spy the marriages of the white gilias, I sniffed the unmistakable odor of burning sage. It is a smell that carries far and indicates usually the nearness of a campoodie, but on the level mesa nothing taller showed than Diana's sage. Over the tops of it, beginning to dusk under a young white moon, trailed a wavering ghost of smoke, and at the end of it I came upon the Pocket Hunter making a dry camp in the friendly scrub. He sat tailorwise in the sand, with his coffee-pot on the coals, his supper ready to hand in the frying-pan, and himself in a mood for talk. His pack burros in hobbles strayed off to hunt for a wetter mouthful than the sage afforded, and gave him no concern.

We came upon him often after that, threading the windy passes, or by water-holes in the desert hills, and got to know much of his way of life. He was a small, bowed man, with a face and manner and speech of no character at all, as if he had that faculty of small hunted things of taking on the protective color of his surroundings. His clothes were of no fashion that I could remember, except that they bore liberal markings of pot black, and he had a curious fashion of going about with his mouth open, which gave him a vacant look until you came near enough to perceive him busy about an endless hummed, wordless tune. He traveled far and took a long time to it, but the simplicity of his kitchen arrangements was elemental. A pot for beans, a coffee-pot, a frying-pan, a tin to mix bread in——he fed the

burros in this when there was need—with these he had been half round our western world and back. He explained to me very early in our acquaintance what was good to take to the hills for food: nothing sticky, for that "dirtied the pots;" nothing with "juice" to it, for that would not pack to advantage; and nothing likely to ferment. He used no gun, but he would set snares by the water-holes for quail and doves, and in the trout country he carried a line. Burros he kept, one or two according to his pack, for this chief excellence, that they would eat potato parings and firewood. He had owned a horse in the foothill country, but when he came to the desert with no forage but mesquite, he found himself under the necessity of picking the beans from the briers, a labor that drove him to the use of pack animals to whom thorns were a relish.

I suppose no man becomes a pocket hunter by first intention. He must be born with the faculty, and along comes the occasion, like the tap on the test tube that induces crystallization. My friend had been several things of no moment until he struck a thousand-dollar pocket in the Lee District and came into his vocation. A pocket, you must know, is a small body of rich ore occurring by itself, or in a vein of poorer stuff. Nearly every mineral ledge contains such, if only one has the luck to hit upon them without too much labor. The sensible thing for a man to do who has found a good pocket is to buy himself into business and keep away from the hills. The logical thing is to set out looking for another one. My friend the Pocket Hunter had been looking twenty years. His working outfit was a shovel, a pick, a gold pan which he kept cleaner than his plate, and a pocket magnifier. When he came to a watercourse he would pan out the gravel of its bed for "colors," and under the glass determine if they had come from far or near, and so spying he would work up the stream until he found where the drift of the gold-bearing outcrop fanned out into the creek; then up the side of the cañon till he came to the proper vein. I think he said the best indication of small pockets was an iron stain, but I could never get the run of miner's talk enough to feel instructed for pocket hunting. He had another method in the waterless hills, where he would work in and out of blind gullies and all windings of the manifold strata that appeared not to have cooled since they had been heaved up. His itinerary began with the east slope of the Sierras of the Snows, where that range swings across to meet the coast hills, and all up that slope to the Truckee River country, where the long cold forbade his progress north. Then he worked back down one or another of the nearly parallel ranges that lie out desertward, and so down to the sink of the Mojave River, burrowing to oblivion in the sand,—a big mysterious land, a lonely, inhospitable land, beautiful, terrible. But he came to no harm in it; the land tolerated him as it might a gopher or a badger. Of all its inhabitants it has the least concern for man.

There are many strange sorts of humans bred in a mining country, each sort despising the queernesses of the other, but of them all I found the Pocket Hunter most acceptable for his clean, companionable talk. There

was more color to his reminiscences than the faded sandy old miners "kyoteing," that is, tunneling like a coyote (kyote in the vernacular) in the core of a lonesome hill. Such a one has found, perhaps, a body of tolerable ore in a poor lead,—remember that I can never be depended on to get the terms right,—and followed it into the heart of country rock to no profit, hoping, burrowing, and hoping. These men go harmlessly mad in time, believing themselves just behind the wall of fortune—most likable and simple men, for whom it is well to do any kindly thing that occurs to you except lend them money. I have known "grub stakers" too, those persuasive sinners to whom you make allowances of flour and pork and coffee in consideration of the ledges they are about to find; but none of these proved so much worth while as the Pocket Hunter. He wanted nothing of you and maintained a cheerful preference for his own way of life. It was an excellent way if you had the constitution for it. The Pocket Hunter had gotten to that point where he knew no bad weather, and all places were equally happy so long as they were out of doors. I do not know just how long it takes to become saturated with the elements so that one takes no account of them. Myself can never get past the glow and exhilaration of a storm, the wrestle of long dust-heavy winds, the play of live thunder on the rocks, nor past the keen fret of fatigue when the storm outlasts physical endurance. But prospectors and Indians get a kind of a weather shell that remains on the body until death.

The Pocket Hunter had seen destruction by the violence of nature and the violence of men, and felt himself in the grip of an All-wisdom that killed men or spared them as seemed for their good; but of death by sickness he knew nothing except that he believed he should never suffer it. He had been in Grape-vine Cañon the year of storms that changed the whole front of the mountain. All day he had come down under the wing of the storm, hoping to win past it, but finding it traveling with him until night. It kept on after that, he supposed, a steady downpour, but could not with certainty say, being securely deep in sleep. But the weather instinct does not sleep. In the night the heavens behind the hill dissolved in rain, and the roar of the storm was borne in and mixed with his dreaming, so that it moved him, still asleep, to get up and out of the path of it. What finally woke him was the crash of pine logs as they went down before the unbridled flood, and the swirl of foam that lashed him where he clung in the tangle of scrub while the wall of water went by. It went on against the cabin of Bill Gerry and laid Bill stripped and broken on a sand bar at the mouth of the Grape-vine, seven miles away. There, when the sun was up and the wrath of the rain spent, the Pocket Hunter found and buried him; but he never laid his own escape at any door but the unintelligible favor of the Powers.

The journeyings of the Pocket Hunter led him often into that mysterious country beyond Hot Creek where a hidden force works mischief, mole-like, under the crust of the earth. Whatever agency is at work in that neighborhood, and it is popularly supposed to be the devil, it changes means and direction without time or season. It creeps up whole hillsides with insidious heat, unguessed until one notes the pine woods dying at the top, and having scorched out a good block of timber returns to steam and spout in caked, forgotten crevices of years before. It will break up sometimes blue-hot and bubbling, in the midst of a clear creek, or make a sucking, scalding quicksand at the ford. These outbreaks had the kind of morbid interest for the Pocket Hunter that a house of unsavory reputation has in a respectable neighborhood, but I always found the accounts he brought me more interesting than his explanations, which were compounded of fag ends of miner's talk and superstition. He was a perfect gossip of the woods, this Pocket Hunter, and when I could get him away from "leads" and "strikes" and "contacts," full of fascinating small talk about the ebb and flood of creeks, the piñon crop on Black Mountain, and the wolves of Mesquite Valley. I suppose he never knew how much he depended for the necessary sense of home and companionship on the beasts and trees, meeting and finding them in their wonted places,— the bear that used to come down Pine Creek in the spring, pawing out trout from the shelters of sod banks, the juniper at Lone Tree Spring, and the quail at Paddy Jack's.

There is a place on Waban, south of White Mountain, where flat, wind-tilted cedars make low tents and coves of shade and shelter, where the wild sheep winter in the snow. Woodcutters and prospectors had brought me word of that, but the Pocket Hunter was accessory to the fact. About the opening of winter, when one looks for sudden big storms, he had attempted a crossing by the nearest path, beginning the ascent at noon. It grew cold, the snow came on thick and blinding, and wiped out the trail

in a white smudge; the storm drift blew in and cut off landmarks, the early
dark obscured the rising drifts. According to the Pocket Hunter's account,
he knew where he was, but couldn't exactly say. Three days before he had
been in the west arm of Death Valley on a short water allowance, ankle-
deep in shifty sand; now he was on the rise of Waban, knee-deep in sodden
snow, and in both cases he did the only allowable thing—he walked on.
That is the only thing to do in a snowstorm in any case. It might have been
the creature instinct, which in his way of life had room to grow, that led
him to the cedar shelter; at any rate he found it about four hours after dark,
and heard the heavy breathing of the flock. He said that if he thought at all
at this juncture he must have thought that he had stumbled on a storm-
belated shepherd with his silly sheep; but in fact he took no note of
anything but the warmth of packed fleeces, and snuggled in between them
dead with sleep. If the flock stirred in the night he stirred drowsily to keep
close and let the storm go by. That was all until morning woke him shining
on a white world. Then the very soul of him shook to see the wild sheep of
God stand up about him, nodding their great horns beneath the cedar roof,
looking out on the wonder of the snow. They had moved a little away from
him with the coming of the light, but paid him no more heed. The light
broadened and the white pavilions of the snow swam in the heavenly
blueness of the sea from which they rose. The cloud drift scattered and
broke billowing in the cañons. The leader stamped lightly on the litter to
put the flock in motion, suddenly they took the drifts in those long light
leaps that are nearest to flight, down and away on the slopes of Waban.
Think of that to happen to a Pocket Hunter! But though he had fallen on
many a wished-for hap, he was curiously inapt at getting the truth about
beasts in general. He believed in the venom of toads, and charms for snake
bites, and—for this I could never forgive him—had all the miner's prejudices against my friend the coyote. Thief, sneak, and son of a thief were the
friendliest words he had for this little gray dog of the wilderness.

Of course with so much seeking he came occasionally upon pockets
of more or less value, otherwise he could not have kept up his way of life;
but he had as much luck in missing great ledges as in finding small ones. He
had been all over the Tonopah country, and brought away float without
happening upon anything that gave promise of what that district was to
become in a few years. He claimed to have chipped bits off the very

outcrop of the California Rand, without finding it worth while to bring away, but none of these things put him out of countenance.

It was once in roving weather, when we found him shifting pack on a steep trail, that I observed certain of his belongings done up in green canvas bags, the veritable "green bag" of English novels. It seemed so incongruous a reminder in this untenanted West that I dropped down beside the trail overlooking the vast dim valley, to hear about the green canvas. He had gotten it, he said, in London years before, and that was the first I had known of his having been abroad. It was after one of his "big strikes" that he had made the Grand Tour, and had brought nothing away from it but the green canvas bags, which he conceived would fit his needs, and an ambition. This last was nothing less than to strike it rich and set himself up among the eminently bourgeois of London. It seemed that the

situation of the wealthy English middle class, with just enough gentility above to aspire to, and sufficient smaller fry to bully and patronize, appealed to his imagination, though of course he did not put it so crudely as that.

It was no news to me then, two or three years after, to learn that he had taken ten thousand dollars from an abandoned claim, just the sort of luck to have pleased him, and gone to London to spend it. The land seemed not to miss him any more than it had minded him, but I missed him and could not forget the trick of expecting him in least likely situations. Therefore it was with a pricking sense of the familiar that I followed a twilight trail of smoke, a year or two later, to the swale of a dripping spring, and came upon a man by the fire with a coffee-pot and frying-pan. I was not surprised to find the Pocket Hunter. No man can be stronger than his destiny.

SHOSHONE LAND

IT IS TRUE I have been in Shoshone Land, but before that, long before, I had seen it through the eyes of Winnenaṕ in a rosy mist of reminiscence, and must always see it with a sense of intimacy in the light that never was. Sitting on the golden slope at the campoodie, looking across the Bitter Lake to the purple tops of Mutarango, the medicine-man drew up its happy places one by one, like little blessed islands in a sea of talk. For he was born a Shoshone, was Winnenaṕ; and though his name, his wife, his children, and his tribal relations were of the Paiutes, his thoughts turned homesickly toward Shoshone Land. Once a Shoshone always a Shoshone. Winnenaṕ lived gingerly among the Paiutes and in his heart despised them. But he could speak a tolerable English when he would, and he always would if it were of Shoshone Land.

He had come into the keeping of the Paiutes as a hostage for the long peace which the authority of the whites made interminable, and, though there was now no order in the tribe, nor any power that could have lawfully restrained him, kept on in the old usage, to save his honor and the word of his vanished kin. He had seen his children's children in the borders of the Paiutes, but loved best his own miles of sand and rainbow-painted hills. Professedly he had not seen them since the beginning of his hostage; but every year about the end of the rains and before the strength of the sun had come upon us from the south, the medicine-man went apart on the mountains to gather herbs, and when he came again I knew by the new fortitude of his countenance and the new color of his reminiscences that he had been alone and unspied upon in Shoshone Land.

To reach that country from the campoodie, one goes south and south, within hearing of the lip-lip-lapping of the great tideless lake, and south by east over a high rolling district, miles and miles of sage and nothing else. So one comes to the country of the painted hills,—old red cones of craters, wasteful beds of mineral earths, hot, acrid springs, and steam jets issuing from a leprous soil. After the hills the black rock, after the craters the spewed lava, ash strewn, of incredible thickness, and full of sharp, winding rifts. There are picture writings carved deep in the face of the cliffs to mark the way for those who do not know it. On the very edge of the black rock the earth falls away in a wide sweeping hollow, which is Shoshone Land.

South the land rises in very blue hills, blue because thickly wooded with ceanothus and manzanita, the haunt of deer and the border of the Shoshones. Eastward the land goes very far by broken ranges, narrow valleys of pure desertness, and huge mesas uplifted to the sky-line, east and east, and no man knows the end of it.

It is the country of the bighorn, the wapiti, and the wolf, nesting place of buzzards, land of cloud-nourished trees and wild things that live without drink. Above all, it is the land of the creosote and the mesquite. The mesquite is God's best thought in all this desertness. It grows in the open, is thorny, stocky, close grown, and iron-rooted. Long winds move in the draughty valleys, blown sand fills and fills about the lower branches, piling pyramidal dunes, from the top of which the mesquite twigs flourish greenly. Fifteen or twenty feet under the drift, where it seems no rain could penetrate, the main trunk grows, attaining often a yard's thickness, resistant as oak. In Shoshone Land one digs for large timber; that is in the southerly, sandy exposures. Higher on the table-topped ranges low trees of juniper and piñon stand each apart, rounded and spreading heaps of greenness. Between them, but each to itself in smooth clear spaces, tufts of tall feathered grass.

This is the sense of the desert hills, that there is room enough and time enough. Trees grow to consummate domes; every plant has its perfect work. Noxious weeds such as come up thickly in crowded fields do not flourish in the free spaces. Live long enough with an Indian, and he or the wild things will show you a use for everything that grows in these borders.

The manner of the country makes the usage of life there, and the land will not be lived in except in its own fashion. The Shoshones live like their trees, with great spaces between, and in pairs and in family groups they set up wattled huts by the infrequent springs. More wickiups than two make a very great number. Their shelters are lightly built, for they travel much and far, following where deer feed and seeds ripen, but they are not more lonely than other creatures that inhabit there.

The year's round is somewhat in this fashion. After the piñon harvest the clans foregather on a warm southward slope for the annual adjustment of tribal difficulties and the medicine dance, for marriage and mourning and vengeance, and the exchange of serviceable information; if, for example, the deer have shifted their feeding ground, if the wild sheep have come back to Waban, or certain springs run full or dry. Here the Shoshones winter flockwise, weaving baskets and hunting big game driven down from the country of the deep snow. And this brief intercourse is all the use they have of their kind, for now there are no wars, and many of their ancient crafts have fallen into disuse. The solitariness of the life breeds in the men, as in the plants, a certain well-roundedness and sufficiency to its own ends. Any Shoshone family has in itself the man-seed, power to multiply and replenish, potentialities for food and clothing and shelter, for healing and beautifying.

When the rain is over and gone they are stirred by the instinct of those that journeyed eastward from Eden, and go up each with his mate and young brood, like birds to old nesting places. The beginning of spring in Shoshone Land—oh the soft wonder of it!—is a mistiness as of incense smoke, a veil of greenness over the whitish stubby shrubs, a web of color on the silver sanded soil. No counting covers the multitude of rayed blossoms that break suddenly underfoot in the brief season of the winter rains, with silky furred or prickly viscid foliage, or no foliage at all. They are morning and evening bloomers chiefly, and strong seeders. Years of scant rains they lie shut and safe in the winnowed sands, so that some species appear to be extinct. Years of long storms they break so thickly into bloom that no horse treads without crushing them. These years the gullies of the hills are rank with fern and a great tangle of climbing vines.

Just as the mesa twilights have their vocal note in the love call of the burrowing owl, so the desert spring is voiced by the mourning doves. Welcome and sweet they sound in the smoky mornings before breeding time, and where they frequent in any great numbers water is confidently looked for. Still by the springs one finds the cunning brush shelters from which the Shoshones shot arrows at them when the doves came to drink.

Now as to these same Shoshones there are some who claim that they have no right to the name, which belongs to a more northerly tribe; but that is the word they will be called by, and there is no greater offense than to call an Indian out of his name. According to their traditions and all proper evidence, they were a great people occupying far north and east of their present bounds, driven thence by the Paiutes. Between the two tribes is the residuum of old hostilities.

Winnenaṕ, whose memory ran to the time when the boundary of the Paiute country was a dead-line to Shoshones, told me once how himself and another lad, in an unforgotten spring, discovered a nesting place of buzzards a bit of a way beyond the borders. And they two burned to rob those nests. Oh, for no purpose at all except as boys rob nests immemorially, for the fun of it, to have and handle and show to other lads as an exceeding treasure, and afterwards discard. So, not quite meaning to, but breathless with daring, they crept up a gully, across a sage brush flat and through a waste of boulders, to the rugged pines where their sharp eyes had made out the buzzards settling.

The medicine-man told me, always with a quaking relish at this point, that while they, grown bold by success, were still in the tree, they sighted a Paiute hunting party crossing between them and their own land. That was mid-morning, and all day on into the dark the boys crept and crawled and slid, from boulder to bush, and bush to boulder, in cactus scrub and on naked sand, always in a sweat of fear, until the dust caked in the nostrils and the breath sobbed in the body, around and away many a mile until they came to their own land again. And all the time Winnenaṕ carried those buzzard's eggs in the slack of his single buckskin garment! Young Shoshones are like young quail, knowing without teaching about feeding and hiding, and learning what civilized children never learn, to be still and to keep on being still, at the first hint of danger or strangeness.

As for food, that appears to be chiefly a matter of being willing.

Desert Indians all eat chuck-wallas, big black and white lizards that have delicate white flesh savored like chicken. Both the Shoshones and the coyotes are fond of the flesh of *Gopherus agassizii*, the turtle that by feeding on buds, going without drink, and burrowing in the sand through the winter, contrives to live a known period of twenty-five years. It seems that most seeds are foodful in the arid regions, most berries edible, and many shrubs good for firewood with the sap in them. The mesquite bean, whether the screw or straight pod, pounded to a meal, boiled to a kind of mush, and dried in cakes, sulphur-colored and needing an axe to cut it, is an excellent food for long journeys. Fermented in water with wild honey and the honeycomb, it makes a pleasant, mildly intoxicating drink.

Next to spring, the best time to visit Shoshone Land is when the deer-star hangs low and white like a torch over the morning hills. Go up past Winnedumah and down Saline and up again to the rim of Mesquite Valley. Take no tent, but if you will, have an Indian build you a wickiup, willows planted in a circle, drawn over to an arch, and bound cunningly with withes, all the leaves on, and chinks to count the stars through. But there was never any but Winnenaṕ who could tell and make it worth telling about Shoshone Land.

And Winnenaṕ will not any more. He died, as do most medicine-men of the Paiutes.

Where the lot falls when the campoodie chooses a medicine-man there it rests. It is an honor a man seldom seeks but must wear, an honor with a condition. When three patients die under his ministrations, the medicine-man must yield his life and his office. Wounds do not count; broken bones and bullet holes the Indian can understand, but measles, pneumonia, and smallpox are witchcraft. Winnenap´ was medicine-man for fifteen years. Besides considerable skill in healing herbs, he used his prerogatives cunningly. It is permitted the medicine-man to decline the case when the patient has had treatment from any other, say the white doctor, whom many of the younger generation consult. Or, if before having seen the patient, he can definitely refer his disorder to some supernatural cause wholly out of the medicine-man's jurisdiction, say to the spite of an evil spirit going about in the form of a coyote, and states the case convincingly, he may avoid the penalty. But this must not be pushed too far. All else failing, he can hide. Winnenaṕ did this the time of the measles epidemic.

Returning from his yearly herb gathering, he heard of it at Black Rock, and turning aside, he was not to be found, nor did he return to his own place until the disease had spent itself, and half the children of the campoodie were in their shallow graves with beads sprinkled over them.

It is possible the tale of Winnenap's patients had not been strictly kept. There had not been a medicine-man killed in the valley for twelve years, and for that the perpetrators had been severely punished by the whites. The winter of the Big Snow an epidemic of pneumonia carried off the Indians with scarcely a warning; from the lake northward to the lava flats they died in the sweat-houses, and under the hands of the medicine-man. Even the drugs of the white physician had no power.

After two weeks of this plague the Paiutes drew to council to consider the remissness of their medicine-men. They were sore with grief and afraid for themselves; as a result of the council, one in every campoodie was sentenced to the ancient penalty. But schooling and native shrewdness had raised up in the younger men an unfaith in old usages, so judgment halted between sentence and execution. At Three Pines the government teacher brought out influential whites to threaten and cajole the stubborn tribes. At Tunawai the conservatives sent into Nevada for that pacific old humbug, Johnson Sides, most notable of Paiute orators, to harangue his people. Citizens of the towns turned out with food and comforts, and so after a season the trouble passed.

But here at Maverick there was no school, no oratory, and no alleviation. One third of the campoodie died, and the rest killed the medicine-men. Winnenap expected it, and for days walked and sat a little apart from his family that he might meet it as became a Shoshone, no doubt suffering the agony of dread deferred. When finally three men came and sat at his fire without greeting he knew his time. He turned a little from them, dropped his chin upon his knees, and looked out over Shoshone Land, breathing evenly. The women went into the wickiup and covered their heads with their blankets.

So much has the Indian lost of savageness by merely desisting from killing, that the executioners braved themselves to their work by drinking and a show of quarrelsomeness. In the end a sharp hatchet-stroke discharged the duty of the campoodie. Afterward his women buried him, and a warm wind coming out of the south, the force of the disease was broken, and even they acquiesced in the wisdom of the tribe. That summer they told me all except the names of the Three.

Since it appears that we make our own heaven here, no doubt we shall have a hand in the heaven of hereafter; and I know what Winnenap's will be like: worth going to if one has leave to live in it according to his liking. It will be tawny gold underfoot, walled up with jacinth and jasper, ribbed with chalcedony, and yet no hymn-book heaven, but the free air and free spaces of Shoshone Land.

JIMVILLE—A BRET HARTE TOWN

JIMVILLE—A BRET HARTE TOWN

WHEN MR. HARTE FOUND himself with a fresh palette and his particular local color fading from the West, he did what he considered the only safe thing, and carried his young impression away to be worked out untroubled by any newer fact. He should have gone to Jimville. There he would have found cast up on the ore-ribbed hills the bleached timbers of more tales, and better ones.

You could not think of Jimville as anything more than a survival, like the herb-eating, bony-cased old tortoise that pokes cheerfully about those borders some thousands of years beyond his proper epoch. Not that Jimville is old, but it has an atmosphere favorable to the type of a half century back, if not "forty-niners," of that breed. It is said of Jimville that getting away from it is such a piece of work that it encourages permanence in the population; the fact is that most have been drawn there by some real likeness or liking. Not however that I would deny the difficulty of getting into or out of that cove of reminder, I who have made the journey so many times at great pains of a poor body. Any way you go at it, Jimville is about three days from anywhere in particular. North or south, after the railroad there is a stage journey of such interminable monotony as induces forgetfulness of all previous states of existence.

The road to Jimville is the happy hunting ground of old stage-coaches bought up from superseded routes the West over, rocking, lumbering, wide vehicles far gone in the odor of romance, coaches that

Vasquez has held up, from whose high seats express messengers have shot or been shot as their luck held. This is to comfort you when the driver stops to rummage for wire to mend a failing bolt. There is enough of this sort of thing to quite prepare you to believe what the driver insists, namely, that all that country and Jimville are held together by wire.

First on the way to Jimville you cross a lonely open land, with a hint in the sky of things going on under the horizon, a palpitant, white, hot land where the wheels gird at the sand and the midday heaven shuts it in breathlessly like a tent. So in still weather; and when the wind blows there is occupation enough for the passengers, shifting seats to hold down the windward side of the wagging coach. This is a mere trifle. The Jimville stage is built for five passengers, but when you have seven, with four trunks, several parcels, three sacks of grain, the mail and express, you begin to understand that proverb about the road which has been reported to you. In time you learn to engage the high seat beside the driver, where you get good air and the best company. Beyond the desert rise the lava flats, scoriæ strewn; sharp-cutting walls of narrow cañons; league-wide, frozen puddles of black rock, intolerable and forbidding. Beyond the lava the mouths that spewed it out, ragged-lipped, ruined craters shouldering to the cloud-line, mostly of red earth, as red as a red heifer. These have some comforting of shrubs and grass. You get the very spirit of the meaning of that country when you see Little Pete feeding his sheep in the red, choked maw of an old vent,—a kind of silly pastoral gentleness that glozes over an elemental violence. Beyond the craters rise worn, auriferous hills of a quiet sort, tumbled together; a valley full of mists; whitish green scrub; and bright, small, panting lizards; then Jimville.

The town looks to have spilled out of Squaw Gulch, and that, in fact, is the sequence of its growth. It began around the Bully Boy and Theresa group of mines midway up Squaw Gulch, spreading down to the smelter at the mouth of the ravine. The freight wagons dumped their loads as near to the mill as the slope allowed, and Jimville grew in between. Above the Gulch begins a pine wood with sparsely grown thickets of lilac, azalea, and odorous blossoming shrubs.

Squaw Gulch is a very sharp, steep, ragged-walled ravine, and that part of Jimville which is built in it has only one street,—in summer paved with bone-white cobbles, in the wet months a frothy yellow flood. All between the ore dumps and solitary small cabins, pieced out with tin cans and packing cases, run footpaths drawing down to the Silver Dollar saloon. When Jimville was having the time of its life the Silver Dollar had those same coins let into the bar top for a border, but the proprietor pried them out when the glory departed. There are three hundred inhabitants in Jimville and four bars, though you are not to argue anything from that.

Hear now how Jimville came by its name. Jim Calkins discovered the Bully Boy, Jim Baker located the Theresa. When Jim Jenkins opened an eating-house in his tent he chalked up on the flap, "Best meals in Jimville, $1.00," and the name stuck.

There was more human interest in the origin of Squaw Gulch, though it tickled no humor. It was Dimmick's squaw from Aurora way. If Dimmick had been anything except New Englander he would have called her a mahala, but that would not have bettered his behavior. Dimmick made a strike, went East, and the squaw who had been to him as his wife took to drink. That was the bald way of stating it in the Aurora country. The milk of human kindness, like some wine, must not be uncorked too much in speech lest it lose savor. This is what they did. The woman would have returned to her own people, being far gone with child, but the drink worked her bane. By the river of this ravine her pains overtook her. There Jim Calkins, prospecting, found her dying with a three days' babe nozzling at her breast. Jim heartened her for the end, buried her, and walked back to Poso, eighteen miles, the child poking in the folds of his denim shirt with small mewing noises, and won support for it from the rough-handed folks of that place. Then he came back to Squaw Gulch, so named from that day, and discovered the Bully Boy. Jim humbly regarded this piece of luck as interposed for his reward, and I for one believed him. If it had been in mediæval times you would have had a legend or a ballad. Bret Harte would have given you a tale. You see in me a mere recorder, for I know what is best for you; you shall blow out this bubble from your own breath.

You could never get into any proper relation to Jimville unless you could slough off and swallow your acquired prejudices as a lizard does his skin. Once wanting some womanly attentions, the stage-driver assured me I might have them at the Nine-Mile House from the lady barkeeper. The phrase tickled all my after-dinner-coffee sense of humor into an anticipation of Poker Flat. The stage-driver proved himself really right, though you are not to suppose from this that Jimville had no conventions and no caste. They work out these things in the personal equation largely. Almost every latitude of behavior is allowed a good fellow, one no liar, a free spender, and a backer of his friends' quarrels. You are respected in as much ground as you can shoot over, in as many pretensions as you can make good.

That probably explains Mr. Fanshawe, the gentlemanly faro dealer of those parts, built for the rôle of Oakhurst, going white-shirted and frock-coated in a community of overalls; and persuading you that whatever shifts and tricks of the game were laid to his deal, he could not practice them on a person of your penetration. But he does. By his own account and the evidence of his manners he had been bred for a clergyman, and he certainly has gifts for the part. You find him always in possession of your point of view, and with an evident though not obtrusive desire to stand well with you. For an account of his killings, for his way with women and the way of women with him, I refer you to Brown of Calaveras and some others of that stripe. His improprieties had a certain sanction of long standing not accorded to the gay ladies who wore Mr. Fanshawe's favors. There were perhaps too many of them. On the whole, the point of the moral distinctions of Jimville appears to be a point of honor, with an absence of humorous appreciation that strangers mistake for dullness. At Jimville they see behavior as history and judge it by facts, untroubled by invention

and the dramatic sense. You glimpse a crude equity in their dealings with Wilkins, who had shot a man at Lone Tree, fairly, in an open quarrel. Rumor of it reached Jimville before Jimville saw him; in fact, he came into the Silver Dollar when we were holding a church fair and bought a pink silk pincushion. I have often wondered what became of it. Some of us shook hands with him, not because we did not know, but because we had not been officially notified, and there were those present who knew how it was themselves. When the sheriff arrived Wilkins had moved on, and Jimville organized a posse and brought him back, because the sheriff was a Jimville man and we had to stand by him.

I said we had the church fair at the Silver Dollar. We had most things there, dances, town meetings, and the kinetoscope exhibition of the Passion Play. The Silver Dollar had been built when the borders of Jimville spread from Minton to the red hill the Defiance twisted through. "Side-Winder" Smith scrubbed the floor for us and moved the bar to the backroom. The fair was designed for the support of the circuit rider who preached to the few that would hear, and buried us all in turn. He was the symbol of Jimville's respectability, although he was of a sect that held dancing among the cardinal sins. The management took no chances on offending the minister; at 11.30 they tendered him the receipts of the evening in the chairman's hat, as a delicate intimation that the fair was closed. The company filed out of the front door and around to the back. Then the dance began formally with no feelings hurt. These were the sort of courtesies, common enough in Jimville, that brought tears of delicate inner laughter.

There were others besides Mr. Fanshawe who had walked out of Mr. Harte's demesne to Jimville and wore names that smacked of the soil,— "Alkali Bill," "Pike" Wilson, "Three Finger," and "Mono Jim;" fierce, shy, profane, sun-dried derelicts of the windy hills, who each owned, or had owned, a mine and was wishful to own one again. They laid up on the worn benches of the Silver Dollar or the Same Old Luck like beached vessels, and their talk ran on endlessly of "strike" and "contact" and "mother lode," and worked around to fights and hold-ups, villainy, haunts, and the hoodoo of the Minietta, told austerely without imagination.

Do not suppose I am going to repeat it all; you who want these things written up from the point of view of people who do not do them every day would get no savor in their speech.

Says Three Finger, relating the history of the Mariposa, "I took it off'n Tom Beatty, cheap, after his brother Bill was shot."

Says Jim Jenkins,"What was the matter of him?"

"Who? Bill? Abe Johnson shot him; he was fooling around Johnson's wife, an' Tom sold me the mine dirt cheap."

"Why didn't he work it himself?"

"Him? Oh, he was laying for Abe and calculated to have to leave the country pretty quick."

"Huh!" says Jim Jenkins, and the tale flows smoothly on.

Yearly the spring fret floats the loose population of Jimville out into the desolate waste hot lands, guiding by the peaks and a few rarely touched water-holes, always, always with the golden hope. They develop prospects and grow rich, develop others and grow poor but never embittered. Say the hills, It is all one, there is gold enough, time enough, and men enough to come after you. And at Jimville they understand the language of the hills.

Jimville does not know a great deal about the crust of the earth, it prefers a "hunch." That is an intimation from the gods that if you go over a brown back of the hills, by a dripping spring, up Coso way, you will find what is worth while. I have never heard that the failure of any particular hunch disproved the principle. Somehow the rawness of the land favors the sense of personal relation to the supernatural. There is not much intervention of crops, cities, clothes, and manners between you and the organizing forces to cut off communication. All this begets in Jimville a state that passes explanation unless you will accept an explanation that passes belief. Along with killing and drunkenness, coveting of women, charity, simplicity, there is a certain indifference, blankness, emptiness if you will, of all vaporings, no bubbling of the pot,—it wants the German to coin a word for that,—no bread-envy, no brother-fervor. Western writers have not sensed it yet; they smack the savor of lawlessness too much upon their tongues, but you have these to witness it is not mean-spiritedness. It is pure Greek in that it represents the courage to sheer off what is not worth while. Beyond that it endures without sniveling, renounces without self-pity, fears no death, rates itself not too great in the scheme of things; so do beasts, so did St. Jerome in the desert, so also in the elder day did gods. Life, its performance, cessation, is no new thing to gape and wonder at.

Here you have the repose of the perfectly accepted instinct which includes passion and death in its perquisites. I suppose that the end of all our hammering and yawping will be something like the point of view of Jimville. The only difference will be in the decorations.

MY NEIGHBOR'S FIELD

MY NEIGHBOR'S FIELD

IT IS ONE of those places God must have meant for a field from all time, lying very level at the foot of the slope that crowds up against Kearsarge, falling slightly toward the town. North and south it is fenced by low old glacial ridges, boulder strewn and untenable. Eastward it butts on orchard closes and the village gardens, brimming over into them by wild brier and creeping grass. The village street, with its double row of unlike houses, breaks off abruptly at the edge of the field in a footpath that goes up the streamside, beyond it, to the source of waters.

The field is not greatly esteemed of the town, not being put to the plough nor affording firewood, but breeding all manner of wild seeds that go down in the irrigating ditches to come up as weeds in the gardens and grass plots. But when I had no more than seen it in the charm of its spring smiling, I knew I should have no peace until I had bought ground and built me a house beside it, with a little wicket to go in and out at all hours, as afterward came about.

Edswick, Roeder, Connor, and Ruffin owned the field before it fell to my neighbor. But before that the Paiutes, mesne lords of the soil, made a campoodie by the rill of Pine Creek; and after, contesting the soil with them, cattle-men, who found its foodful pastures greatly to their advantage; and bands of blethering flocks shepherded by wild, hairy men of little speech, who attested their rights to the feeding ground with their long staves upon each other's skulls. Edswick homesteaded the field about the time the wild tide of mining life was roaring and rioting up Kearsarge, and where the village now stands built a stone hut, with loopholes to make good his claim against cattle-men or Indians. But Edswick died and Roeder became master of the field. Roeder owned cattle on a thousand hills, and made it a recruiting ground for his bellowing herds before beginning the long drive to market across a shifty desert. He kept the field fifteen years, and afterward falling into difficulties, put it out as security against certain sums. Connor, who held the securities, was cleverer than Roeder and not so busy. The money fell due the winter of the Big Snow, when all the trails were forty feet under drifts, and Roeder was away in San Francisco selling his cattle. At the set time Connor took the law by the forelock and was adjudged possession of the field. Eighteen days later Roeder arrived on snowshoes, both feet frozen, and the money in his pack. In the long suit at law ensuing, the field fell to Ruffin, that clever one-armed lawyer with the tongue to wile a bird out of the bush, Connor's counsel, and was sold by him to my neighbor, whom from envying his possession I call Naboth.

Curiously, all this human occupancy of greed and mischief left no mark on the field, but the Indians did, and the unthinking sheep. Round its corners children pick up chipped arrow points of obsidian, scattered through it are kitchen middens and pits of old sweathouses. By the south corner, where the campoodie stood, is a single shrub of "hoopee" (*Lycium andersonii*), maintaining itself hardly among alien shrubs, and near by, three low rakish trees of hackberry, so far from home that no prying of mine has been able to find another in any cañon east or west. But the berries of both were food for the Paiutes, eagerly sought and traded for as far south as Shoshone Land. By the fork of the creek where the shepherds camp is a single clump of mesquite of the variety called "screw bean." The seed must have shaken there from some sheep's coat, for this is not the habitat of mesquite, and except for other single shrubs at sheep camps, none grows freely for a hundred and fifty miles south or east.

Naboth has put a fence about the best of the field, but neither the Indians nor the shepherds can quite forego it. They make camp and build their wattled huts about the borders of it, and no doubt they have some sense of home in its familiar aspect.

As I have said, it is a low-lying field, between the mesa and the town, with no hillocks in it, but a gentle swale where the waste water of the creek goes down to certain farms, and the hackberry-trees, of which the tallest might be three times the height of a man, are the tallest things in it. A mile up from the water gate that turns the creek into supply pipes for the town, begins a row of long-leaved pines, threading the watercourse to the foot of Kearsarge. These are the pines that puzzle the local botanist, not easily determined, and unrelated to other conifers of the Sierra slope; the same pines of which the Indians relate a legend mixed of brotherliness and the retribution of God. Once the pines possessed the field, as the worn stumps of them along the streamside show, and it would seem their secret purpose to regain their old footing. Now and then some seedling escapes the devastating sheep a rod or two down-stream. Since I came to live by the field one of these has tiptoed above the gully of the creek, beckoning the procession from the hills, as if in fact they would make back toward that skyward-pointing finger of granite on the opposite range, from which, according to the legend, when they were bad Indians and it a great chief, they ran away. This year the summer floods brought the round, brown, fruitful cones to my very door, and I look, if I live long enough, to see them come up greenly in my neighbor's field.

It is interesting to watch this retaking of old ground by the wild plants, banished by human use. Since Naboth drew his fence about the field and restricted it to a few wild-eyed steers, halting between the hills and the shambles, many old habitués of the field have come back to their haunts. The willow and brown birch, long ago cut off by the Indians for wattles, have come back to the streamside, slender and virginal in their spring greenness, and leaving long stretches of the brown water open to the sky. In stony places where no grass grows, wild olives sprawl; close-twigged, blue-gray patches in winter, more translucent greenish gold in spring than any aureole. Along with willow and birch and brier, the clematis, that shyest plant of water borders, slips down season by season to within a hundred yards of the village street. Convinced after three years that it would come no nearer, we spent time fruitlessly pulling up roots to plant in the garden. All this while, when no coaxing or care prevailed upon any transplanted slip to grow, one was coming up silently outside the fence near the wicket, coiling so secretly in the rabbit-brush that its presence was never suspected until it flowered delicately along its twining length. The horehound comes through the fence and under it, shouldering the pickets off the railings; the brier rose mines under the horehound; and no care, though I own I am not a close weeder, keeps the small pale moons of the primrose from rising to the night moth under my apple-trees. The first summer in the new place, a clump of cypripediums came up by the irrigating ditch at the bottom of the lawn. But the clematis will not come inside, nor the wild almond.

I have forgotten to find out, though I meant to, whether the wild almond grew in that country where Moses kept the flocks of his father-in-law, but if so one can account for the burning bush. It comes upon one with a flame-burst as of revelation; little hard red buds on leafless twigs, swelling unnoticeably, then one, two, or three strong suns, and from tip to tip one soft fiery glow, whispering with bees as a singing flame. A twig of finger size will be furred to the thickness of one's wrist by pink five-petaled bloom, so close that only the blunt-faced wild bees find their way in it. In this latitude late frosts cut off the hope of fruit too often for the wild almond to multiply greatly, but the spiny, tap-rooted shrubs are resistant to most plant evils.

It is not easy always to be attentive to the maturing of wild fruit. Plants are so unobtrusive in their material processes, and always at the significant moment some other bloom has reached its perfect hour. One can never fix the precise moment when the rosy tint the field has from the wild almond passes into the inspiring blue of lupines. One notices here and there a spike of bloom, and a day later the whole field royal and ruffling lightly to the wind. Part of the charm of the lupine is the continual stir of its plumes to airs not suspected otherwise. Go and stand by any crown of bloom and the tall stalks do but rock a little as for drowsiness, but look off across the field, and on the stillest days there is always a trepidation in the purple patches.

From midsummer until frost the prevailing note of the field is clear gold, passing into the rusty tone of bigelovia going into a decline, a succession of color schemes more admirably managed than the transformation scene at the theatre. Under my window a colony of cleome made a soft web of bloom that drew me every morning for a long still time; and one day I discovered that I was looking into a rare fretwork of fawn and straw colored twigs from which both bloom and leaf had gone, and I could not say if it had been for a matter of weeks or days. The time to plant cucumbers and set out cabbages may be set down in the almanac, but never seed-time nor blossom in Naboth's field.

Certain winged and mailed denizens of the field seem to reach their heyday along with the plants they most affect. In June the leaning towers of the white milkweed are jeweled over with red and gold beetles, climbing dizzily. This is that milkweed from whose stems the Indians flayed fibre to make snares for small game, but what use the beetles put it to except for a displaying ground for their gay coats, I could never discover. The white butterfly crop comes on with the bigelovia bloom, and on warm mornings makes an airy twinkling all across the field. In September young linnets grow out of the rabbit-brush in the night. All the nests discoverable in the neighboring orchards will not account for the numbers of them. Somewhere, by the same secret process by which the field matures a million more seeds than it needs, it is maturing red-hooded linnets for their devouring. All the purlieus of bigelovia and artemisia are noisy with them for a month. Suddenly as they come as suddenly go the fly-by-nights, that pitch and toss on dusky barred wings above the field of summer twilights. Never one of these nighthawks will you see after linnet time, though the hurtle of their wings makes a pleasant sound across the dusk in their season.

For two summers a great red-tailed hawk has visited the field every afternoon between three and four o'clock, swooping and soaring with the airs of a gentleman adventurer. What he finds there is chiefly conjectured,

so secretive are the little people of Naboth's field. Only when leaves fall and the light is low and slant, one sees the long clean flanks of the jackrabbits, leaping like small deer, and of late afternoons little cotton-tails scamper in the runways. But the most one sees of the burrowers, gophers, and mice is the fresh earthwork of their newly opened doors, or the pitiful small shreds the butcher-bird hangs on spiny shrubs.

It is a still field, this of my neighbor's, though so busy, and admirably compounded for variety and pleasantness,—a little sand, a little loam, a grassy plot, a stony rise or two, a full brown stream, a little touch of humanness, a footpath trodden out by moccasins. Naboth expects to make town lots of it and his fortune in one and the same day; but when I take the trail to talk with old Seyavi at the campoodie, it occurs to me that though the field may serve a good turn in those days it will hardly be happier. No, certainly not happier.

THE MESA TRAIL

THE MESA TRAIL

THE MESA TRAIL begins in the campoodie at the corner of Naboth's field, though one may drop into it from the wood road toward the cañon, or from any of the cattle paths that go up along the streamside; a clean, pale, smooth-trodden way between spiny shrubs, comfortably wide for a horse or an Indian. It begins, I say, at the campoodie, and goes on toward the twilight hills and the borders of Shoshone Land. It strikes diagonally across the foot of the hill-slope from the field until it reaches the larkspur level, and holds south along the front of Oppapago, having the high ranges to the right and the foothills and the great Bitter Lake below it on the left. The mesa holds very level here, cut across at intervals by the deep washes of dwindling streams, and its treeless spaces uncramp the soul.

Mesa trails were meant to be traveled on horseback, at the jigging coyote trot that only western-bred horses learn successfully. A foot-pace carries one too slowly past the units in a decorative scheme that is on a scale with the country round for bigness. It takes days' journeys to give a note of variety to the country of the social shrubs. These chiefly clothe the benches and eastern foot-slopes of the Sierras,—great spreads of artemisia, *coleogyne,* and spinosa, suffering no other woody stemmed thing in their purlieus; this by election apparently, with no elbowing; and the several shrubs have each their clientèle of flowering herbs. It would be worth knowing how much the devastating sheep have had to do with driving the tender plants to the shelter of the prickle-bushes. It might have begun earlier, in the time Seyavi of the campoodie tells of, when antelope ran on the mesa like sheep for numbers, but scarcely any foot-high herb rears itself except from the midst of some stout twigged shrub; larkspur in the *coleogyne,* and for every spinosa the purpling coils of phacelia. In the shrub shelter, in the season, flock the little stemless things whose blossom time is as short as a marriage song. The larkspurs make the best showing, being tall and sweet, swaying a little above the shrubbery, scattering pollen dust which Navajo brides gather to fill their marriage baskets. This were an easier task than to find two of them of a shade. Larkspurs in the botany are blue, but if you were to slip rein to the stub of some black sage and set about proving it you would be still at it by the hour when the white gilias set their pale disks to the westering sun. This is the gilia the children call "evening snow," and it is no use trying to improve on children's names for wild flowers.

From the height of a horse you look down to clean spaces in a shifty yellow soil, bare to the eye as a newly sanded floor. Then as soon as ever the hill shadows begin to swell out from the sidelong ranges, come little flakes of whiteness fluttering at the edge of the sand. By dusk there are tiny drifts in the lee of every strong shrub, rosy-tipped corollas as riotous in the sliding mesa wind as if they were real flakes shaken out of a cloud, not sprung from the ground on wiry three-inch stems. They keep awake all night, and all the air is heavy and musky sweet because of them.

Farther south on the trail there will be poppies meeting ankle deep, and singly, peacock-painted bubbles of calochortus blown out at the tops of tall stems. But before the season is in tune for the gayer blossoms the best display of color is in the lupin wash. There is always a lupin wash somewhere on a mesa trail,—a broad, shallow, cobble-paved sink of

vanished waters, where the hummocks of *Lupinus ornatus* run a delicate gamut from silvery green of spring to silvery white of winter foliage. They look in fullest leaf, except for color, most like the huddled huts of the campoodie, and the largest of them might be a man's length in diameter. In their season, which is after the gilias are at their best, and before the larkspurs are ripe for pollen gathering, every terminal whorl of the lupin sends up its blossom stalk, not holding any constant blue, but paling and purpling to guide the friendly bee to virginal honey sips, or away from the perfected and depleted flower. The length of the blossom stalk conforms to the rounded contour of the plant, and of these there will be a million moving indescribably in the airy current that flows down the swale of the wash.

There is always a little wind on the mesa, a sliding current of cooler air going down the face of the mountain of its own momentum, but not to disturb the silence of great space. Passing the wide mouths of cañons, one gets the effect of whatever is doing in them, openly or behind a screen of cloud,—thunder of falls, wind in the pine leaves, or rush and roar of rain. The rumor of tumult grows and dies in passing, as from open doors gaping on a village street, but does not impinge on the effect of solitariness. In quiet weather mesa days have no parallel for stillness, but the night silence breaks into certain mellow or poignant notes. Late afternoons the burrowing owls may be seen blinking at the doors of their hummocks with

perhaps four or five elfish nestlings arow, and by twilight begin a soft *whoo-oo-ing,* rounder, sweeter, more incessant in mating time. It is not possible to disassociate the call of the burrowing owl from the late slant light of the mesa. If the fine vibrations which are the golden-violet glow of spring twilights were to tremble into sound, it would be just that mellow double note breaking along the blossom-tops. While the glow holds one sees the thistle-down flights and pouncings after prey, and on into the dark hears their soft *pus-ssh!* clearing out of the trail ahead. Maybe the pin-point shriek of field mouse or kangaroo rat that pricks the wakeful pauses of the night is extorted by these mellow-voiced plunderers, though it is just as like to be the work of the red fox on his twenty-mile constitutional.

Both the red fox and the coyote are free of the night hours, and both killers for the pure love of slaughter. The fox is not great talker, but the coyote goes garrulously through the dark in twenty keys at once, gossip, warning, and abuse. They are light treaders, the split-feet, so that the solitary camper sees their eyes about him in the dark sometimes, and hears the soft intake of breath when no leaf has stirred and no twig snapped underfoot. The coyote is your real lord of the mesa, and so he makes sure you are armed with no long black instrument to spit your teeth into his vitals at a thousand yards, is both bold and curious. Not so bold, however, as the badger and not so much of a curmudgeon. This short-legged meat-eater loves half lights and lowering days, has no friends, no enemies, and disowns his offspring. Very likely if he knew how hawk and crow dog him for dinners, he would resent it. But the badger is not very well contrived for looking up or far to either side. Dull afternoons he may be met nosing a trail hot-foot to the home of ground rat or squirrel, and is with difficulty persuaded to give the right of way. The badger is a pot-hunter and no sportsman. Once at the hill, he dives for the central chamber, his sharp-clawed, splayey feet splashing up the sand like a bather in the surf. He is a swift trailer, but not so swift or secretive but some small sailing hawk or lazy crow, perhaps one or two of each, has spied upon him and come drifting down the wind to the killing.

No burrower is so unwise as not to have several exits from his dwelling under protecting shrubs. When the badger goes down, as many of the furry people as are not caught napping come up by the back doors, and the hawks make short work of them. I suspect that the crows get nothing but the gratification of curiosity and the pickings of some secret store of seeds unearthed by the badger. Once the excavation begins they walk about expectantly, but the little gray hawks beat slow circles about the doors of exit, and are wiser in their generation, though they do not look it.

There are always solitary hawks sailing above the mesa, and where some blue tower of silence lifts out of the neighboring range, an eagle hanging dizzily, and always buzzards high up in the thin, translucent air making a merry-go-round. Between the coyote and the birds of carrion the mesa is kept clear of miserable dead.

The wind, too, is a besom over the treeless spaces, whisking new sand over the litter of the scant-leaved shrubs, and the little doorways of the burrowers are as trim as city fronts. It takes man to leave unsightly scars on the face of the earth. Here on the mesa the abandoned campoodies of the Paiutes are spots of desolation long after the wattles of the huts have warped in the brush heaps. The campoodies are near the watercourses, but never in the swale of the stream. The Paiute seeks rising ground, depending on air and sun for purification of his dwelling, and when it becomes wholly untenable, moves.

A campoodie at noontime, when there is no smoke rising and no stir of life, resembles nothing so much as a collection of prodigious wasps' nests. The huts are squat and brown and chimneyless, facing east, and the inhabitants have the faculty of quail for making themselves scarce in the underbrush at the approach of strangers. But they are really not often at home during midday, only the blind and incompetent left to keep the camp. These are working hours, and all across the mesa one sees the women whisking seeds of *chía* into their spoon-shaped baskets, these

88

emptied again into the huge conical carriers, supported on the shoulders by a leather band about the forehead.

Mornings and late afternoons one meets the men singly and afoot on unguessable errands, or riding shaggy, browbeaten ponies, with game slung across the saddle-bows. This might be deer or even antelope, rabbits, or, very far south towards Shoshone Land, lizards.

There are myriads of lizards on the mesa, little gray darts, or larger salmon-sided ones that may be found swallowing their skins in the safety of a prickle-bush in early spring. Now and then a palm's breadth of the trail gathers itself together and scurries off with a little rustle under the brush, to resolve itself into sand again. This is pure witchcraft. If you succeed in catching it in transit, it loses its power and becomes a flat, horned, toad-like creature, horrid looking and harmless, of the color of the soil; and the curio dealer will give you two bits for it, to stuff.

Men have their season on the mesa as much as plants and four-footed things, and one is not like to meet them out of their time. For example, at the time of *rodeos,* which is perhaps April, one meets free riding vaqueros who need no trails and can find cattle where to the layman no cattle exist. As early as February bands of sheep work up from the south to the high Sierra pastures. It appears that shepherds have not changed more than sheep in the process of time. The shy hairy men who heard the tractile flocks might be, except for some added clothing, the very brethren of David. Of necessity they are hardy, simple livers, superstitious, fearful, given to seeing visions, and almost without speech. It needs the bustle of shearings and copious libations of sour, weak wine to restore the human faculty. Petite Pete, who works a circuit up from the Ceriso to Red Butte and around by way of Salt Flats, passes year by year on the mesa trail, his thick hairy chest thrown open to all weathers, twirling his long staff, and dealing brotherly with his dogs, who are possibly as intelligent, certainly handsomer.

A flock's journey is seven miles, ten if pasture fails, in a windless blur of dust, feeding as it goes, and resting at noons. Such hours Pete weaves a little screen of twigs between his head and the sun—the rest of him is as impervious as one of his own sheep—and sleeps while his dogs have the flocks upon their consciences. At night, wherever he may be, there Pete camps, and fortunate the trail-weary traveler who falls in with him. When the fire kindles and savory meat seethes in the pot, when there is a drowsy blether from the flock, and far down the mesa the twilight twinkle of shepherd fires, when there is a hint of blossom underfoot and a heavenly whiteness on the hills, one harks back without effort to Judæa and the Nativity. But one feels by day anything but good will to note the shorn shrubs and cropped blossom-tops. So many seasons' effort, so many suns and rains to make a pound of wool! And then there is the loss of ground-inhabiting birds that must fail from the mesa when few herbs ripen seed.

Out West, the west of the mesas and the unpatented hills, there is more sky than any place in the world. It does not sit flatly on the rim of earth, but begins somewhere out in the space in which the earth is poised, hollows more, and is full of clean winey winds. There are some odors, too, that get into the blood. There is the spring smell of sage that is the warning that sap is beginning to work in a soil that looks to have none of the juices of life in it; it is the sort of smell that sets one thinking what a long furrow the plough would turn up here, the sort of smell that is the beginning of new leafage, is best at the plant's best, and leaves a pungent trail where wild cattle crop. There is the smell of sage at sundown, burning sage from campoodies and sheep camps, that travels on the thin blue wraiths of smoke; the kind of smell that gets into the hair and garments, is not much liked except upon long acquaintance, and every Paiute and shepherd smells of it indubitably. There is the palpable smell of the bitter dust that comes up from the alkali flats at the end of the dry seasons, and the smell of rain from the wide-mouthed cañons. And last the smell of the salt grass country, which is the beginning of other things that are the end of the mesa trail.

THE BASKET MAKER

THE BASKET MAKER

"A MAN," SAYS SEYAVI of the campoodie, "must have a woman, but a woman who has a child will do very well."

That was perhaps why, when she lost her mate in the dying struggle of his race, she never took another, but set her wit to fend for herself and her young son. No doubt she was often put to it in the beginning to find food for them both. The Paiutes had made their last stand at the border of the Bitter Lake; battle-driven they died in its waters, and the land filled with cattle-men and adventurers for gold: this while Seyavi and the boy lay up in the caverns of the Black Rock and ate tule roots and fresh-water clams that they dug out of the slough bottoms with their toes. In the interim, while the tribes swallowed their defeat, and before the rumor of war died out, they must have come very near to the bare core of things. That was the time Seyavi learned the sufficiency of mother wit, and how much more easily one can do without a man than might at first be supposed.

To understand the fashion of any life, one must know the land it is lived in and the procession of the year. This valley is a narrow one, a mere trough between hills, a draught for storms, hardly a crow's flight from the sharp Sierras of the Snows to the curled, red and ochre, uncomforted, bare ribs of Waban. Midway of the groove runs a burrowing, dull river, nearly a hundred miles from where it cuts the lava flats of the north to its widening in a thick, tideless pool of a lake. Hereabouts the ranges have no foothills, but rise up steeply from the bench lands above the river. Down from the Sierras, for the east ranges have almost no rain, pour glancing white floods toward the lowest land, and all beside them lie the campoodies, brown wattled brush heaps, looking east.

In the river are mussels, and reeds that have edible white roots, and in the soddy meadows tubers of joint grass; all these at their best in the spring. On the slope the summer growth affords seeds; up the steep the one-leafed pines, an oily nut. That was really all they could depend upon, and that only at the mercy of the little gods of frost and rain. For the rest it was cunning against cunning, caution against skill, against quacking hordes of wild-fowl in the tulares, against pronghorn and bighorn and deer. You can guess, however, that all this warring of rifles and bowstrings, this influx of overlording whites, had made game wilder and hunters fearful of being hunted. You can surmise also, for it was a crude time and the land was raw, that the women became in turn the game of the conquerors.

There used to be in the Little Antelope a she dog, stray or outcast, that had a litter in some forsaken lair, and ranged and foraged for them, slinking savage and afraid, remembering and mistrusting humankind, wistful, lean, and sufficient for her young. I have thought Seyavi might have had days like that, and have had perfect leave to think, since she will not talk of it. Paiutes have the art of reducing life to its lowest ebb and yet saving it alive on grasshoppers, lizards, and strange herbs; and that time

must have left no shift untried. It lasted long enough for Seyavi to have evolved the philosophy of life which I have set down at the beginning. She had gone beyond learning to do for her son, and learned to believe it worth while.

In our kind of society, when a woman ceases to alter the fashion of her hair, you guess that she has passed the crisis of her experience. If she goes on crimping and uncrimping with the changing mode, it is safe to suppose she has never come up against anything too big for her. The Indian woman gets nearly the same personal note in the pattern of her baskets. Not that she does not make all kinds, carriers, water-bottles, and cradles,—these are kitchen ware,—but her works of art are all of the same piece. Seyavi made flaring, flat-bottomed bowls, cooking pots really, when cooking was done by dropping hot stones into water-tight food baskets, and for decoration a design in colored bark of the procession of plumed crests of the valley quail. In this pattern she had made cooking pots in the golden spring of her wedding year, when the quail went up two and two to their resting places about the foot of Oppapago. In this fashion she made them when, after pillage, it was possible to reinstate the housewifely crafts. Quail ran then in the Black Rock by hundreds,—so you will still find them in fortunate years,—and in the famine time the women cut their long hair to make snares when the flocks came morning and evening to the springs.

Seyavi made baskets for love and sold them for money, in a generation that preferred iron pots for utility. Every Indian woman is an artist,—sees, feels, creates, but does not philosophize about her processes. Seyavi's bowls are wonders of technical precision, inside and out, the palm finds no fault with them, but the subtlest appeal is in the sense that warns us of humanness in the way the design spreads into the flare of the bowl. There used to be an Indian woman at Olancha who made bottle-neck trinket baskets in the rattlesnake pattern, and could accommodate the design to the swelling bowl and flat shoulder of the basket without sensible disproportion, and so cleverly that you might own one a year without thinking how it was done; but Seyavi's baskets had a touch beyond cleverness. The weaver and the warp lived next to the earth and were saturated with the same elements. Twice a year, in the time of white butterflies and again when young quail ran neck and neck in the chaparral, Seyavi cut willows for basketry by the creek where it wound toward the river against the sun and sucking winds. It never quite reached the river except in far-between times of summer flood, but it always tried, and the willows encouraged it as much as they could. You nearly always found them a little farther down than the trickle of eager water. The Paiute fashion of counting time appeals to me more than any other calendar. They have no stamp of heathen gods nor great ones, nor any succession of moons as have red men of the East and North, but count forward and back by the progress of the season; the time of *taboose,* before the trout begin to leap, the end of the piñon harvest, about the beginning of deep snows. So they get nearer the sense of the season, which runs early or late according as the rains are forward or delayed. But whenever Seyavi cut willows for baskets was always a golden time, and the soul of the weather went into the wood. If you had ever owned one of Seyavi's golden russet cooking bowls with the pattern of plumed quail, you would understand all this without saying anything.

Before Seyavi made baskets for the satisfaction of desire,——for that is a house-bred theory of art that makes anything more of it,——she danced and dressed her hair. In those days, when the spring was at flood and the blood pricked to the mating fever, the maids chose their flowers, wreathed themselves, and danced in the twilights, young desire crying out to young desire. They sang what the heart prompted, what the flower expressed, what boded in the mating weather.

"And what flower did you wear, Seyavi?"

"I, ah,——the white flower of twining (clematis), on my body and my hair, and so I sang:——

> "I am the white flower of twining,
> Little white flower by the river,
> Oh, flower that twines close by the river;
> Oh, trembling flower!
> So trembles the maiden heart."

So sang Seyavi of the campoodie before she made baskets, and in her later days laid her arms upon her knees and laughed in them at the recollection. But it was not often she would say so much, never understanding the keen hunger I had for bits of lore and the "fool talk" of her people. She had fed her young son with meadowlarks' tongues, to make him quick of speech;

but in late years was loath to admit it, though she had come through the period of unfaith in the lore of the clan with a fine appreciation of its beauty and significance.

"What good will your dead get, Seyavi, of the baskets you burn?" said I, coveting them for my own collection.

Thus Seyavi, "As much good as yours of the flowers you strew."

Oppapago looks on Waban, and Waban on Coso and the Bitter Lake, and the campoodie looks on these three; and more, it sees the beginning of winds along the foot of Coso, the gathering of clouds behind the high ridges, the spring flush, the soft spread of wild almond bloom on the mesa. These first, you understand, are the Paiute's walls, the other his furnishings. Not the wattled hut is his home, but the land, the winds, the hill front, the stream. These he cannot duplicate at any furbisher's shop as you who live within doors, who, if your purse allows, may have the same home at Sitka and Samarcand. So you see how it is that the homesickness of an Indian is often unto death, since he gets no relief from it; neither wind nor weed nor sky-line, nor any aspect of the hills of a strange land sufficiently like his own. So it was when the government reached out for the Paiutes, they gathered into the Northern Reservation only such poor tribes as could devise no other end of their affairs. Here, all along the river, and south to Shoshone Land, live the clans who owned the earth, fallen into the deplorable condition of hangers-on. Yet you hear them laughing at the hour when they draw in to the campoodie after labor, when there is a smell of meat and the steam of the cooking pots goes up against the sun. Then the children lie with their toes in the ashes to hear tales; then they are merry, and have the joys of repletion and the nearness of their kind. They have their hills, and though jostled are sufficiently free to get some fortitude for what will come. For now you shall hear of the end of the basket maker.

In her best days Seyavi was most like Deborah, deep bosomed, broad in the hips, quick in counsel, slow of speech, esteemed of her people. This was that Seyavi who reared a man by her own hand, her own wit, and none other. When the townspeople began to take note of her—and it was some years after the war before there began to be any towns—she was then in the quick maturity of primitive women; but when I knew her she seemed already old. Indian women do not often live to great age, though they look incredibly steeped in years. They have the wit to win sustenance from the raw material of life without intervention, but they have not the sleek look of the women whom the social organization conspires to nourish. Seyavi had somehow squeezed out of her daily round a spiritual ichor that kept the skill in her knotted fingers long after the accustomed time, but that also failed. By all counts she would have been about sixty years old when it came her turn to sit in the dust on the sunny side of the wickiup, with little strength left for anything but looking. And in time she paid the toll of the smoky huts and became blind. This is a thing so long expected by the Paiutes that when it comes they find it neither bitter nor sweet, but tolerable because common. There were three other blind women in the campoodie, withered fruit on a bough, but they had memory and speech. By noon of the sun there were never any left in the campoodie but these or some mother of weanlings, and they sat to keep the ashes warm upon the hearth. If it were cold, they burrowed in the blankets of the hut; if it were warm, they followed the shadow of the wickiup around. Stir much out of their places they hardly dared, since one might not help another; but they called, in high, old cracked voices, gossip and reminder across the ash heaps.

The Basket Maker

Then, if they have your speech or you theirs, and have an hour to spare, there are things to be learned of life not set down in any books, folk tales, famine tales, love and long-suffering and desire, but no whimpering. Now and then one or another of the blind keepers of the camp will come across to where you sit gossiping, tapping her way among the kitchen middens, guided by your voice that carries far in the clearness and stillness of mesa afternoons. But suppose you find Seyavi retired into the privacy of her blanket, you will get nothing for that day. There is no other privacy possible in a campoodie. All the processes of life are carried on out of doors or behind the thin, twig-woven walls of the wickiup, and laughter is the only corrective for behavior. Very early the Indian learns to possess his countenance in impassivity, to cover his head with his blanket. Something to wrap around him is as necessary to the Paiute as to you your closet to pray in.

So in her blanket Seyavi, sometime basket maker, sits by the unlit hearths of her tribe and digests her life, nourishing her spirit against the time of the spirit's need, for she knows in fact quite as much of these matters as you who have a larger hope, though she has none but the certainty that having borne herself courageously to this end she will not be reborn a coyote.

THE STREETS OF THE MOUNTAINS

THE STREETS OF THE MOUNTAINS

ALL STREETS OF the mountains lead to the citadel; steep or slow they go up to the core of the hills. Any trail that goes otherwhere must dip and cross, sidle and take chances. Rifts of the hills open into each other, and the high meadows are often wide enough to be called valleys by courtesy; but one keeps this distinction in mind,—valleys are the sunken places of the earth, cañons are scored out by the glacier ploughs of God. They have a better name in the Rockies for these hill-fenced open glades of pleas-antness; they call them parks. Here and there in the hill country one comes upon blind gullies fronted by high stony barriers. These head also for the heart of the mountains; their distinction is that they never get anywhere.

All mountain streets have streams to thread them, or deep grooves where a stream might run. You would do well to avoid that range uncom-forted by singing floods. You will find it forsaken of most things but beauty and madness and death and God. Many such lie east and north away from the mid Sierras, and quicken the imagination with the sense of purposes not revealed, but the ordinary traveler brings nothing away from them but an intolerable thirst.

The river cañons of the Sierras of the Snows are better worth while than most Broadways, though the choice of them is like the choice of streets, not very well determined by their names. There is always an amount of local history to be read in the names of mountain highways where one touches the successive waves of occupation of discovery, as in the old villages where the neighborhoods are not built but grow. Here you have the Spanish Californian in *Cero Gordo* and piñon; Symmes and Shepherd, pioneers both; Tunawai, probably Shoshone; Oak Creek, Kearsarge,—easy to fix the date of that christening,—Tinpah, Paiute that; Mist Cañon and Paddy Jack's. The streets of the west Sierras sloping toward the San Joaquin are long and winding, but from the east, my country, a day's ride carries one to the lake regions. The next day reaches the passes of the high divide, but whether one gets passage depends a little on how many have gone that road before, and much on one's own powers. The passes are steep and windy ridges, though not the highest. By two and three thousand feet the snow-caps overtop them. It is even possible to wind through the Sierras without having passed above timber-line, but one misses a great exhilaration.

The shape of a new mountain is roughly pyramidal, running out into long shark-finned ridges that interfere and merge into other thunder-splintered sierras. You get the saw-tooth effect from a distance, but the near-by granite bulk glitters with the terrible keen polish of old glacial ages. I say terrible; so it seems. When those glossy domes swim into the alpenglow, wet after rain, you conceive how long and imperturbable are the purposes of God.

Never believe what you are told, that midsummer is the best time to go up the streets of the mountain—well—perhaps for the merely idle or sportsmanly or scientific; but for seeing and understanding, the best time is when you have the longest leave to stay. And here is a hint if you would attempt the stateliest approaches; travel light, and as much as possible live off the land. Mulligatawny soup and tinned lobster will not bring you the favor of the woodlanders.

Every cañon commends itself for some particular pleasantness; this for pines, another for trout, one for pure bleak beauty of granite buttresses, one for its far-flung irised falls; and as I say, though some are easier going, leads each to the cloud shouldering citadel. First, near the cañon mouth you get the low-heading full-branched, one-leaf pines. That is the sort of tree to know at sight, for the globose, resin-dripping cones have palatable, nourishing kernels, the main harvest of the Paiutes. That perhaps accounts for their growing accommodatingly below the limit of deep snows, grouped sombrely on the valleyward slopes. The real procession of the pines begins in the rifts with the long-leafed *Pinus jeffreyi*, sighing its soul away upon the wind. And it ought not to sigh in such good company. Here begins the manzanita, adjusting its tortuous stiff stems to the sharp waste of boulders, its pale olive leaves twisting edgewise to the sleek, ruddy, chestnut stems; begins also the meadowsweet, burnished laurel, and the million unregarded trumpets of the coral-red pentstemon. Wild life is likely to be busiest about the lower pine borders. One looks in hollow trees and hiving rocks for wild honey. The drone of bees, the chatter of jays, the hurry and stir of squirrels, is incessant; the air is odorous and hot. The roar of the stream fills up the morning and evening intervals, and at night the deer feed in the buckthorn thickets. It is worth watching the year round in the purlieus of the long-leafed pines. One month or another you get sight or trail of most roving mountain dwellers as they follow the limit of forbidding snows, and more bloom than you can properly appreciate.

Whatever goes up or comes down the streets of the mountains, water has the right of way; it takes the lowest ground and the shortest passage. Where the rifts are narrow, and some of the Sierra cañons are not a stone's throw from wall to wall, the best trail for foot or horse winds considerably above the watercourses; but in a country of cone-bearers there is usually a good strip of swardy sod along the cañon floor. Pine woods, the short-leafed Balfour and Murryana of the high Sierras, are sombre, rooted in the litter of a thousand years, hushed, and corrective to the spirit. The trail passes insensibly into them from the black pines and a thin belt of firs. You look back as you rise, and strain for glimpses of the tawny valley, blue glints of the Bitter Lake, and tender cloud films on the farther ranges. For such pictures the pine branches make a noble frame. Presently they close in wholly; they draw mysteriously near, covering your tracks, giving up the trail indifferently, or with a secret grudge. You get a kind of impatience with their locked ranks, until you come out lastly on some high, windy dome and see what they are about. They troop thickly up the open ways, river banks, and brook borders; up open swales of dribbling springs; swarm over old moraines; circle the peaty swamps and part and meet about clean still lakes; scale the stony gullies; tormented, bowed, persisting to the door of the storm chambers, tall priests to pray for rain. The spring winds lift clouds of pollen dust, finer than frankincense, and trail it out over high altars, staining the snow. No doubt they understand this work better than we; in fact they know no other. "Come," say the churches of the valleys, after a season of dry years, "let us pray for rain." They would do better to plant more trees.

It is a pity we have let the gift of lyric improvisation die out. Sitting islanded on some gray peak above the encompassing wood, the soul is lifted up to sing the Iliad of the pines. They have no voice but the wind, and no sound of them rises up to the high places. But the waters, the evidences of their power, that go down the steep and stony ways, the outlets of ice-bordered pools, the young rivers swaying with the force of their running, they sing and shout and trumpet at the falls, and the noise of it far outreaches the forest spires. You see from these conning towers how they call and find each other in the slender gorges; how they fumble in the meadows, needing the sheer nearing walls to give them countenance and show the way; and how the pine woods are made glad by them.

Nothing else in the streets of the mountains gives such a sense of pageantry as the conifers; other trees, if they are any, are home dwellers, like the tender fluttered, sisterhood of quaking asp. They grow in clumps by spring borders, and all their stems have a permanent curve toward the down slope, as you may also see in hillside pines, where they have borne the weight of sagging drifts.

Well up from the valley, at the confluence of cañons, are delectable summer meadows. Fireweed flames about them against the gray boulders; streams are open, go smoothly about the glacier slips and make deep bluish pools for trout. Pines raise statelier shafts and give themselves room to grow,—gentians, shinleaf, and little grass of Parnassus in their golden checkered shadows; the meadow is white with violets and all outdoors keeps the clock. For example, when the ripples at the ford of the creek raise a clear half tone,—sign that the snow water has come down from the heated high ridges,—it is time to light the evening fire. When it drops off a note—but you will not know it except the Douglas squirrel tells you with his high, fluty chirrup from the pines' aerial gloom—sign that some star watcher has caught the first far glint of the nearing sun. Whitney cries it from his vantage tower; it flashes from Oppapago to the front of William-son; LeConte speeds it to the westering peaks. The high rills wake and run, the birds begin. But down three thousand feet in the cañon, where you stir the fire under the cooking pot, it will not be day for an hour. It goes on, the play of light across the high places, rosy, purpling, tender, glint and glow, thunder and windy flood, like the grave, exulting talk of elders above a merry game.

Who shall say what another will find most to his liking in the streets of the mountains. As for me, once set above the country of the silver firs, I must go on until I find white columbine. Around the amphitheatres of the lake regions and above them to the limit of perennial drifts they gather flock-wise in splintered rock wastes. The crowds of them, the airy spread of sepals, the pale purity of the petal spurs, the quivering swing of bloom, obsesses the sense. One must learn to spare a little of the pang of inexpressible beauty, not to spend all one's purse in one shop. There is always another year, and another.

Lingering on in the alpine regions until the first full snow, which is often before the cessation of bloom, one goes down in good company. First snows are soft and clogging and make laborious paths. Then it is the roving inhabitants range down to the edge of the wood, below the limit of early storms. Early winter and early spring one may have sight or track or deer and bear and bighorn, cougar and bobcat, about the thickets of buckthorn on open slopes between the black pines. But when the ice crust is firm above the twenty foot drifts, they range far and forage where they will. Often in midwinter will come, now and then, a long fall of soft snow piling three or four feet above the ice crust, and work a real hardship for the

dwellers of these streets. When such a storm portends the weather-wise blacktail will go down across the valley and up to the pastures of Waban where no more snow falls than suffices to nourish the sparsely growing pines. But the bighorn, the wild sheep, able to bear the bitterest storms with no signs of stress, cannot cope with the loose shifty snow. Never such a storm goes over the mountains that the Indians do not catch them floundering belly deep among the lower rifts. I have a pair of horns, inconceivably heavy, that were borne as late as a year ago by a very monarch of the flock whom death overtook at the mouth of Oak Creek after a week of wet snow. He met it as a king should, with no vain effort or trembling, and it was wholly kind to take him so with four of his following rather than that the night prowlers should find him.

There is always more life abroad in the winter hills than one looks to find, and much more in evidence than in summer weather. Light feet of hare that make no print on the forest litter leave a wondrously plain track in the snow. We used to look and look at the beginning of winter for the birds to come down from the pine lands; looked in the orchard and stubble; looked north and south on the mesa for their migratory passing, and wondered that they never came. Busy little grosbeaks picked about the kitchen doors, and woodpeckers tapped the eaves of the farm buildings, but we saw hardly any other of the frequenters of the summer cañons. After a while when we grew bold to tempt the snow borders we found them in the street of the mountains. In the thick pine woods where the overlapping boughs hung with snow-wreaths make wind-proof shelter tents, in a very community of dwelling, winter the bird-folk who get their living from the persisting cones and the larvæ harboring bark. Ground inhabiting species seek the dim snow chambers of the chaparral. Consider how it must be in a hill-slope overgrown with stout-twigged, partly evergreen shrubs, more than man high, and as thick as a hedge. Not all the cañon's sifting of snow can fill the intricate spaces of the hill tangles. Here and there an overhanging rock, or a stiff arch of buckthorn, makes an opening to communicating rooms and runways deep under the snow.

The light filtering through the snow walls is blue and ghostly, but serves to show seeds of shrubs and grass, and berries, and the wind-built walls are warm against the wind. It seems that live plants, especially if they are evergreen and growing, give off heat; the snow wall melts earliest from within and hollows to thinness before there is a hint of spring in the air. But you think of these things afterward. Up in the street it has the effect of being done consciously; the buckthorns lean to each other and the drift to them, the little birds run in and out of their appointed ways with the greatest cheerfulness. They give almost no tokens of distress, and even if the winter tries them too much you are not to pity them. You of the house habit can hardly understand the sense of the hills. No doubt the labor of being comfortable gives you an exaggerated opinion of yourself, an exaggerated pain to be set aside. Whether the wild things understand it or not they adapt themselves to its processes with the greater ease. The business that goes on in the street of the mountain is tremendous, world-formative. Here go birds, squirrels, and red deer, children crying small wares and playing in the street, but they do not obstruct its affairs. Summer is their holiday; "Come now," says the lord of the street, "I have need of a great work and no more playing."

But they are left borders and breathing-space out of pure kindness. They are not pushed out except by the exigencies of the nobler plan which they accept with a dignity the rest of us have not yet learned.

WATER BORDERS

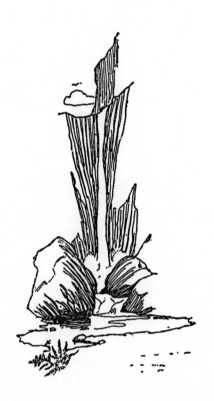

WATER BORDERS

I LIKE THAT NAME the Indians give to the mountain of Lone Pine, and find it pertinent to my subject,—Oppapago, The Weeper. It sits eastward and solitary from the lordliest ranks of the Sierras, and above a range of little, old, blunt hills, and has a bowed, grave aspect as of some woman you might have known, looking out across the grassy barrows of her dead. From twin gray lakes under its noble brow stream down incessant white and tumbling waters. "Mahala all time cry," said Winnenaṕ, drawing furrows in his rugged, wrinkled cheeks.

The origin of mountain streams is like the origin of tears, patent to the understanding but mysterious to the sense. They are always at it, but one so seldom catches them in the act. Here in the valley there is no cessation of waters even in the season when the niggard frost gives them scant leave to run. They make the most of their midday hour, and tinkle all night thinly under the ice. An ear laid to the snow catches a muffled hint of their eternal busyness fifteen or twenty feet under the cañon drifts, and long before any appreciable spring thaw, the sagging edges of the snow bridges mark out the place of their running. One who ventures to look for it finds the immediate source of the spring freshets—all the hill fronts furrowed with the reek of melting drifts, all the gravelly flats in a swirl of waters. But later, in June or July, when the camping season begins, there runs the stream away full and singing, with no visible reinforcement other than an icy trickle from some high, belated clot of snow. Oftenest the stream drops bodily from the bleak bowl of some alpine lake; sometimes breaks out of a hillside as a spring where the ear can trace it under the rubble of loose stones to the neighborhood of some blind pool. But that leaves the lakes to be accounted for.

The lake is the eye of the mountain, jade green, placid, unwinking, also unfathomable. Whatever goes on under the high and stony brows is guessed at. It is always a favorite local tradition that one or another of the blind lakes is bottomless. Often they lie in such deep cairns of broken boulders that one never gets quite to them, or gets away unhurt. One such drops below the plunging slope that the Kearsarge trail winds over, perilously, nearing the pass. It lies still and wickedly green in its sharp-lipped cup, and the guides of that region love to tell of the packs and pack animals it has swallowed up.

But the lakes of Oppapago are perhaps not so deep, less green than gray, and better befriended. The ousel haunts them, while still hang about their coasts the thin undercut drifts that never quite leave the high altitudes. In and out of the bluish ice caves he flits and sings, and his singing heard from above is sweet and uncanny like the Nixie's chord. One finds butterflies, too, about these high, sharp regions which might be called desolate, but will not by me who love them. This is above timber-line but not too high for comforting by succulent small herbs and golden tufted grass. A granite mountain does not crumble with alacrity, but once resolved to soil makes the best of it. Every handful of loose gravel not wholly

water leached affords a plant footing, and even in such unpromising surroundings there is a choice of locations. There is never going to be any communism of mountain herbage, their affinities are too sure. Full in the runnels of snow water on gravelly, open spaces in the shadow of a drift, one looks to find buttercups, frozen knee-deep by night, and owning no desire but to ripen their fruit above the icy bath. Soppy little plants of the portulaca and small, fine ferns shiver under the drip of falls and in dribbling crevices. The bleaker the situation, so it is near a stream border, the better the cassiope loves it. Yet I have not found it on the polished glacier slips, but where the country rock cleaves and splinters in the high windy headlands that the wild sheep frequents, hordes and hordes of the white bells swing over matted, mossy foliage. On Oppapago, which is also called Sheep Mountain, one finds not far from the beds of cassiope the ice-worn, stony hollows where the bighorns cradle their young. These are above the wolf's quest and the eagle's wont, and though the heather beds are softer, they are neither so dry nor so warm, and here only the stars go by. No other animal of any pretensions makes a habitat of the alpine regions. Now and then one gets a hint of some small, brown creature, rat or mouse kind, that slips secretly among the rocks; no others adapt themselves to desert-ness of aridity or altitude so readily as these ground inhabiting, graminiv-orous species. If there is an open stream the trout go up the lake as far as the water breeds food for them, but the ousel goes farthest, for pure love of it.

Since no lake can be at the highest point, it is possible to find plant life higher than the water borders; grasses perhaps the highest, gilias, royal blue trusses of polymonium, rosy plats of Sierra primroses. What one has to get used to in flowers at high altitudes is the bleaching of the sun. Hardly do they hold their virgin color for a day, and this early fading before their function is performed gives them a pitiful appearance not according with their hardihood. The color scheme runs along the high ridges from blue to rosy purple, carmine and coral red; along the water borders it is chiefly white and yellow where the mimulus makes a vivid note, running into red when the two schemes meet and mix about the borders of the meadows, at the upper limit of the columbine.

Here is the fashion in which a mountain stream gets down from the perennial pastures of the snow to its proper level and identity as an irri-gating ditch. It slips stilly by the glacier scoured rim of an ice bordered pool, drops over sheer, broken ledges to another pool, gathers itself, plunges headlong on a rocky ripple slope, finds a lake again, reinforced, roars downward to a pothole, foams and bridles, glides a tranquil reach in some still meadow, tumbles into a sharp groove between hill flanks, curdles under the stream tangles, and so arrives at the open country and steadier going. Meadows, little strips of alpine freshness, begin before the timber-line is reached. Here one treads on a carpet of dwarf willows, downy catkins of creditable size and the greatest economy of foliage and stems. No other plant of high altitudes knows its business so well. It hugs the ground, grows roots from stem joints where no roots should be, grows a slender leaf or two and twice as many erect full catkins that rarely, even in that short growing season, fail of fruit. Dipping over banks in the inlets of the creeks, the fortunate find the rosy apples of the miniature manzanita, barely, but always quite sufficiently, borne above the spongy sod. It does not do to be anything but humble in the alpine regions, but not fearful. I have pawed about for hours in the chill sward of meadows where one might properly expect to get one's death, and got no harm from it, except it might be Oliver Twist's complaint. One comes soon after this to shrubby willows, and where willows are trout may be confidently looked for in most Sierra streams. There is no accounting for their distribution; though provident anglers have assisted nature of late, one still comes upon roaring brown waters where trout might very well be, but are not.

The highest limit of conifers—in the middle Sierras, the white bark pine—is not along the water border. They come to it about the level of the heather, but they have no affinity for dampness as the tamarack pines. Scarcely any bird-note breaks the stillness of the timber-line, but chipmunks inhabit here, as may be guessed by the gnawed ruddy cones of the pines, and lowering hours the woodchucks come down to the water. On a little spit of land running into Windy Lake we found one summer the evidence of a tragedy; a pair of sheep's horns not fully grown caught in the crotch of a pine where the living sheep must have lodged them, and the skull bones crumbled away from the weathered horn cases. We hoped it was not too far out of the running of night prowlers to have put a speedy end to the long agony, but we could not be sure. I never liked the spit of Windy Lake again.

It seems that all snow nourished plants count nothing so excellent in their kind as to be forehanded with their bloom, working secretly to that end under the high piled winters. The heathers begin by the lake borders, while little sodden drifts still shelter under their branches. I have seen the tiniest of them (*Kalmia glauca*) blooming, and with well-formed fruit, a foot away from a snowbank from which it could hardly have emerged within a week. Somehow the soul of the heather has entered into the blood of the English-speaking. "And oh! is that heather?" they say; and the most indifferent ends by picking a sprig of it in a hushed, wondering way. One must suppose that the root of their respective races issued from the glacial borders at about the same epoch, and remember their origin.

Among the pines where the slope of the land allows it, the streams run into smooth, brown, trout-abounding rills across open flats that are in reality filled lake basins. These are the displaying grounds of the gentians—blue—blue—eye-blue, perhaps, virtuous and likable flowers. One is not surprised to learn that they have tonic properties. But if your meadow should be outside the forest reserve, and the sheep have been there, you will find little but the shorter, paler *G. newberryii,* and in the matted sods of the little tongues of greenness that lick up among the pines along the watercourses, white, scentless, nearly stemless, alpine violets.

At about the nine thousand foot level and in the summer there will be hosts of rosy-winged dodecatheon, called shooting-stars, outlining the crystal runnels in the sod. Single flowers have often a two-inch spread of petal, and the full, twelve blossomed heads above the slender pedicels have the airy effect of wings.

It is about this level one looks to find the largest lakes with thick ranks of pines bearing down on them, often swamped in the summer floods and paying the inevitable penalty for such encroachment. Here in wet coves of the hills harbors that crowd of bloom that makes the wonder of the Sierra cañons.

They drift under the alternate flicker and gloom of the windy rooms of pines, in gray rock shelters, and by the ooze of blind springs, and their juxtapositions are the best imaginàble. Lilies come up out of fern beds, columbine swings over meadowsweet, white rein-orchids quake in the leaning grass. Open swales, where in wet years may be running water, are plantations of false hellebore (*Veratrum californicum*), tall, branched candelabra of greenish bloom above the sessile, sheathing, boat-shaped leaves, semi-translucent in the sun. A stately plant of the lily family, but why "false?" It is frankly offensive in its character, and its young juices deadly as any hellebore that ever grew.

Like most mountain herbs it has an uncanny haste to bloom. One hears by night, when all the wood is still, the crepitatious rustle of the unfolding leaves and the pushing flower-stalk within, that has open blossoms before it has fairly uncramped from the sheath. It commends itself by a certain exclusiveness of growth, taking enough room and never elbowing; for if the flora of the lake region has a fault it is that there is too much of it. We have more than three hundred species from Kearsarge Cañon alone, and if that does not include them all it is because they were already collected otherwise.

One expects to find lakes down to about nine thousand feet, leading into each other by comparatively open ripple slopes and white cascades. Below the lakes are filled basins that are still spongy swamps, or substantial meadows, as they get down and down.

Here begin the stream tangles. On the east slopes of the middle Sierras the pines, all but an occasional yellow variety, desert the stream borders about the level of the lowest lakes, and the birches and tree-willows begin. The firs hold on almost to the mesa levels,—there are no foothills on this eastern slope,—and whoever has firs misses nothing else. It goes without saying that a tree that can afford to take fifty years to its first fruiting will repay acquaintance. It keeps, too, all that half century, a virginal grace of outline, but having once flowered, begins quietly to put away the things of its youth. Year by year the lower rounds of boughs are shed, leaving no scar; year by year the star-branched minarets approach the sky. A fir-tree loves a water border, loves a long wind in a draughty cañon, loves to spend itself secretly on the inner finishings of its burnished, shapely cones. Broken open in mid-season, the petal-shaped scales show a crimson satin surface, perfect as a rose.

The birch—the brown-bark western birch characteristic of lower stream tangles—is a spoil sport. It grows thickly to choke the stream that feeds it; grudges it the sky and space for angler's rod and fly. The willows do better; painted-cup, cypripedium, and the hollow stalks of span-broad white umbels, find a footing among their stems. But in general the steep plunges, the white swirls, green and tawny pools, the gliding hush of waters between the meadows and the mesas afford little fishing and few flowers.

One looks for these to begin again when once free of the rifted cañon walls; the high note of babble and laughter falls off to the steadier mellow tone of a stream that knows its purpose and reflects the sky.

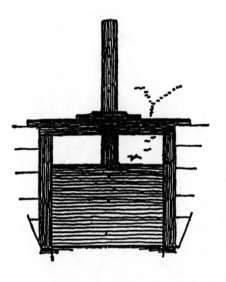

OTHER WATER BORDERS

IT IS THE PROPER DESTINY of every considerable stream in the west to become an irrigating ditch. It would seem the streams are willing. They go as far as they can, or dare, toward the tillable lands in their own boulder fenced gullies—but how much farther in the man-made waterways. It is difficult to come into intimate relations with appropriated waters; like very busy people they have no time to reveal themselves. One needs to have known an irrigating ditch when it was a brook, and to have lived by it, to mark the morning and evening tone of its crooning, rising and falling to the excess of snow water; to have watched far across the valley, south to the Eclipse and north to the Twisted Dyke, the shining wall of the village water gate; to see still blue herons stalking the little glinting weirs across the field.

Perhaps to get into the mood of the waterways one needs to have seen old Amos Judson asquat on the headgate with his gun, guarding his water-right toward the end of a dry summer. Amos owned the half of Tule Creek and the other half pertained to the neighboring Greenfields ranch. Years of a "short water crop," that is, when too little snow fell on the high pine ridges, or, falling, melted too early, Amos held that it took all the water that came down to make his half, and maintained it with a Winchester and a deadly aim. Jesus Montaña, first proprietor of Green-fields,—you can see at once that Judson had the racial advantage,—contesting the right with him, walked into five of Judson's bullets and his eternal possessions on the same occasion. That was the Homeric age of settlement and passed into tradition. Twelve years later one of the Clarks, holding Greenfields, not so very green by now, shot one of the Judsons. Perhaps he hoped that also might become classic, but the jury found for manslaughter. It had the effect of discouraging the Greenfields claim, but Amos used to sit on the headgate just the same, as quaint and lone a figure as the sandhill crane watching for water toads below the Tule drop. Every subsequent owner of Greenfields bought it with Amos in full view. The last of these was Diedrick. Along in August of that year came a week of low water. Judson's ditch failed and he went out with his rifle to learn why. There on the headgate sat Diedrick's frau with a long-handled shovel across her lap and all the water turned into Diedrick's ditch; there she sat knitting through the long sun, and the children brought out her dinner. It was all up with Amos; he was too much of a gentleman to fight a lady— that was the way he expressed it. She was a very large lady, and a long-handled shovel is no mean weapon. The next year Judson and Diedrick put in a modern water gauge and took the summer ebb in equal inches. Some of the water-right difficulties are more squalid than this, some more tragic; but unless you have known them you cannot very well know what the water thinks as it slips past the gardens and in the long slow sweeps of the canal. You get that sense of brooding from the confined and sober floods, not all at once but by degrees, as one might become aware of a middle-aged and serious neighbor who has had that in his life to make him so. It is the repose of the completely accepted instinct.

With the water runs a certain following of thirsty herbs and shrubs. The willows go as far as the stream goes, and a bit farther on the slightest provocation. They will strike root in the leak of a flume, or the dribble of an overfull bank, coaxing the water beyond its appointed bounds. Given a new waterway in a barren land, and in three years the willows have fringed all its miles of banks; three years more and they will touch tops across it. It is perhaps due to the early usurpation of the willows that so little else finds growing-room along the large canals. The birch beginning far back in the cañon tangles is more conservative; it is shy of man haunts and needs to have the permanence of its drink assured. It stops far short of the summer limit of waters, and I have never known it to take up a position on the banks beyond the ploughed lands. There is something almost like pre-meditation in the avoidance of cultivated tracts by certain plants of water borders. The clematis, mingling its foliage secretly with its host, comes down with the stream tangles to the village fences, skips over to corners of little used pasture lands and the plantations that spring up about waste water pools; but never ventures a footing in the trail of spade or plough; will not be persuaded to grow in any garden plot. On the other hand, the horehound, the common European species imported with the colonies, hankers after hedgerows and snug little borders. It is more widely dis-tributed than many native species, and may be always found along the ditches in the village corners, where it is not appreciated. The irrigating

ditch is an impartial distributer. It gathers all the alien weeds that come west in garden and grass seeds and affords them harbor in its banks. There one finds the European mallow (*Malva rotundifolia*) spreading out to the streets with the summer overflow, and every spring a dandelion or two, brought in with the blue grass seed, uncurls in the swardy soil. Farther than either of these have come the lilies that the Chinese coolies cultivate in adjacent mud holes for their foodful bulbs. The *seegoo* establishes itself very readily in swampy borders, and the white blossom spikes among the arrow-pointed leaves are quite as acceptable to the eye as any native species.

In the neighborhood of towns founded by the Spanish Californians, whether this plant is native to the locality or not, one can always find aromatic clumps of *yerba buena,* the "good herb" (*Micromeria douglassii*). The virtue of it as a febrifuge was taught to the mission fathers by the neophytes, and wise old dames of my acquaintance have worked astonishing cures with it and the succulent *yerba mansa.* This last is native to wet meadows and distinguished enough to have a family all to itself.

Where the irrigating ditches are shallow and a little neglected, they choke quickly with watercress that multiplies about the lowest Sierra springs. It is characteristic of the frequenters of water borders near man haunts, that they are chiefly of the sorts that are useful to man, as if they made their services an excuse for the intrusion. The joint-grass of soggy pastures produces edible, nut-flavored tubers, called by the Indians *taboose.* The common reed of the ultramontane marshes (here *Phragmites vulgaris*), a very stately, whispering reed, light and strong for shafts or arrows, affords sweet sap and pith which makes a passable sugar.

It seems the secrets of plant powers and influences yield themselves most readily to primitive peoples, at least one never hears of the knowledge coming from any other source. The Indian never concerns himself, as the botanist and the poet, with the plant's appearances and relations, but with what it can do for him. It can do much, but how do you suppose he finds it out; what instincts or accidents guide him? How does a cat know when to eat catnip? Why do western bred cattle avoid loco weed, and strangers eat it and go mad? One might suppose that in a time of famine the Paiutes digged wild parsnip in meadow corners and died from eating it, and so learned to produce death swiftly and at will. But how did they learn, repenting in the last agony, that animal fat is the best antidote for its virulence; and who taught them that the essence of joint pine (*Ephedra nevadensis*), which looks to have no juice in it of any sort, is efficacious in stomachic disorders. But they so understand and so use. One believes it to be a sort of instinct atrophied by disuse in a complexer civilization. I remember very well when I came first upon a wet meadow of *yerba mansa,* not knowing its name or use. It *looked* potent; the cool, shiny leaves, the succulent, pink stems and fruity bloom. A little touch, a hint, a word, and I should have known what use to put them to. So I felt, unwilling to leave it until we had come to an understanding. So a musician might have felt in the presence of an instrument known to be within his province, but beyond his power. It was with the relieved sense of having shaped a long surmise that I watched the Señora Romero make a poultice of it for my burned hand.

On, down from the lower lakes to the village weirs, the brown and golden disks of *helenum* have beauty as a sufficient excuse for being. The plants anchor out on tiny capes, or mid-stream islets, with the nearly sessile radicle leaves submerged. The flowers keep up a constant trepidation in time with the hasty water beating at their stems, a quivering, instinct with life, that seems always at the point of breaking into flight; just as the babble of the watercourses always approaches articulation but never quite achieves it. Although of wide range the helenum never makes itself common through profusion, and may be looked for in the same places from year to year. Another lake dweller that comes down to the ploughed lands is the red columbine (*C. truncata*). It requires no encouragement other than shade, but grows too rank in the summer heats and loses its wildwood grace. A common enough orchid in these parts is the false lady's slipper (*Epipactis gigantea*), one that springs up by any water where there is sufficient growth of other sorts to give it countenance. It seems to thrive best in an atmosphere of suffocation.

The middle Sierras fall off abruptly eastward toward the high valleys. Peaks of the fourteen thousand class, belted with sombre swathes of pine, rise almost directly from the bench lands with no foothill approaches. At the lower edge of the bench or mesa the land falls away, often by a fault, to the river hollows, and along the drop one looks for springs or intermittent swampy swales. Here the plant world resembles a little the lake gardens, modified by altitude and the use the town folk put it to for pasture. Here are cress, blue violets, potentilla, and, in the damp of the willow fence-rows, white false asphodels. I am sure we make too free use of this word *false* in naming plants—false mallow, false lupine, and the like. The asphodel is at least no falsifier, but a true lily by all the heaven-set marks, though small of flower and run mostly to leaves, and should have a name that gives it credit for growing up in such celestial semblance. Native to the mesa meadows is a pale iris, gardens of it acres wide, that in the spring season of full bloom make an airy fluttering as of azure wings. Single flowers are too thin and sketchy of outline to affect the imagination, but the full fields have the misty blue of mirage waters rolled across desert sand, and quicken the senses to the anticipation of things ethereal. A very poet's flower, I thought; not fit for gathering up, and proving a nuisance in the pastures, therefore needing to be the more loved. And one day I caught Winnenap drawing out from mid leaf a fine strong fibre for making snares. The borders of the iris fields are pure gold, nearly sessile buttercups and a creeping-stemmed composite of a redder hue. I am convinced that English-speaking children will always have buttercups. If they do not light upon the original companion of little frogs they will take the next best and cherish it accordingly. I find five unrelated species loved by that name, and as many more and as inappropriately called cowslips.

By every mesa spring one may expect to find a single shrub of the buckthorn, called of old time *Cascara sagrada*—the sacred bark. Up in the cañons, within the limit of the rains, it seeks rather a stony slope, but in the dry valleys is not found away from water borders.

In all the valleys and along the desert edges of the west are considerable areas of soil sickly with alkali-collecting pools, black and evil-smelling like old blood. Very little grows hereabout but thick-leaved pickle weed. Curiously enough, in this stiff mud, along roadways where there is frequently a little leakage from canals, grows the only western representative of the true heliotropes (*Heliotropium curassavicum*). It has flowers of faded white, foliage of faded green, resembling the "live-for-ever" of old gardens and graveyards, but even less attractive. After so much schooling in the virtues of water-seeking plants, one is not surprised to learn that its mucilaginous sap has healing powers.

Last and inevitable resort of overflow waters is the tulares, great wastes of reeds (*Juncus*) in sickly, slow streams. The reeds, called tules, are ghostly pale in winter, in summer deep poisonous-looking green, the waters thick and brown; the reed beds breaking into dingy pools, clumps of rotting willows, narrow winding water lanes and sinking paths. The tules grow inconceivably thick in places, standing man-high above the water; cattle, no, not any fish nor fowl can penetrate them. Old stalks succumb slowly; the bed soil is quagmire, settling with the weight as it fills and fills. Too slowly for counting they raise little islands from the bog and reclaim the land. The waters pushed out cut deeper channels, gnaw off the edges of the solid earth.

The tulares are full of mystery and malaria. That is why we have meant to explore them and have never done so. It must be a happy mystery. So you would think to hear the redwinged blackbirds proclaim it clear March mornings. Flocks of them, and every flock a myriad, shelter in the dry, whispering stems. They make little arched runways deep into the

heart of the tule beds. Miles across the valley one hears the clamor of their high, keen flutings in the mating weather.

Wild fowl, quacking hordes of them, nest in the tulares. Any day's venture will raise from open shallows the great blue heron on his hollow wings. Chill evenings the mallard drakes cry continually from the glassy pools, the bittern's hollow boom rolls along the water paths. Strange and farflown fowl drop down against the saffron, autumn sky. All day wings beat above it hazy with speed; long flights of cranes glimmer in the twilight. By night one wakes to hear the clanging geese go over. One wishes for, but gets no nearer speech from those the reedy fens have swallowed up. What they do there, how fare, what find, is the secret of the tulares.

NURSLINGS OF THE SKY

CHOOSE A HILL COUNTRY for storms. There all the business of the weather is carried on above your horizon and loses its terror in familiarity. When you come to think about it, the disastrous storms are on the levels, sea or sand or plains. There you get only a hint of what is about to happen, the fume of the gods rising from their meeting place under the rim of the world; and when it breaks upon you there is no stay nor shelter. The terrible mewings and mouthings of a Kansas wind have the added terror of viewlessness. You are lapped in them like uprooted grass; suspect them of a personal grudge. But the storms of hill countries have other business. They scoop watercourses, manure the pines, twist them to a fine fibre, fit the firs to be masts and spars, and, if you keep reasonably out of the track of their affairs, do you no harm.

They have habits to be learned, appointed paths, seasons, and warnings, and they leave you in no doubt about their performances. One who builds his house on a water scar or the rubble of a steep slope must take chances. So they did in Overtown who built in the wash of Argus water, and at Kearsarge at the foot of a steep, treeless swale. After twenty years Argus water rose in the wash against the frail houses, and the piled snows of Kearsarge slid down at a thunder peal over the cabins and the camp, but you could conceive that it was the fault of neither the water nor the snow.

The first effect of cloud study is a sense of presence and intention in storm processes. Weather does not happen. It is the visible manifestation of the Spirit moving itself in the void. It gathers itself together under the heavens; rains, snows, yearns mightily in wind, smiles; and the Weather Bureau, situated advantageously for that very business, taps the record on his instruments and going out on the streets denies his God, not having gathered the sense of what he has seen. Hardly anybody takes account of the fact that John Muir,* who knows more of mountain storms than any other, is a devout man.

Of the high Sierras choose the neighborhood of the splintered peaks about the Kern and King's river divide for storm study, or the short, wide-mouthed cañons opening eastward on high valleys. Days when the hollows are steeped in a warm, winey flood the clouds come walking on the floor of heaven, flat and pearly gray beneath, rounded and pearly white above. They gather flock-wise, moving on the level currents that roll about the peaks, lock hands and settle with the cooler air, drawing a veil about those places where they do their work. If their meeting or parting takes place at sunrise or sunset, as it often does, one gets the splendor of the apocalypse. There will be cloud pillars miles high, snow-capped, glorified, and preserving an orderly perspective before the unbarred door of the sun, or perhaps mere ghosts of clouds that dance to some pied piper of an unfelt wind. But be it day or night, once they have settled to their work, one sees from the valley only the blank wall of their tents stretched along the ranges. To get the real effect of a mountain storm you must be inside.

One who goes often into a hill country learns not to say: What if it should rain? It always does rain somewhere among the peaks: the unusual thing is that one should escape it. You might suppose that if you took any account of plant contrivances to save their pollen powder against showers. Note how many there are deep-throated and bell-flowered like the pent-stemons, how many have nodding pedicels as the columbine, how many grow in copse shelters and grow there only. There is keen delight in the quick showers of summer cañons, with the added comfort, born of experience, of knowing that no harm comes of a wetting at high altitudes. The day is warm; a white cloud spies over the cañon wall, slips up behind the

* John Muir (1838–1914), explorer, naturalist, and writer. He influenced Congress to pass Yosemite National Park Bill in 1890 and founded the Sierra Club in 1892. He was author of *The Mountains of California* (1894) and other books.

ridge to cross it by some windy pass, obscures your sun. Next you hear the rain drum on the broad-leaved hellebore, and beat down the mimulus beside the brook. You shelter on the lee of some strong pine with shut-winged butterflies and merry, fiddling creatures of the wood. Runnels of rain water from the glacier-slips swirl through the pine needles into rivulets; the streams froth and rise in their banks. The sky is white without cloud; the sky is gray with rain; the sky is clear. The summer showers leave no wake.

Such as these follow each other day by day for weeks in August weather. Sometimes they chill suddenly into wet snow that packs about the lake gardens clear to the blossom frills, and melts away harmlessly. Sometimes one has the good fortune from a hearther-grown headland to watch a rain-cloud forming in mid-air. Out over meadow or lake region begins a little darkling of the sky,—no cloud, no wind, just a smokiness such as spirits materialize from in witch stories.

It rays out and draws to it some floating films from secret cañons. Rain begins, "slow dropping veil of thinnest lawn;" a wind comes up and drives the formless thing across a meadow, or a dull lake pitted by the glancing drops, dissolving as it drives. Such rains relieve like tears.

The same season brings the rains that have work to do, ploughing storms that alter the face of things. These come with thunder and the play of live fire along the rocks. They come with great winds that try the pines for their work upon the seas and strike out the unfit. They shake down avalanches of splinters from sky-line pinnacles and raise up sudden floods like battle fronts in the cañons against towns, trees, and boulders. They would be kind if they could, but have more important matters. Such storms, called cloud-bursts by the country folk, are not rain, rather the spillings of Thor's cup, jarred by the Thunderer. After such a one the water that comes up in the village hydrants miles away is white with forced bubbles from the wind-tormented streams.

All that storms do to the face of the earth you may read in the geographies, but not what they do to our contemporaries. I remember one night of thunderous rain made unendurably mournful by the houseless cry of a cougar whose lair, and perhaps his family, had been buried under a slide of broken boulders on the slope of Kearsarge. We had heard the heavy detonation of the slide about the hour of the alpenglow, a pale rosy interval in a darkling air, and judged he must have come from hunting to the ruined cliff and paced the night out before it, crying a very human woe. I remember, too, in that same season of storms, a lake made milky white for days, and crowded out of its bed by clay washed into it by a fury of rain, with the trout floating in it belly up, stunned by the shock of the sudden flood. But there were trout enough for what was left of the lake next year and the beginning of a meadow about its upper rim. What taxed me most in the wreck of one of my favorite cañons by cloud-burst was to see a bobcat mother mouthing her drowned kittens in the ruined lair built in the wash, far above the limit of accustomed waters, but not far enough for the unexpected. After a time you get the point of view of gods about these things to save you from being too pitiful.

The great snows that come at the beginning of winter, before there is yet any snow except the perpetual high banks, are best worth while to watch. These come often before the late bloomers are gone and while the migratory birds are still in the piney woods. Down in the valley you see little but the flocking of blackbirds in the streets, or the low flight of mallards over the tulares, and the gathering of clouds behind Williamson. First there is a waiting stillness in the wood; the pine-trees creak although there is no wind, the sky glowers, the firs rock by the water borders. The noise of the creek rises insistently and falls off a full note like a child abashed by sudden silence in the room. This changing of the stream-tone following tardily the changes of the sun on melting snows is most meaningful of wood notes. After it runs a little trumpeter wind to cry the wild creatures to their holes. Sometimes the warning hangs in the air for days with increasing stillness. Only Clark's crow and the strident jays make light of it; only they can afford to. The cattle get down to the foothills and ground inhabiting creatures make fast their doors. It grows chill, blind clouds fumble in the cañons; there will be a roll of thunder, perhaps, or a flurry of rain, but mostly the snow is born in the air with quietness and the sense of strong white pinions softly stirred. It increases, is wet and clogging, and makes a white night of midday.

There is seldom any wind with first snows, more often rain, but later, when there is already a smooth foot or two over all the slopes, the drifts begin. The late snows are fine and dry, mere ice granules at the wind's will.

Keen mornings after a storm they are blown out in wreaths and banners from the high ridges sifting into the cañons.

Once in a year or so we have a "big snow." The cloud tents are widened out to shut in the valley and an outlying range or two and are drawn tight against the sun. Such a storm begins warm, with a dry white mist that fills and fills between the ridges, and the air is thick with formless groaning. Now for days you get no hint of the neighboring ranges until the snows begin to lighten and some shouldering peak lifts through a rent. Mornings after the heavy snows are steely blue, two-edged with cold, divinely fresh and still, and these are times to go up to the pine borders. There you may find floundering in the unstable drifts "tainted wethers" of the wild sheep, faint from age and hunger; easy prey. Even the deer make slow going in the thick fresh snow, and once we found a wolverine going blind and feebly in the white glare.

No tree takes the snow stress with such ease as the silver fir. The star-whorled, fan-spread branches droop under the soft wreaths—droop and press flatly to the trunk; presently the point of overloading is reached, there is a soft sough and muffled drooping, the boughs recover, and the weighting goes on until the drifts have reached the midmost whorls and covered up the branches. When the snows are particularly wet and heavy they spread over the young firs in green-ribbed tents wherein harbor winter loving birds.

All storms of desert hills, except wind storms, are impotent. East and

east of the Sierras they rise in nearly parallel ranges, desertward, and no rain breaks over them, except from some far-strayed cloud or roving wind from the California Gulf, and these only in winter. In summer the sky travails with thunderings and the flare of sheet lightnings to win a few blistering big drops, and once in a lifetime the chance of a torrent. But you have not known what force resides in the mindless things until you have known a desert wind. One expects it at the turn of the two seasons, wet and dry, with electrified tense nerves. Along the edge of the mesa where it drops off to the valley, dust devils begin to rise white and steady, fanning out at the top like the genii out of the Fisherman's bottle. One supposes the Indians might have learned the use of smoke signals from these dust pillars as they learn most things direct from the tutelage of the earth. The air begins to move fluently, blowing hot and cold between the ranges. Far

south rises a murk of sand against the sky; it grows, the wind shakes itself, and has a smell of earth. The cloud of small dust takes on the color of gold and shuts out the neighborhood, the push of the wind is unsparing. Only man of all folk is foolish enough to stir abroad in it. But being in a house is really much worse; no relief from the dust, and a great fear of the creaking timbers. There is no looking ahead in such a wind, and the bite of the small sharp sand on exposed skin is keener than any insect sting. One might sleep, for the lapping of the wind wears one to the point of exhaustion very soon, but there is dread, in open sand stretches sometimes justified, of being over blown by the drift. It is hot, dry, fretful work, but by going along the ground with the wind behind, one may come upon strange things in its tumultuous privacy. I like these truces of wind and heat that the desert makes, otherwise I do not know how I should come by so many acquaintances with furtive folk. I like to see hawks sitting daunted in shallow holes, not daring to spread a feather, and doves in a row by the prickle-bushes, and shut-eyed cattle, turned tail to the wind in a patient doze. I like the smother of sand among the dunes, and finding small coiled snakes in open places, but I never like to come in a wind upon the silly sheep. The wind robs them of what wit they had, and they seem never to have learned the self-induced hypnotic stupor with which most wild things endure weather stress. I have never heard that the desert winds brought harm to any other than the wandering shepherds and their flocks. Once below Pastaria Little Pete showed me bones sticking out of the sand where a flock of two hundred had been smothered in a bygone wind. In many places the four-foot posts of a cattle fence had been buried by the wind-blown dunes.

It is enough occupation, when no storm is brewing, to watch the cloud currents and the chambers of the sky. From Kearsarge, say, you look over Inyo and find pink soft cloud masses asleep on the level desert air; south of you hurries a white troop late to some gathering of their kind at the back of Oppapago; nosing the foot of Waban, a woolly mist creeps south. In the clean, smooth paths of the middle sky and highest up in air, drift, unshepherded, small flocks ranging contrarily. You will find the proper names of these things in the reports of the Weather Bureau—cirrus, cumulus, and the like—and charts that will teach by study when to sow and take up crops. It is astonishing the trouble men will be at to find out when to plant potatoes, and gloze over the eternal meaning of the skies. You have to beat out for yourself many mornings on the windy headlands the sense of the fact that you get the same rainbow in the cloud drift over Waban and the spray of your garden hose. And not necessarily then do you live up to it.

THE LITTLE TOWN OF THE

GRAPE VINES

THE LITTLE TOWN OF THE

GRAPE VINES

THERE ARE STILL some places in the west where the quails cry "*cuidado*"; where all the speech is soft, all the manners gentle; where all the dishes have *chile* in them, and they make more of the Sixteenth of September than they do of the Fourth of July. I mean in particular El Pueblo de Las Uvas. Where it lies, how to come at it, you will not get from me; rather would I show you the heron's nest in the tulares. It has a peak behind it, glinting above the tamarack pines, above a breaker of ruddy hills that have a long slope valley-wards and the shoreward steep of waves toward the Sierras.

Below the Town of the Grape Vines, which shortens to Las Uvas for common use, the land dips away to the river pastures and the tulares. It shrouds under a twilight thicket of vines, under a dome of cottonwood-trees, drowsy and murmurous as a hive. Hereabouts are some strips of tillage and the headgates that dam up the creek for the village weirs; upstream you catch the growl of the arrastra. Wild vines that begin among the willows lap over to the orchard rows, take the trellis and roof-tree.

There is another town above Las Uvas that merits some attention, a town of arches and airy crofts, full of linnets, blackbirds, fruit birds, small sharp hawks, and mockingbirds that sing by night. They pour out piercing, unendurably sweet cavatinas above the fragrance of bloom and musky smell of fruit. Singing is in fact the business of the night at Las Uvas as sleeping is for midday. When the moon comes over the mountain wall new-washed from the sea, and the shadows lie like lace on the stamped floors of the patios, from recess to recess of the vine tangle runs the thrum of guitars and the voice of singing.

At Las Uvas they keep up all the good customs brought out of Old Mexico or bred in a lotus-eating land; drink, and are merry and look out for something to eat afterward; have children, nine or ten to a family, have cock-fights, keep the siesta, smoke cigarettes and wait for the sun to go down. And always they dance; at dusk on the smooth adobe floors, afternoons under the trellises where the earth is damp and has a fruity smell. A betrothal, a wedding, or a christening, or the mere proximity of a guitar is sufficient occasion; and if the occasion lacks, send for the guitar and dance anyway.

All this requires explanation. Antonio Sevadra, drifting this way from Old Mexico with the flood that poured into the Tappan district after the first notable strike, discovered La Golondrina. It was a generous lode and Tony a good fellow; to work it he brought in all the Sevadras, even to the twice-removed; all the Castros who were his wife's family, all the Saises, Romeros, an Eschobars,—the relations of his relations-in-law. There you have the beginning of a pretty considerable town. To these accrued much of the Spanish California float swept out of the southwest by eastern enterprise. They slacked away again when the price of silver went down, and the ore dwindled in La Golondrina. All the hot eddy of mining life swept away from that corner of the hills, but there were always those too idle, too poor to move, or too easily content with El Pueblo de Las Uvas.

Nobody comes nowadays to the town of the grape vines except, as we say, "with the breath of crying," but of these enough. All the low sills run over with small heads. Ah, ah! There is a kind of pride in that if you did but know it, to have your baby every year or so as the time sets, and keep a full breast. So great a blessing as marriage is easily come by. It is told of Ruy Garcia that when he went for his marriage license he lacked a dollar of the clerk's fee, but borrowed it of the sheriff, who expected reëlection and exhibited thereby a commendable thrift.

Of what account is it to lack meal or meat when you may have it of any neighbor? Besides, there is sometimes a point of honor in these things. Jesus Romero, father of ten, had a job sacking ore in the Marionette which he gave up of his own accord. "Eh, why?" said Jesus, "for my fam'ly."

"It is so, señora," he said solemnly, "I go to the Marionette, I work, I eat meat—pie—frijoles—good, ver' good. I come home sad'day nigh' I see my fam'ly. I play lil' game poker with the boys, have lil' drink wine, my money all gone. My fam'ly have no money, nothing eat. All time I work at mine I eat, good, ver' good grub. I think sorry for my fam'ly. No, no, señora, I no work no more that Marionette, I stay with my fam'ly." The wonder of it is, I think, that the family had the same point of view.

Every house in the town of the vines has its garden plot, corn and brown beans and a row of peppers reddening in the sun; and in damp borders of the irrigating ditches clumps of *yerba santa,* horehound, catnip, and spikenard, wholesome herbs and curative, but if no peppers then nothing at all. You will have for a holiday dinner, in Las Uvas, soup with meat balls and chile in it, chicken with chile, rice with chile, fried beans with more chile, enchilada, which is corn cake with a sauce of chile and tomatoes, onion, grated cheese, and olives, and for a relish chile *tepines* passed about in a dish, all of which is comfortable and corrective to the stomach. You will have wine which every man makes for himself, of good body and inimitable bouquet, and sweets that are not nearly so nice as they look.

There are two occasions when you may count on that kind of a meal; always on the Sixteenth of September, and on the two-yearly visits of Father Shannon. It is absurd, of course, that El Pueblo de Las Uvas should have an Irish priest, but Black Rock, Minton, Jimville, and all that country round do not find it so. Father Shannon visits them all, waits by the Red Butte to confess the shepherds who go through with their flocks, carries a blessing to small and isolated mines, and so in the course of a year or so works around to Las Uvas to bury and marry and christen. Then all the little graves in the *Campo Santo* are brave with tapers, the brown pine headboards blossom like Aaron's rod with paper roses and bright cheap prints of Our Lady of Sorrows. Then the Señora Sevadra, who thinks herself elect of heaven for that office, gathers up the original sinners, the little Elijias, Lolas, Manuelitas, Josés, and Felipés, by dint of adjurations and sweets smuggled into small perspiring palms, to fit them for the Sacrament.

I used to peek in at them, never so softly, in Doña Ina's living-room; Raphael-eyed little imps, going sidewise on their knees to rest them from the bare floor, candles lit on the mantel to give a religious air, and a great sheaf of wild bloom before the Holy Family. Come Sunday they set out the altar in the schoolhouse, with the fine-drawn altar cloths, the beaten silver candlesticks, and the wax images, chief glory of Las Uvas, brought up mule-back from Old Mexico forty years ago. All in white the communicants go up two and two in a hushed, sweet awe to take the body of their Lord, and Tomaso, who is priest's boy, tries not to look unduly puffed up by his office. After that you have dinner and a bottle of wine that ripened on the sunny slope of Escondito. All the week Father Shannon has shriven his people, who bring clean conscience to the betterment of appetite, and the Father sets them an example. Father Shannon is rather big about the middle to accommodate the large laugh that lives in him, but a most shrewd searcher of hearts. It is reported that one derives comfort from his confessional, and I for my part believe it.

The celebration of the Sixteenth, though it comes every year, takes as long to prepare for as Holy Communion. The señoritas have each a new dress apiece, the señoras a new *rebosa*. The young gentlemen have new silver trimmings to their sombreros, unspeakable ties, silk handkerchiefs, and new leathers to their spurs. At this time when the peppers glow in the gardens and the young quail cry "*cuidado,*" "have a care!" you can hear the *plump, plump* of the *metate* from the alcoves of the vines where comfortable old dames, whose experience gives them the touch of art, are pounding out corn for tamales.

The Little Town of the Grape Vines

School-teachers from abroad have tried before now at Las Uvas to have school begin on the first of September, but got nothing else to stir in the heads of the little Castros, Garcias, and Romeros but feasts and cock-fights until after the Sixteenth. Perhaps you need to be told that this is the anniversary of the Republic, when liberty awoke and cried in the provinces of Old Mexico. You are aroused at midnight to hear them shouting in the streets, "*Vive la Libertad!*" answered from the houses and the recesses of the vines, "*Vive la Mexico!*" At sunrise shots are fired commemorating the tragedy of unhappy Maximilian, and then music, the noblest of national hymns, as the great flag of Old Mexico floats up the flag-pole in the bare little plaza of shabby Las Uvas. The sun over Pine Mountain greets the eagle of Montezuma before it touches the vineyards and the town, and the day begins with a great shout. By and by there will be a reading of the Declaration of Independence and an address punctured by *vives;* all the town in its best dress, and some exhibits of horsemanship that make lathered bits and bloody spurs; also a cock-fight.

By night there will be dancing, and such music! old Santos to play the flute, a little lean man with a saintly countenance, young Garcia whose guitar has a soul, and Carrasco with the violin. They sit on a high platform above the dancers in the candle flare, backed by the red, white, and green of Old Mexico, and play fervently such music as you will not hear otherwise.

At midnight the flag comes down. Count yourself at a loss if you are not moved by that performance. Pine Mountain watches whitely over-head, shepherd fires glow strongly on the glooming hills. The plaza, the bare glistening pole, the dark folk, the bright dresses, are lit ruddily by a bonfire. It leaps up to the eagle flag, dies down, the music begins softly and aside. They play airs of old longing and exile; slowly out of the dark the flag drops down, bellying and falling with the midnight draught. Sometimes a hymn is sung, always there are tears. The flag is down; Tony Sevadra has received it in his arms. The music strikes a barbaric swelling tune, another flag begins a slow ascent,—it takes a breath or two to realize that they are both, flag and tune, the Star Spangled Banner,—a volley is fired, we are back, if you please, in California of America. Every youth who has the blood of patriots in him lays ahold on Tony Sevadra's flag, happiest if he can get a corner of it. The music goes before, the folk fall in two and two, singing. They sing everything, America, the Marseillaise, for the sake of the French shepherds hereabout, the hymn of Cuba, and the Chilian national air to comfort two families of that land. The flag goes to Doña Ina's, with the candlesticks and the altar cloths, then Las Uvas eats tamales and dances the sun up the slope of Pine Mountain.

You are not to suppose that they do not keep the Fourth, Washington's Birthday, and Thanksgiving at the town of the grape vines. These make excellent occasions for quitting work and dancing, but the Sixteenth is the holiday of the heart. On Memorial Day the graves have garlands and new pictures of the saints tacked to the headboards. There is great virtue in an *Ave* said in the Camp of the Saints. I like that name which the Spanish speaking people give to the garden of the dead, *Campo Santo,* as if it might be some bed of healing from which blind souls and sinners rise up whole and praising God. Sometimes the speech of simple folk hints at truth the understanding does not reach. I am persuaded only a complex soul can get any good of a plain religion. Your earthborn is a poet and a symbolist. We breed in an environment of asphalt pavements a body of people whose creeds are chiefly restrictions against other people's way of life, and have kitchens and latrines under the same roof that houses their God. Such as these go to church to be edified, but at Las Uvas they go for pure worship and to entreat their God. The logical conclusion of the faith that every good gift cometh from God is the open hand and the finer courtesy. The meal done without buys a candle for the neighbor's dead child. You do foolishly to suppose that the candle does no good.

At Las Uvas every house is a piece of earth——thick walled, white-

washed adobe that keeps the even temperature of a cave; every man is an accomplished horseman and consequently bow-legged; every family keeps dogs, flea-bitten mongrels that loll on the earthen floors. They speak a purer Castilian than obtains in like villages of Mexico, and the way they count relationship everybody is more or less akin. There is not much villainy among them. What incentive to thieving or killing can there be when there is little wealth and that to be had for the borrowing! If they love too hotly, as we say "take their meat before grace," so do their betters. Eh, what! shall a man be a saint before he is dead? And besides, Holy Church takes it out of you one way or another before all is done. Come away, you who are obsessed with your own importance in the scheme of things, and have got nothing you did not sweat for, come away by the brown valleys and full-bosomed hills to the even-breathing days, to the kindliness, earthiness, ease of El Pueblo de Las Uvas.

LOST BORDERS

CONTENTS

There's a little creek in Inyo, singing by beyond the town,
Through the pink wild-almond tangle and the birches slim and brown,
Where all night we'll watch the star-beams in the shallow, open rills,
And the hot, bright moons of August skulking low along the hills;
And the Word will wake in Inyo——never printed in a page——
With the wind that wakes the morning on a thousand miles of sage.

I

THE LAND

WHEN THE Paiute nations broke westward through the Sierra wall they cut off a remnant of the Shoshones, and forced them south as far as Death Valley and the borders of the Mojaves, they penned the Washoes in and around Tahoe, and passing between these two, established themselves along the snow-fed Sierra creeks. And this it was proper they should do, for the root of their name-word is Pah, meaning water, to distinguish them from their brothers the Utes of the Great Basin.

In time they passed quite through the sawcut cañons by Kern and Kings rivers and possessed all the east slope of the San Joaquin, but chiefly they settled by small clans and family groups where the pines leave off and the sage begins and the desert abuts on the great Sierra fault. On the northeast they touched the extreme flanks of the Utes, and with them and the southerly tribes swept a wide arc about that region of mysterious desertness of which you shall presently hear more particularly.

The boundaries between the tribes and between the clans within the tribe were plainly established by natural landmarks—peaks, hillcrests, creeks, and chains of water-holes—beginning at the foot of the Sierra and continuing eastward past the limit of endurable existence. Out there, a week's journey from everywhere, the land was not worth parcelling off, and the boundaries which should logically have been continued until they met the cañon of the Colorado ran out in foolish wastes of sand and inextricable disordered ranges. Here you have the significance of the Indian name for that country—Los Borders. And you can always trust Indian names to express to you the largest truth about any district in the shortest phrases.

But there is more in the name than that. For law runs with the boundary, not beyond it; it is as fast to the given landmarks as a limpet to its scar on the rock. I am convinced most men make law for the comfortable feel of it, defining them to themselves; they shoulder along like blindworms, rearing against restrictions, turning thereward for security as climbing plants to the warmth of a nearing wall. They pinch themselves with regulations to make sure of being sentient, and organize within organizations.

Out there, then, where the law and the landmarks fail together, the souls of little men fade out at the edges, leak from them as water from wooden pails warped asunder.

Out there where the borders of conscience break down, where there is no convention, and behavior is of little account except as it gets you your desire, almost anything might happen; does happen, in fact, though I shall have trouble making you believe it. Out there where the boundary of soul and sense is as faint as a trail in a sand-storm, I have seen things happen that I do not believe myself. That is what you are to expect in a country where the names mean something. Ubehebe, Pharanagat, Resting Springs, Dead Man's Gulch, Funeral Mountains—these beckon and allure. There is always a tang of reality about them like the smart of wood smoke to the eyes, that warns of neighboring fires.

Riding through by the known trails, the senses are obsessed by the coil of a huge and senseless monotony; straight, white, blinding, alkali flats, forsaken mesas; skimpy shrubs growing little and less, starved knees of hills sticking out above them; black clots of pines high upon rubbishy mountain-heads—days and days of this, as if Nature herself had obscured the medium to escape you in her secret operations.

One might travel weeks on end and not come on any place or occasion whereby men may live, and drop suddenly into close hives of them digging, jostling, drinking, lusting, and rejoicing. Every story of that country is colored by the fashion of the life there, breaking up in swift, passionate intervals between long, dun stretches, like the land that out of hot sinks of desolation heaves up great bulks of granite ranges with opal shadows playing in their shining, snow-piled curves. Out there beyond the borders are the Shivering Dunes, heaps upon heaps of blinding sand all acrawl in the wind, drifting and reforming with a faint, stridulent rustle, and black, wall-sided box-cañons that give the stars at midday, scored over with picture-writings of a forgotten race. There are lakes there of a pellucid clearness like ice, closed over with man-deep crystals of pure salt. Long Tom Bassit told me a story of one of these which he had from a man who saw it. It was of an emigrant train all out of its reckoning, laboring in a long, hollow trough of desolation between waterless high ranges, arriving at such a closed salt-pit, too much spent to go around it and trusting the salt crust to hold under their racked wagons and starveling teams. But when they had come near the middle of the lake, the salt thinned out abruptly, and, the forward rank of the party breaking through, the bodies were caught under the saline slabs and not all of them recovered. There was a woman among them, and the Man-who-saw had cared—cared enough to go back years afterward, when, after successive oven-blast summers, the salt held solidly over all the lake, and he told Tom Bassit how, long before he reached the point, he saw the gleam of red in the woman's dress, and found her at last, lying on her side, sealed in the crystal, rising as ice rises to the surface of choked streams. Long Tom wished me to make a story of it. I did once at a dinner, but I never got through with it. There, about the time the candles began to burn their shades and red track of the light on the wine-glasses barred the cloth, with the white, disdainful shoulders and politely incredulous faces leaning through the smoke of cigarettes, it had a garish sound. Afterward I came across the proof of the affair in the records of the emigrant party, but I never tried telling it again.

That is why in all that follows I have set down what the Borderers thought and felt; for that you have a touchstone in your *own* heart, but I should get no credit with you if I were to tell what really became of Loring, and what happened to the man who went down into the moaning pit of Sand Mountain.

Curiously, in that country, you can get anybody to believe any sort of a tale that has gold in it, like the Lost Mine of Fisherman's Peak and the

Duke o' Wild Rose. Young Woodin* brought me a potsherd once from a kitchen-midden in Shoshone Land. It might have been, for antiquity, one of those Job scraped himself withal, but it was dotted all over with colors and specks of pure gold from the riverbed from which the sand and clay were scooped. Said he:

"You ought to find a story about this somewhere."

I was sore then about not getting myself believed in some elementary matters, such as that horned toads are not poisonous, and that Indians really have the bowels of compassion. Said I:

"I will do better than that, I will *make* a story."

We sat out a whole afternoon under the mulberry-tree, with the landscape disappearing in shimmering heat-waves around us, testing our story for likelihood and proving it. There was an Indian woman in the tale, not pretty, for they are mostly not that in life, and the earthenware pot, of course, and a lost river bedded with precious sand. Afterward my friend went to hold down some claims in the Coso country, and I north to the lake region where the red firs are, and we told the pot-of-gold story as often we were permitted. One night when I had done with it, a stranger by our camp-fire said the thing was well known in his country. I said, "Where was that?"

"Coso," said he, and that was the first I had heard of my friend.

Next winter, at Lone Pine, a prospector from Panamint-way wanted to know if I had ever heard of the Indian-pot Mine which was lost out toward Pharump. I said I had a piece of the pot, which I showed him. Then I wrote the tale for a magazine of the sort that gets taken in camps and at miners' boarding-houses, and several men were at great pains to explain to me where my version varied from the accepted one of the hills. By this time, you understand, I had begun to believe the story myself. I had a spasm of conscience, though, when Tennessee told me that he thought he knew the very squaw of the story, and when the back of the winter was broken he meant to make a little "pasear" in search of the lost river. But Tennessee died before spring, and spared my confessing. Now it only needs that some one should find another shard of the gold-besprinkled pot to

---

* Woodin was a doctor in the Owens Valley with whom Mary Austin found intellectual companionship during her years as the mother of young Ruth.

fix the tale in the body of desert myths. Well—it had as much fact behind it as the Gunsight, and is more interesting than the Bryfogle, which began with the finding of a dead man, clothless as the desert dead mostly are, with a bag of nuggets clutched in his mummied hands.

First and last, accept no man's statement that he knows this Country of Lost Borders well. A great number having lost their lives in the process of proving where it is not safe to go, it is now possible to pass through much of the district by guide-posts and well-known water-holes, but the best part of it remains locked, inviolate, or at best known only to some far-straying Indian, sheepherder, or pocket hunter, whose account of it does not get into the reports of the Geological Survey. But a boast of knowledge is likely to prove as hollow as the little yellow gourds called apples of Death Valley.

Pure desertness clings along the pits of the long valleys and the formless beds of vanished lakes. Every hill that lifts as high as the cloud-line has some trees upon it, and deer and bighorn to feed on the tall, tufted, bunch grass between the boulders. In the year when Tonopah, turning upon itself like a swarm, trickled prospectors all over that country from Hot Creek to the Armagosa, Indians brought me word that the men had camped so close about the water-holes that the bighorn died of thirst on the headlands, turned always in the last agony toward the man-infested springs.

That is as good a pointer as any if you go waterless in the country of Lost Borders: where you find cattle dropped, skeleton or skin dried, the heads almost invariably will be turned toward the places where water-holes should be. But no such reminders will fend men from its trails. This is chiefly, I am persuaded, because there is something incomprehensible to the man-mind in the concurrence of death and beauty. Shall the tender opal mist betray you? the airy depth of mountain blueness, the blazonry of painted wind-scoured buttes, the far peaks molten with the alpen glow, cooled by the rising of the velvet violet twilight tide, and the leagues and leagues of stars? As easy for a man to believe that a beautiful woman can be cruel. Mind you, it is men who go mostly into the desert, who love it past all reasonableness, slack their ambitions, cast off old usages, neglect their families because of the pulse and beat of a life laid bare to its thews and sinews. Their woman hate with implicitness the life like the land, stretching interminably whity-brown, dim and shadowy blue hills that hem it, glimmering pale waters of mirage that creep and crawl about its edges. There was a woman once at Agua Hedionda—but you wouldn't believe that either.

If the desert were a woman, I know well what like she would be: deep-breasted, broad in the hips, tawny, with tawny hair, great masses of it lying smooth along her perfect curves, full lipped like a sphinx, but not heavy-lidded like one, eyes sane and steady as the polished jewel of her skies, such a countenance as should make men serve without desiring her, such a largeness to her mind as should make their sins of no account, passionate, but not necessitous, patient—and you could not move her, no, not if you had all the earth to give, so much as one tawny hair's-breadth beyond her own desires. If you cut very deeply into any soul that has the mark of the land upon it, you find such qualities as these—as I shall presently prove to you.

II

THE HOODOO OF THE MINNIETTA

ALL THE TRAILS in this book begin at Lone Pine, winding east by south and east again, though you will look long without finding the places where things happened in them unless you are susceptible to those influences that contribute to the fixed belief of mining countries, that the hot essences of greed and hate and lust are absorbed, as it were, by the means that provoke them, and inhere in houses, lands, or stones to work mischief to the possessor. This is common in new and untamed lands where destinies are worked out in plain sight. Manuel de Borba could not persuade Narcisse Duplin to accept as a gift the knife with which he killed Mariana, and no miner acquainted with its hoodoo will have anything to do with the Minnietta.

It lies out in the stark, wide light, on the red flanks of Coso, a crumbling tunnel, a ruined smelter, and a row of sun-warped cabins under tall, skeleton-white cliffs; and no man in these days visits it of his own intention.

Antone discovered it in a forgotten year. No one knew his other name; at Panimint he was called Dutchy, after the use of mining camps, from which you gather that he might have been a German, a Swede, Norwegian, Dane, or even a Dutchman. He was a foreigner, very sick when he came to the hills, sicker when he left them, and he discovered the ledge in a three weeks' prospecting trip, from which he returned to Jake

Hogan's cabin with his pockets full of ore, elate, penniless, and utterly overworn.

He talked it all out with Hogan, on into the night, with the candle guttering in a bottle and the winking specimens spread out on the table between them. The ore was heavy and dull, and had the greasy feel of richness. Antone promised himself great things between the pains of a racking cough. He talked on afterward in his bunk, maunderingly, as his fever rose, to which succeeded the stupor of exhaustion. That was why, three days later, not being able to attend to it himself, Antone asked Hogan to have the ore assayed and bring him the report. And the report was so little in the eye of his expectation that a week later, loathing the filthy cabin and the ill-cooked food, feeling death in his throat, all his thought set toward home, Antone accepted the two hundred dollars which Hogan offered him for all right and interest in his claim. Hogan saw him off considerately on the Mojave stage, and immediately gathered his pack to set out for a certain gully faced by tall, white cliffs, where the outcrop was heavy and dull with a greasy feel. Within a month it was known in all Panimint and Coso and as far north as Cero Gordo that Jake Hogan had made a good strike at the Minnietta.

Long afterward, when rage had made him drunk, Hogan, as he cursed the Minnietta, his wickedness, as it were, an added poison to his curse, told how one night while Antone lay sick, when the assayer had given him the full count of the ore, amazed by its richness, he had walked long in the one street barred with blocks of light from the dance-houses roaring full of song, and the light of the furnaces glowing low and evilly along the ground, walking up and down and contriving how he might impose on Antone the report of some other assay, and how, when he had done so successfully, he had bought the claim for a song. That, said Hogan, when he cursed the men who had done him out of the Minnietta, was the sort of man he was, as much as to say, being a toad, he spat venom and was not to be trod upon. But at the time he must have thought more cheerfully of his offence.

Hogan organized a stock company to open the mine and build a smelter, and began to grow rich amazingly. Jigging burro trains went up and down with water; eighteen-mule freighters trailed in with supplies in a wake of tawny dust. Beflounced and fluttered women, last indubitable evidence of a prosperous camp, preened themselves in the cabins set askew under the white cliffs.

It is not given to every man to deal successfully with mining stock-companies. Hogan, prospecting a grub stake, and Hogan, owner of the Minnietta putting out its thousands a week, were much the same person. Because he was ignorant Hogan did not understand his stock-company when he had organized it, and because he had come into his property by stealth, feared to lose it by conspiracy. Before the end of the second year Hogan and the Minnietta Mining and Milling Company were taking away each other's characters openly in court.

Hogan got a judgment that gave him little less than half that he asked; contumaciously carried it to a higher court and got a reversal of judgment that gave him nothing at all. So at the last he went out of the Minnietta with little more than he had brought into it—folly and shame, you understand, peering with painted faces from the little cabins under the cliff, had had their pickings of him—and going, cursed it with fluency and all his might. Tunnel and shaft and winze, he cursed it, sheave and cross-cut, pulley and belt and blast and fall rope under the hoist, as he had made it he cursed it in every part. Those who heard him maintain that in the cursing of Hogan was wrought the Hoodoo of the Minnietta; but, in fact, it began in the fake assay which Hogan carried to Antone in his bed, a villany of which he despoiled himself in his cursing, with the wantonness by which a man, checked in an evil, reveals the iniquity in which he shaped it.

After that the Minnietta Mining and Milling Company was not uniformly prosperous; the price of silver went down, or the quality of the ore fell off, and there were months at a time when the mine was shut down while the directors settled their private squabbles. Now and then, and always at inopportune moments, the company had streaks of economy. In one of these they happened upon McKenna for superintendent, whose particular qualification was that he was cheap, and being no spender at the best of times, was not always careful to draw his salary at the end of the month. This is very bad business for a mining country, as McKenna came to know when the next shutdown found him with a salary some fifteen months in arrears. He said uncomplimentary things about the management, but did not unnecessarily harass the directors, because he held his job on half pay until work began again, all of which was still unpaid when the mine reopened with a small force in April.

By this time, you understand, the Minnietta Mining and Milling Company was in a rather bad way. When the ore was of high grade, or the price of silver went up a few points, it would work the mine at a profit; when neither of these things happened it ran at a loss, and McKenna was their chief creditor. All this time the flux of mining life slacked throughout that district, slacked and dribbled away down the trails of desolate gulches, poured off quick, as it had come, like the sudden rains that burst over those ranges, leaving it scarred with dump and shaft and track. Houses full of cheap, garish furniture of the camps warped apart in the sun, rabbits ran in and out of the sagging sills. Five days' desolation lay between the world and the Minnietta.

During the shut-down McKenna stayed and looked after the mine, he said because it owned him so much he could not afford to neglect it; but really because the desert had him, cat-like, between her paws. So he stayed on and tinkered about repairs for the mill and the smelter. After one such session he was observed to go about in the tumultuous silence of a man with a doubtful project, also he ceased to vex the management greatly about his arrears of salary. And that was about a year before the Minnietta was shut down altogether.

In the course of time, McKenna, as the chief creditor, brought suit, attached the property of the Company, an got a judgment by default. At that time he could have had the whole district on the same terms, for something had happened, or was about to happen, in some other quarter which made the value of silver to the ton about half the cost of working it. The first thing McKenna did when he came into possession was to rip up the smelter.

This was before the cyanide process was discovered, and the smelter was of the rudest description—and McKenna had repaired it. Four great bars of virgin silver, half the length of a man's body and of incredible thickness, he took out of it in the way of leakings. McKenna used it to put the property in working order. The thing which was about to happen in Germany, or Argentina, or wherever, had not happened, or if it had, not with the anticipated effect. Silver went up. McKenna looked to the management himself, grew sleek, and married a wife. But the Hoodoo worked.

In the second year Mrs. McKenna had a child, and it died. Did I say somewhere that women mostly hate the desert? Women, unless they have very large and simple souls, need cover; clothes, you know, and furniture, social observances to screen them, conventions to get behind; life when it leaps upon them, large and naked, shocks them into disorder. Mrs. McKenna, at the Minnietta, had the armlong grave under the skeleton cliffs, and McKenna, with no screen to his commonness. Her mind travelled back and forth from these and down the gulch to a vista of treeless discolored hills. Finally, for very emptiness, it fixed upon McKenna's assistant. The assistant was also common, but he had a little veil of unfamiliarity—and Mrs. McKenna was the only woman within three days. I do not say that what happened wouldn't have happened without the Hoodoo, given the conditions, any woman, and the man; but it served to take McKenna's mind off the mine, and the Hoodoo cut in between. After a while Mrs. McKenna and the superintendent went out of the story by way of the Mojave stage, and McKenna, leaving the mine in charge of Jordan, whom he had promoted from his foreman's job to be superintendent, was supposed to have gone in search of his wife. Whether he found her, or if the Hoodoo stayed by him in the place where he had gone, nobody ever heard. I think myself it inheres where it was bred, in the hollow of the comfortless thick hills. He was, however, bound to lose the mine in some such case as he had got it.

Jordan was the man McKenna had to help him when he ripped up the smelter; he knew exactly how the Minnietta came into his employer's hands and thought well of it. In every mining camp there are men incurably unable to be lessoned by the logic of events. McKenna was certain not to come near the mine again; might reasonably wish to be quit of it. This he might have done profitably, except for the Hoodoo, for the grade of the ore was increasingly rich. Jordan, as a practical miner, was much about the tunnel, and being left to himself too much, had time for thought, and, as I have said, he was the sort of man who admired the sort of thing McKenna had done. Along in the early summer the direction of the work in the main gallery was altered at never so slight an angle, and in due course of time was boarded over.

Jordan reported to McKenna that as the main lead appeared to be nearly worked out, it would be better to put the mine on the market before the fact became generally known. Eventually this was done. The selling price was not large, but considering what McKenna thought he knew of the property, and what the purchasers tipped by Jordan did know, it was satisfactory to both parties. In some unexplained way the Minnietta came shortly into the hands of his former foreman, Dan Jordan, who ripped up the siding and uncovered a body of high-grade ore.

The Minnietta is a nearly horizontal vein in a crumbling country rock that necessitates timbering and an elaborate system of props and siding. The new owner had all the petty, fiddling ways of a man accustomed to days' wages. He bought second-hand timbers from abandoned mines, and took unnecessary risks in the matter of siding, and the men grumbled.

Jordan did not get on well with his men; he gave himself airs, and suspected an attempt to cry down his new dignities. He was swelled and sullen with pride of his prosperity. By this time the conviction of the Hoodoo was well abroad in that country, and men were few and fearful who could be hired to work in the Minnietta. When there was a good twenty thousand on the dump the men refused to go into the tunnel again until certain things were remedied. Jordan, who did not believe in it, cursed the Hoodoo, cursed the hands, and went down into the tunnel, trailing abuse behind him for the men who followed timorously far at his back.

"Better keep this side the cut, sir," said one of them, respectfully enough, "them props ain't no ways safe." Jordan kicked the prop scornfully for all answer—and when the men, starting back from the sound of falling, dared to come up with him, they found him quite dead, his skull crushed, and buried under the crumbling rock.

After that the Minnietta passed in due course to Jordan's heirs, two families of cousins who knew nothing of silver mines except that they were supposed to be eminently desirable.

Now, as they had come into the property through no fault of theirs, if the Hoodoo were nothing more than the logical tendency of evil-doing to draw to and consume the evil-doer, they should have been beyond its reach. This would have been the case if, as you suppose, the Hoodoo were a myth begotten of a series of fortuitous events. But you, between the church and the police, whose every emanation of the soul is shred to tatters by the yammering of kin and neighbor, what do you know of the great, silent spaces across which the voice of law and opinion reaches small as the rustle of blown sand? There the castings of a man's soul lie in whatever shape of hate and rage he threw them from him.

There are places in Lost Valley where in the early fifties emigrant trains went through—places so void of wind and jostling weather that the wheel-tracks show upon the sand, plain from that single passing; other places where, as at the Minnietta, the reek of men's passions lies in the hollow desertness like an infection, as if every timber had absorbed mischief instead of moisture, and every bolt gives it off in lieu of rust.

If it were not so there is no reason why the heirs of Dan Jordan should have gone to law about it while the price of silver went down and down. They stripped themselves in litigation while the timbers sagged in the tunnel and the cuts choked with rubble. The ore on the dump, by no means worth twenty thousand by this time, went to a lawyer who had been a very decent sort until he became dissolute through prosperity and neglected his family. The battens of the mill, warped through successive summers, fell off, and the boards shrunk from each other and curled at the edges like the lips of men dead and sundried in the desert. But if they should come together, or the price of silver go up, say three points, unless they be able to charge the enterprise with some counter-passion of nobility or sacrifice, they stand a chance to prove, in their own persons, how the Hoodoo works.

It is curious, though, and if we considered it long enough would no doubt be terribly disconcerting, to see how little account, when it deals with men singly, the desert takes of nobility as we conceive it between the walls. Clear out beyond the Borders the only unforgivable offence is incompetence; and conscience, in as far as it is a hereditary prejudice in favor of a given line of behavior, is not sort of baggage to take into the wilderness, which has its own exigencies and occasions, and will not be lived in except upon its own conditions. The case of Saunders is in point.

III

A CASE OF CONSCIENCE

SAUNDERS WAS an average Englishman with a lung complaint. He tried Ashfork, Arizona, and Indio, and Catalina. Then he drifted north through the San Jacinta mountains and found what he was looking for. Back in England he had left so many of the things a man wishes to go on with, that he bent himself with great seriousness to his cure. He bought a couple of pack-burros, a pair of cayaques, and a camp kit. With these, a Shakespeare, a prayer-book, and a copy of *Ingoldsby Legends,** he set out on foot to explore the coast of Lost Borders. The prayer-book he had from his mother; I believe he read it regularly night and morning, and the copy of *Ingoldsby Legends* he gave me in the second year of his exile. It happened about that time I was wanting the *Ingoldsby Legends,* three hundred miles from a library, and book money hard to come by. Now there is nearly always a copy of *Ingoldsby Legends* in the vicinity of an Englishman. Englishmen think them amusing, though I do not know why. So I asked my friend, the barkeeper at the Last Chance, to inquire for it of the next Englishman who hit the town. I had to write the name out plainly so the barkeeper could remember it. The first who came was an agent for a London mining syndicate, and he left an address of a book-shop where it could be bought. The next was a remittance man, and of course he hadn't

*This collection of English narrative ballads and tales by Richard Harris Barham (pseud. Thomas Ingoldsby) was first published in 1840.

anything. If he had he would have put it in soak. That means he would have put the book up for its value in bad drink, and I write it as a part of our legitimate speech, because it says so exactly what had occurred: that particular Englishman had put everything, including his honor and his immortal soul, in soak. And the third was Saunders. He was so delighted to find an appreciator of the *Ingoldsby Legends* in the wilderness, that he offered to come to the house and render the obscure passages, and that was the beginning of my knowing about what went on later at Ubehebe.

Saunders had drifted about from water-hole to water-hole, living hardily, breathing the driest, cleanest air, sleeping and waking with the ebb and flow of light that sets in a mighty current around the world. He went up in summer to the mountain heads under the foxtail pines, and back in winter to watch the wild almond bloom by Resting Springs. He saw the Medicine dance of the Shoshones, and hunted the bighorn on Funeral Mountains, and dropped a great many things out of his life without making himself unhappy. But he kept the conscience he had brought with him. Of course it was a man's conscience that allowed him to do a great many things that by the code and the commandments are as wrong as any others, but in the end the wilderness was too big for him, and forced him to a violation of what he called his sense of duty.

In the course of time, Saunders came to a range of purplish hills lying west from Lost Valley, because of its rounded, swelling, fair twin peaks called Ubehebe (Maiden's Breast). It is a good name. Saunders came there in the spring, when the land is lovely and alluring, soft with promise and austerely virgin. He lingered in and about its pleasant places until the month of the Deer-Star, and it was then, when he would come up a week's journey to Lone Pine, for supplies, he began to tell me about Turwhasé, the gray-eyed Shoshone. He thought I would be interested, and I was, though for more reasons than Saunders at first supposed. There is a story current and confirmed, I believe, by proper evidence, that a man of one of the emigrant trains that suffered so much, and went so far astray in the hell trap of Death Valley, wandering from his party in search of water, for want of which he was partly crazed, returned to them no more and was accounted dead. But wandering in the witless condition of great thirst, he was found by the Shoshones, and by them carried to their campody in the secret places of the hills. There, though he never rightly knew himself, he showed some skill and excellences of the white men, and for that, and for his loose wit, which was fearful to them, he was kept and reverenced as a Coyote-man and a Medicine-maker of strange and fitful powers. And at the end of fifteen years his friends found him and took him away. As witness of his sojourning, there is now and then born to the descendants of that campody a Shoshone with gray eyes.

When Saunders began to tell me about Turwhasé, I knew to what it must come, though it was not until his mother wrote me that I could take any notice of it. Some too solicitous person had written her that Saunders had become a squaw-man. She thought he had married Turwhasé, and would bring home a handful of little half-breeds to inherit the estate.

She never knew how near Saunders came to doing that very thing, nor to say truth did I when I wrote her that her son was not married, and that she had nothing to fear; but with the letter I was able to get out of Saunders as much as I did not already know of the story.

I suppose at bottom the things a man loves a woman for are pretty much the same, though it is only when he talks to you of a woman not of his own class that he is willing to tell you what those things are. Saunders loved Turwhasé: first, because he was lonely and had to love somebody; then because of the way the oval of her cheek melted into the chin, and for the lovely line that runs from the waist to the knee, and for her soft, bubbling laughter; and kept on loving her because she made him comfortable.

I suppose the white strain that persisted in her quickened her aptitude for white ways. Saunders taught her to cook. She was never weary nor afraid. She was never out of temper, except when she was jealous, and that was rather amusing. Saunders told me himself how she glowed and blossomed under his caress, and wept when he neglected her. He told me everything I had the courage to know. When a man has gone about the big wilderness with slow death and sure camping on his trail, there is not much worth talking about except the things that are. Turwhasé had the art to provoke tenderness and the wish to protect, and the primitive woman's capacity for making no demands upon it. And this, in fine, is how these women take our men from us, and why, at the last, they lose them.

If you ask whether we discussed the ethics of Saunders' situation— at first there didn't appear to be any. Turwhasé was as much married as if

Church and State had witnessed it; as for Saunders, society, life itself, had cast him off. He was unfit for work or marrying; being right-minded in regard to his lung complaint, he drank from no man's cup nor slept in any bed but his own. And if society had no use for him, how had it a right to say what he should do out there in the bloomy violet spaces at Maiden's Breast? Yet, at the last, the Englishman found, or thought he found, a moral issue.

Maiden's Breast—virgin land, clear sun, unsullied airs, Turwhasé. Isn't there a hint all through of the myth of the renewal of life in a virgin embrace? A great many myths come true in the big wilderness. Saunders went down to Los Angeles once in the year to a consulting physician to please his mother, not because he hoped for anything. He came back from one such journey looking like a sleepwalker newly awakened. He had been told that the diseased portion of his lung was all sloughed away, and if nothing happened to him in six months more of Ubehebe, he might go home! It was then Saunders' conscience began to trouble him, for by this time, you understand, Turwhasé had a child—a daughter, small and gold-colored and gray-eyed. By a trick of inheritance the eyes were like Saunders' mother's, and in the long idle summer she had become a plaything of which he was extremely fond. The mother, of course, was hopeless. She had never left off her blanket, and like all Indian women when they mature, had begun to grow fat. Oh, I *said* he had a man's conscience! Turwhasé must be left behind, but what to do about the daughter lay heavily on Saunders' mind.

It made an obstinate ripple in his complacency like a snag in the current of his thought, which set toward England. Out there by the water-holes, where he had expected to leave his bones, life had been of a simplicity that did not concern itself beyond the happy day. Now the old needs and desires awoke and cried in him, and along with them the old, obstinate Anglo-Saxon prejudice that makes a man responsible for his offspring. Saunders must have had a bad time of it with himself before he came to a decision that he must take the child to England. It would be hard on Turwhasé; if it came to that, it would be hard on him—there would be explanations. As matters stood he looked to make a very good marriage at home, and the half-breed child would be against him. All his life she would be against him. But then it was a question of duty. Duty is a potent fetish of

Englishmen, but the wilderness has a word bigger than that. Just how Turwhasé took his decision about the child I never heard, but as I know Indian women, I suppose she must have taken it quietly at first, said no, and considered it done with; then, as she saw his purpose clear, sat wordless in her blanket, all its folds drawn forward as a sign of sullenness, her thick hair falling on either side to screen her grief; neither moved to attend him, nor ate nor slept; and at last broke under it and seemed to accept, put the child from her as though it was already not hers, and made no more of it.

If there was in this acquiescence a gleam in her gray eye that witnessed she had found the word, Saunders was not aware of it.

As to what he felt himself in regard to Turwhasé I am equally uninformed. I've a notion, though, that men do not give themselves time to feel in such instances; they just get it over with. All I was told was, that when at last he felt himself strong for it, Saunders put the child before him on the horse—she was then about two years old—and set out from Ubehebe. He went all of one day down a long box cañon, where at times his knees scraped the walls on either side, and over the tortuous roots of the mountain blown bare of the sand. The evening of the next day saw the contour of the Maiden's Breast purpling in the east, fading at last in the blurred horizon. He rode all day on glittering pale sands and down steep and utterly barren barrancas. All through that riding something pricked between his shoulders, troubled his sleep with expectancy, haunted him with a suggestion of impossible espionage. The child babbled at first, or slept in his arm; he hugged it to him and forgot that its mother was a Shoshone. It cried in the night and began to refuse its food. Great tears of fatigue stood upon its cheeks; it shook with long, quivering sobs, crying silently as Indian children do when they are frightened. Saunders' arm ached with the weight of it; his heart with the perplexity. The little face looked up at him, hard with inscrutable savagery. When he came to the Inyo range and the beaten trail, he distrusted his judgment; his notion of rearing the child in England began to look ridiculous. By the time he had cleared the crest and saw the fields and orchards far below him, it appeared preposterous. And the hint of following hung like some pestiferous insect about his trail.

In all the wide, uninterrupted glare no speck as of a moving body swam within his gaze. By what locked and secret ways the presence kept pace with him, only the vultures hung high under the flaring heaven could have known.

At the hotel at Keeler that night he began to taste the bitterness he had chosen. Men, white men, mining men, mill superintendents, well-dressed, competent, looked at the brat which had Shoshone written plainly all over it, and looked away unsmiling; being gentlemen, they did not so much as look at one another. Sanders gave money to the women at the hotel to keep his daughter all night out of his sight. Riding next day toward Lone Pine between the fenced lands, farms and farmhouses, schools, a church, he began to understand that there was something more than mere irresponsibility in the way of desert-faring men who formed relations such as this and left them off with the land, as they left the clothes they wore there and its tricks of speech.

He was now four days from Ubehebe. The child slept little that night; sat up in bed, listened; would whisper its mother's name over and over, questioning, expectant; left off, still as a young quail, if Saunders moved or noticed it. It occurred to him that the child might die, which would be the best thing for it.

Coming out of his room in the early morning he stumbled over something soft in a blanket. It unrolled of itself and stood up—Turwhasé! The child gave a little leap in his arms and was still, pitifully, breathlessly still. The woman stretched out her own arms, her eyes were red and devouring.

"My baby!" she said. "Give it to me!" Without a word Saunders held it out to her. The little dark arms went around her neck, prehensile and clinging; the whole little body clung, the lines of the small face softened with a sigh of unutterable content. Turwhasé drew up her blanket and held it close.

"Mine!" she said, fiercely. "Mine, not yours!"

Saunders did not gainsay her; he drew out all the money he had and poured it in her bosom. Turwhasé laughed. With a flirt of her blanket she scattered the coins on the ground; she turned with dignity and began to walk desertward. You could see by the slope of the shoulders under the blanket and the swing of her hips, as she went, that she was all Indian.

Saunders reached down to me from the platform of the train that morning for a last goodby. He was looking very English, smug and freshly shaven.

"I am convinced," he said, "that it really wouldn't have done, you know." I believe he thought he had come to that conclusion by himself.

WHAT I LIKE MOST about the speech of the campody is that there are no confidences. When they talk there of the essential performances of life, it is because they are essential and therefore worth talking about. Only Heaven, who made my heart, knows why it should have become a pit, bottomless and insatiable for the husks of other people's experiences, as if it were not, as I declare it, filled to the brim with the entertainment of its own affairs; as if its mere proximity were an advertisement for it, there must be always some one letting fall confidences as boys drop stones in wells, to listen afterward in some tale of mine for the faint, reverberating sound. But this is the mark of sophistication, that they always appear *as* confidences, always with that wistful back-stroke of the ego toward a personal distinction. "I don't know why I am telling you this—I shouldn't like to have you repeat it"—and then the heart loosening intimacy of speech and its conscious easement.

But in a campody it is possible to speak of the important operations of life without shamefacedness. Mid-afternoons of late fall and winter weather—for though you may speak to your brother man without curtailment, it is not well to do so in summer when the snakes are about, for the snakes are two-tongued and carry word to the gods, who, if they are to be of use to you, must not know too much of your affairs—in mid-afternoon then, when the women weave baskets and grind at the metate, and the men make nets and snares, there is good talk and much to be learned by it. Such times the sky is hard like polished turquoise set in the tawny matrix of the earth, the creek goes thinly over the stones, and the very waters of mirage are rolled back to some shut fountain in the skies; the *plump, plump!* of the metate beats on under the talk of the women like the comfortable pulse of not too insistent toil.

When Indian women talk together, and they are great gossips, three things will surely come to the surface in the course of the afternoon—children, marriage, and the ways of the whites. This last appears as a sort of pageant, which, though it is much of it sheer foolishness, is yet charged with a mysterious and compelling portent. They could never, for example, though they could give you any number of fascinating instances, get any rational explanation of the effect of their familiar clear space and desertness upon the white man adventuring in it. It was as if you had discovered in your parlor-furniture an inexplicable power of inciting your guest to strange behavior. And what in the conduct of men most interests women of the campody, or women anywhere for that matter, is their relation to women. If this, which appears to have rooted about the time the foundations of the earth were laid, is proved amenable to the lack of shade, scarcity of vegetation, and great spaces disinterested of men—not these of course, but the Power moving nakedly in the room of these things—it only goes to show that the relation is more incidental than we are disposed to think it. There is nothing in the weather and the distance between water-holes to affect a man's feeling for his children, as I have already explained to you in the case of Saunders and Mr. Wills. But there where the Borders run out, through all the talk of the women, white women, too, who get no better understanding of the thing they witness to, through the thin web of their lives moves the vast impersonal rivalry of desertness. But because of what I said in the beginning I can tell you no more of that than I had from Tiawa in the campody of Sacabuete, where there are no confidences.

IV

THE PLOUGHED LANDS

TIAWA CAME FROM a Shoshone camp of three wickiups somewhere between Toquina and Fish Lake Valley. When she was young and comely she had come out of that country at the heels of a white man, and wrestled with the wilderness for the love of Curly Gavin. Gavin had been swamper for Ike Mallory's eighteen-mule team, and when the news of rich strikes in the Ringold district made red flares like rockets on Mallory's horizon, he grub-staked Curly to go with Burke and Estes to prospect the Toquina. Gavin had a lot of reddish curls and a lot of good-nature and small vices; the rest of him was sheer grit. The party was out three weeks, made some fair prospects, and had a disagreement. As to that, there was never any clear account, only it became immensely important to Gavin's own mind that he should get back to Maverick and record the location of some claims before Burke and Estes had a chance at them. Accordingly he left the others at Mud Springs, and, with one day's ration of water, set out by what he believed to be a short cut for home; and he had never been loose in the wilderness before! It was spring of the year after a winter of strong rains, and a bloom on the world, all the air soft as shed petals. Every inch of the moon-white soil had a flower in it, purple or golden; mornings the light made a luminous mist about the long wands of the creosote, at noon it slid and shimmered on the slopes as the hills breathed evenly in sleep. It is as easy, I say, to believe that such a land could neglect men to their death, as for man to believe that a lovely woman can be unkind. Gavin, for one, did not believe it.

By noon of the second day he began to suspect he had missed the trail—by night he was sure of it, and thinking to behave very sensibly walked back by the stars to recover the lost landmarks. By that time his water was quite gone. There came a time soon after that when the one consuming desire of the man was to get shut of the whole affair, the swimming earth that swung and tilted about the pivot of his feet, the hell-bent sun, the tormenting thirst, the glare of the sand that ate into his eyes. He was horribly bored; he wanted the thing to quit, to let him rest.

"Have done, curse you!" he shouted to it. As if the land had heard him, it reeled and sank; a grateful blackness swallowed all his sense. It was about that time Tiawa's father, hunting chuckwallas, found him and led him to his camp.

In the interval before Gavin was quite himself again, Tiawa tended him. When he rose in his delirium to go to record those claims, she dropped her strong arms about him and eased him to the ground, rocking him in her bosom. So long as he did not know her, her tenderness had scope and power. But Gavin was annoyed when, as soon as he was able to travel, though not properly fit for it, he asked for a guide and got Tiawa. By the usage of her people it was Tiawa's right, because she loved him. She could do that—these gentle savages who will not be seen walking abreast with their women grant them the right to love unasked and unashamed. *They* have no place, let me tell you, in the acceptance or rejection of a proffered love, for the snigger of the sophisticated male. Tiawa was pretty—so slim and round of limb, so smoothly brown and lustrous eyed! Gavin had no scruples, you may be sure; he was merely in the grip of another mistress who might or might not loose his bonds.

Well do I know the way of that tawny-throated one. If she but turns toward our valley with her hot breath to blow back the winter's rains, you hear the prophecy of that usurpation in the flat trumpeting of the bucks that bell the does; there will be few young that season in the lairs along Salt Creek, the quail will not mate; and this, mind you, if she no more than turns toward us her fulgent, splendid smiling for the three months between the piñon harvest and the time of taboose. Judge, then, what she would do to man.

Said Tiawa's father, who knew something of white men, and had looked between Gavin's eyes where the mark of the desert was set: "My daughter, when you have brought him as far as the ploughed lands, best you come home again."

Tiawa had put on her best bead necklace for the journey, and her cheeks were smooth with vermilion earth. She did not mean to come back. Tiawa told me this at Sacabuete, middle aged and fat, smiling above the metate as she paused in her grinding, for she had married a Paiute after Gavin left her, and made him very comfortable.

"But I did not know then," she said, "that a white man could take service from such as we and not requite it. If I had done the half of that for a Shoshone he would have loved me, for there were not two sticks laid together on that journey that I had not the doing of it."

They made a dry camp the first night, and when Gavin from sheer weakness lay down along the sand, and Tiawa had brought him food, before the glow was gone from the top of Toquina, when the evening star was lit and the heaven was clear and tender, he turned his back on Tiawa and stretched himself to sleep. On her side of the fire, Tiawa, dry-eyed and hot with shame, lay and pondered the reasons for these things. He was white, therefore he could accept her service without regarding the love that prompted it, and sleep upon it compunctionless. In the morning he spoke to her kindly, and she hoped again, for her desire was toward him and the spring was in her blood; but the obsession of his errand was on Gavin's mind, and he did not know. The morning wind blew out the strands of her thick hair, and shaped her garments to her loveliest curves as she brushed against him in the trail; every turn of her soft throat and the glint of her lustrous eyes was of love, but the sun-glare was heavy in his eyes, and he did not see. At the end of the third day, being at the end of her woman's devices, Tiawa bethought her of the gods. When it was full dark, before the moon was up, she went a little aside from the camp and made a medicine of songs. She swung and swayed to the postures of desire, beat upon the full, young, aching breast, and sang to the gods for the satisfaction of her love. Her voice reached him heavy with world-old anguish of women.

"Aw, shut up, can't you!" said Gavin. "I want to go to sleep!"

The desert had him. He had come into it fearlessly and unguarded, and it struck home; but Tiawa, who did not know any better, thought only that she had lost. She took off her bead collar because it had failed her, and wiped the vermilion from her cheeks. Only service remained, and that flowed from her as naturally as the long wands of the creosote flowed upon the wind. By day she went before him in the trails, by night at nameless water-holes she cooked his food. She did not know the places on the map where Gavin wished to go. She had set out by her father's direction for the shortest cut to the Ploughed Lands, and as they neared her heart sank inwardly as she remembered her father's word. For the Ploughed Lands meant the end of her Indian world. It meant white people, towns, farms at least—things, the desire of which had hurried Gavin mindlessly along the trail, the comfortable, long-turned furrow in which his life ran wontedly, the Ploughed Lands where he had no need of her.

Out here toward Toquina in the stark cañons, in the thin-sown pastures, she knew the way of subsistence; there in the fat, well-watered fields, unless Gavin accepted her when they came to the Ploughed Lands, she must go back. It is only our pitiful civilization, you understand, that attempts to magnify the love of man by shaming its end. In her own country Tiawa could venture much, as she pitted herself against the wilderness, but in the end she lay all night with her face between her arms weeping tearlessly. About noon of the last day they sighted the planted fields. From a hill-crest looking down they saw the dark smears of green on the golden valley, and out beyond these the line of willows, the thin gleam of the irrigating ditch like a blade from which the foiled desert started back. The rest of that day's trudging was down and down. Tiawa went before, and Gavin, breathing more evenly in the cooled air, felt the grip of the desert loosen on him with the tension of a spring released. He perceived suddenly that the woman was lovely and young. She was not so round by now, for they had come a long way with scant rations; but by the mark of her service upon her, he was suddenly aware that she loved him.

"Give me that pack," said Gavin; "you've carried it long enough."

The intent was kind, but to the girl it was the intimation of dismissal; he had refused her love, and now he would not even have her service. His tongue was freed of the spell of the silent places, and he talked as they went, pointing out this ranch and that as they went down.

About sunset they came to the out-curve of the canal and the farthest corner of an alfalfa field, and made their camp there. For the last time Tiawa laid the sticks together under the cooking-pot. For the last time; so it seemed to Tiawa. Lights began to come out in the ranch houses, faint and far. Tiawa thought of the little fires by the huts in Toquina; tears in her heart welled and brimmed about her eyes. Just then Gavin called her. She turned, and by the faint stars, by the dying flicker of their fire, she saw incredibly that he smiled. And to such as Tiawa, you understand, the smile of a white man—a man with ruddy curls, broad in the shoulders and young—is as the favor of the gods.

"Tiawa?"

"Great One!" she whispered.

Still smiling, he stretched out his arm to her and hollowed it in invitation . . . for he had come to the Ploughed Lands. He was his own man again.

In the end—as I have already explained to you—Gavin went back to his own kind, and Tiawa married a Paiute and grew fat, for mostly in encounter with the primal forces woman gets the worst of it except now and then, when there are children in question, she becomes a primal force herself.

Great souls that go into the desert come out mystics—saints and prophets—declaring unutterable things: Buddha, Mahomet, and the Gallilean, convincing of the casual nature of human relations, because the desert itself has no use for the formal side of man's affairs. What need, then, of so much pawing over precedent and discoursing upon it, when the open country lies there, a sort of chemist's cup for resolving obligations? Say whether, when all decoration is eaten away, there remains any bond, and what you shall do about it.

V

THE RETURN OF MR. WILLS

MRS. WILLS had lived seventeen years with Mr. Wills, and when he left her for three, those three were so much the best of her married life that she wished he had never come back. And the only real trouble with Mr. Wills was that he should never have moved West. Back East I suppose they breed such men because they need them, but they ought really to keep them there.

I am quite certain that when Mr. Wills was courting Mrs. Wills he parted his hair in the middle, and the breast-pocket of his best suit had a bright silk lining which Mr. Wills pulled up to simulate a silk handkerchief. Mrs. Wills had a certain draggled prettiness, and a way of tossing her head which came back to her after Mr. Wills left, which made you think she might have been the prettiest girl of her town. They were happy enough at first, when Mr. Wills was a grocery clerk, assistant Sunday-school superintendent, and they owned a cabinet organ and four little Willses. It might have been that Mr. Wills thought he could go right on being the same sort of a man in the West—he was clerk at the Bed Rock Emporium, and had brought the organ and the children; or it might have been at bottom he thought himself a very different sort of man, and meant to be it if he got a chance.

There is a sort of man bred up in close communities, like a cask, to whom the church, public opinion, the social note, are a sort of hoop to hold him in serviceable shape. Without these there are a good many ways of going to pieces. Mr. Wills' way was Lost Mines.

Being clerk at the Emporium, where miners and prospectors bought their supplies, he heard a lot of talk about mines, and was too new to it to understand that the man who has the most time to stop and talk about it has the least to do with mining. And of all he heard, the most fascinating to Mr. Wills, who was troubled with an imagination, was of the lost mines: incredibly rich ledges, touched and not found again. To go out into the unmapped hills on the mere chance of coming across something was, on the face of it, a risky business; but to look for a mine once located, sampled and proved, definitely situated in a particular mountain range or a certain cañon, had a smack of plausibility. Besides that, an ordinary prospect might or might not prove workable, but the lost mines were always amazingly rich. Of all the ways in the West for a man to go to pieces this is the most insidious. Out there beyond the towns the long Wilderness lies brooding, imperturbable; she puts out to adventurous minds glittering fragments of fortune or romance, like the lures men use to catch antelopes—clip! then she has them. If Mr. Wills had gambled or drank, his wife could have gone to the minister about it, his friends could have done something. There was a church in Maverick of twenty-seven members, and the Willses had brought letters to it, but except for the effect it had on Mrs. Wills, it would not be worth mentioning. Though he might never have found it out in the East, Mr. Wills belonged to the church, not because of what it meant to himself, but for what it meant to other people. Back East it had meant social standing, repute, moral impeccability. To other people in Maverick it meant a weakness which was excused in you so long as you did not talk about it. Mr. Wills did not, because there was so much else to talk about in connection with lost mines.

He began by grub-staking Pedro Ruiz to look for the Lost Ledge of Fisherman's Peak, and that was not so bad, for it had not been lost more than thirty years, the peak was not a hundred miles from Maverick, and, besides, I have a piece of the ore myself. Then he was bitten by the myth of the Gunsight, of which there was never anything more tangible than a dime's worth of virgin silver, picked up by a Jayhawker, hammered into a sight for a gun; and you had to take the gun on faith at that, for it and the man who owned it had quite disappeared; and afterward it was the Duke o'

The Return of Mr. Wills

Wild Rose, which was never a mine at all, merely an arrow-mark on a map left by a penniless lodger found dead in a San Francisco hotel. Grub-staking is expensive, even to a clerk at the Bed Rock Emporium getting discounts on the grub, and grub-staked prospectors are about as dependable as the dreams they chase, often pure fakes, lying up at seldom-visited water-holes while the stake lasts, returning with wilder tales and clews more alluring. It was a late conviction that led Mr. Wills, when he put the last remnant of his means into the search for the White Cement mines, to resign his clerkship and go in charge of the expedition himself. There is no doubt whatever that there is a deposit of cement on Bald Mountain, with lumps of gold sticking out of it like plums in a pudding. It lies at the bottom of a small gulch near the middle fork of Owens River, and is overlaid by pumice. There is a camp kit buried somewhere near, and two skeletons. There is also an Indian in that vicinity who is thought to be able to point out the exact location—if he would. It is quite the sort of thing to appeal to the imagination of Mr. Wills, and he spent two years proving that he could not find it. After that he drifted out toward the Lee district to look for Lost Cabin mine, because a man who had immediate need of twenty dollars, had, for that amount, offered Wills some exact and unpublished information as to its location. By that time Wills' movements had ceased to interest anybody in Maverick. He could be got to believe anything about any sort of a prospect, providing it was lost.

The only visible mark left by all this was on Mrs. Wills. Everybody in a mining-town, except the minister and professional gamblers who wear frock-coats, dresses pretty much alike, and Wills very soon got to wear in his face the guileless, trustful fixity of the confirmed prospector. It seemed as if the desert had overshot him and struck at Mrs. Wills, and Richard Wills, Esther Wills, Benjy Wills, and the youngest Wills, who was called Mugsey. Desertness attacked the door-yard and the house; even the cabinet organ had a weathered look. During the time of the White Cement obsession the Wills family appeared to be in need of a grub-stake themselves. Mrs. Wills' eyes were like the eyes of trail-weary cattle; her hands grew to have that pitiful way of catching the front of her dress of the woman not so much a slattern as hopeless. It was when her husband went out after Lost Cabin she fell into the habit of sitting down to a cheap novel with the dishes unwashed, a sort of drugging of despair common among women of the camps. All this time Mr. Wills was drifting about from camp to camp of the desert borders, working when it could not be avoided, but mostly on long, fruitless trudges among the unmindful ranges. I do not know if the man was honest with himself; if he knew by this time that the clew of a lost mine was the baldest of excuses merely to be out and away from everything that savored of definiteness and responsibility. The fact was, the desert had got him. All the hoops were off the cask. The mind of Mr. Wills faded out at the edges like the desert horizon that melts in mists and mirages, and finally he went on an expedition from which he did not come back.

He had been gone nearly a year when Mrs. Wills gave up expecting him. She had grown so used to the bedraggled crawl of life that she might never have taken any notice of the disappearance of Mr. Wills had not the Emporium refused to make any more charges in his name. There had been a great many dry water-holes on the desert that year, and more than the usual complement of sun-dried corpses. In a general way this accounted for Mr. Wills, though nothing transpired of sufficient definiteness to justify Mrs. Wills in putting on a widow's dress, and, anyway, she could not have afforded it.

Mrs. Wills and the children went to work, and work was about the only thing in Maverick of which there was more than enough. It was a matter of a very few months when Mrs. Wills made the remarkable discovery that after the family bills were paid at the end of the month, there was a little over. A very little. Mrs. Wills had lived so long with the tradition that a husband is a natural provider that it took some months longer to realize that she not only did not need Mr. Wills, but got on better without him. This was about the time she was able to have the sitting-room repapered and put up lace curtains. And the next spring the children planted roses in the front yard. All up and down the wash of Salt Creek there were lean coyote mothers, and wild folk of every sort could have taught her that nature never makes the mistake of neglecting to make the child-bearer competent to provide. But Mrs. Wills had not been studying life in the lairs. She had most of her notions of it from the church and her parents, and all under the new sense of independence and power she had an ache of forlornness and neglect. As a matter of fact she filled out, grew stronger, had a spring in her walk. She was not pining for Mr. Wills; the desert had him—for whatever conceivable use, it was more than Mrs. Wills could put him to—let the desert keep what it had got.

It was in the third summer that she regained a certain air that made me think she must have been pretty when Mr. Wills married her. And no woman in a mining-town can so much as hint at prettiness without its being found out. Mrs. Wills had a good many prejudices left over from the time when Mr. Wills had been superintendent of the Sunday-school, and would not hear of divorce. Yet, as the slovenliness of despair fell away from her, as she held up her head and began to have company to tea, it is certain somebody would have broached it to her before the summer was over; but by that time Mr. Wills came back.

It happened that Benjy Wills, who was fourteen and driving the Bed Rock delivery wagon, had a runaway accident in which he had behaved very handsomely and gotten a fractured skull. News of it went by way of the local paper to Tonopah, and from there drifted south to the Funeral Mountains and the particular prospect that Mr. Wills was working on a grub-stake. He had come to that. Perhaps as much because he had found there was nothing in it, as from paternal anxiety, he came home the evening of the day the doctor had declared the boy out of danger.

It was my turn to sit up that night, I remember, and Mrs. Meyer, who had the turn before, was telling me about the medicines. There was a neighbor woman who had come in by the back door with a bowl of custard, and the doctor standing in the sitting-room with Mrs. Wills, when Mr. Wills came in through the black block of the doorway with his hand before his face to ward off the light—and perhaps some shamefaced-ness—who knows?

I saw Mrs. Wills quiver, and her hand went up to her bosom as if some one had struck her. I have seen horses start and check like that as they came over the Pass and the hot blast of the desert took them fairly. It was the stroke of desolation. I remember turning quickly at the doctor's curt signal to shut the door between the sitting-room and Benjy.

"Don't let the boy see you to-night, Wills," said the doctor, with no hint of a greeting; "he's not to be excited." With that he got himself off as quickly as possible, and the neighbor woman and I went out and sat on the back steps a long time, and tried to talk about everything but Mr. Wills. When I went in, at last, he was sitting in the Morris chair, which had come with soap-wrappers, explaining to Mrs. Meyer about the rich prospect he had left to come to his darling boy. But he did not get so much as a glimpse of his darling boy while I was in charge.

Mr. Wills settled on his family like a blight. For a man who has prospected lost mines to that extent is positively not good for anything else. It was not only as if the desert had sucked the life out of him and cast him back, but as if it would have Mrs. Wills in his room. As the weeks went on you could see a sort of dinginess creeping up from her dress to her hair and her face, and it spread to the house and the doorway. Mr. Wills had enjoyed the improved condition of his home, though he missed the point of it; his wife's cooking tasted good to him after miner's fare, and he was proud of his boys. He didn't want any more of the desert. Not he. "There's no place like home," said Mr. Wills, or something to that effect.

But he had brought the desert with him on his back. If it had been at any other time than when her mind was torn with anxiety for Benjy, Mrs. Wills might have made a fight against it. But the only practical way to separate the family from the blight was to divorce Mr. Wills, and the church to which Mrs. Wills belonged admitted divorce only in the event of there being another woman.

Mrs. Wills rose to the pitch of threatening, I believe, about the time Mr. Wills insisted on his right to control the earnings of his sons. But the minister called; the church put out its hand upon her poor, staggered soul that sunk aback. The minister himself was newly from the East, and did not understand that the desert is to be dealt with as a woman and a wanton; he was thinking of it as a place on the map. Therefore, he was not of the slightest use to Mrs. Wills, which did not prevent him from commanding her behavior. And the power of the wilderness lay like a wasting sickness on the home.

About that time Mrs. Wills took to novel-reading again; the eldest son drifted off up Tonopah way; and Benjy began to keep back a part of the wages he brought home. And Mr. Wills is beginning to collect misinformation about the exact locality where Peg-leg Smith is supposed to have found the sunburnt nuggets. He does not mention the matter often, being, as he says, done with mines; but whenever the Peg-leg comes up in talk I can see Mrs. Wills chirk up a little, her gaze wandering to the inscrutable grim spaces, not with the hate you might suppose, but with something like hope in her eye, as if she had guessed what I am certain of—that in time its insatiable spirit will reach out and take Mr. Wills again.

And this time, if I know Mrs. Wills, he will not come back.

VI

THE LAST ANTELOPE

THERE WERE SEVEN notches in the juniper by the Lone Tree Spring for the seven seasons that Little Pete had summered there, feeding his flocks in the hollow of the Ceriso. The first time of coming he had struck his axe into the trunk, meaning to make firewood, but thought better of it, and thereafter chipped it in sheer friendliness, as one claps an old acquaintance, for by the time the flock has worked up the treeless windy stretch from the Little Antelope to the Ceriso, even a lone juniper has a friendly look. And Little Pete was a friendly man, though shy of demeanor, so that with the best will in the world for wagging his tongue, he could scarcely pass the time of day with good countenance; the soul of a jolly companion with the front and bearing of one of his own sheep.

He loved his dogs as brothers; he was near akin to the wild things; he communed with the huddled hills, and held intercourse with the stars, saying things to them in his heart that his tongue stumbled over and refused. He knew his sheep by name, and had respect to signs and seasons; his lips moved softly as he walked, making no sound. Well—what would you? a man must have fellowship in some sort.

Whoso goes a-shepherding in the desert hills comes to be at one with his companions, growing brutish or converting them. Little Pete human-ized his sheep. He perceived lovable qualities in them, and differentiated the natures and dispositions of inanimate things.

The Last Antelope

Not much of this presented itself on slight acquaintance, for, in fact, he looked to be of rather less account than his own dogs. He was under-sized and hairy, and had a roving eye; probably he washed once a year at the shearing as the sheep were washed. About his body he wore a twist of sheepskin with the wool outward, holding in place the tatters of his clothing. On hot days when he wreathed leaves about his head, and wove him a pent of twigs among the scrub in the middle of his flock, he looked a faun or some wood creature come out of pagan times, though no pagan, as was clearly shown by the medal of the Sacred Heart that hung on his hairy chest, worn open to all weathers. Where he went about sheep-camps and shearing there were sly laughter and tapping of foreheads, but those who kept the tale of his flocks spoke well of him and increased his wage.

Little Pete kept to the same round year by year, breaking away from La Liebre after the spring shearing, south around the foot of Piños, swinging out to the desert in the wake of the quick, strong rains, thence to Little Antelope in July to drink a bottle for *La Quatorze,** and so to the Ceriso by the time the poppy fires were burned quite out and the quail trooped at noon about the tepid pools. The Ceriso is not properly mesa nor valley, but a long-healed crater miles wide, rimmed about with the jagged edge of the old cone.

It rises steeply from the tilted mesa, overlooked by Black Mountain, darkly red as the red cattle that graze among the honey-colored hills. These are blunt and rounded, tumbling all down from the great crater and the mesa edge toward the long, dim valley of Little Antelope. Its outward slope is confused with the outlines of the hills, tumuli of blind cones, and the old lava flow that breaks away from it by the west gap and the ravine of the spring; within, its walls are deeply guttered by the torrent of winter rains.

In its cup-like hollow, the sink of its waters, salt and bitter as all pools without an outlet, waxes and wanes within a wide margin of bleaching reeds. Nothing taller shows in all the Ceriso, and the wind among them fills all the hollow with an eerie whispering. One spring rills down by the gorge of an old flow on the side toward Little Antelope, and, but for the lone

* Bastille Day, the national French holiday on July 14, commemorates the fall of the Bastille in 1789.

juniper that stood by it, there is never a tree until you come to the foot of Black Mountain.

The flock of Little Pete, a maverick strayed from some rodeo, a prospector going up to Black Mountain, and a solitary antelope were all that passed through the Ceriso at any time. The antelope had the best right. He came as of old habit; he had come when the lightfoot herds ranged from here to the sweet, mist-watered cañons of the Coast Range, and the bucks went up to the windy mesas what time the young ran with their mothers, nose to flank. They had ceased before the keen edge of slaughter that defines the frontier of men.

All that a tardy law had saved to the district of Little Antelope was the buck that came up the ravine of the Lone Tree Spring at the set time of the year when Little Pete fed his flock in the Ceriso, and Pete averred that they were glad to see each other. True enough, they were each the friendliest thing the other found there; for though the law ran as far as the antelope ranged, there were hill-dwellers who took no account of it— namely, the coyotes. They hunted the buck in season and out, bayed him down from the feeding-grounds, fended him from the pool, pursued him by relay races, ambushed him in the pitfalls of the black rock.

There were seven coyotes ranging the east side of the Ceriso at the time when Little Pete first struck his axe into the juniper-tree, slinking, sly-footed, and evil-eyed. Many an evening the shepherd watched them running lightly in the hollow of the crater, the flash-flash of the antelope's white rump signalling the progress of the chase. But always the buck outran or outwitted them, taking to the high, broken ridges where no split foot could follow his seven-leagued bounds. Many a morning Little Pete, tending his cooking-pot by a quavering sagebrush fire, saw the antelope feeding down toward the Lone Tree Spring, and looked his sentiments. The coyotes had spoken theirs all in the night with derisive voices; never was there any love lost between a shepherd and a coyote. The pronghorn's chief recommendation to an acquaintance was that he could outdo them.

After the third summer, Pete began to perceive a reciprocal friend-liness in the antelope. Early mornings the shepherd saw him rising from his lair, or came often upon the warm pressed hollow where he had lain within cry of his coyote-scaring fire. When it was midday in the misty hollow and the shadows drawn close, stuck tight under the juniper and the sage, they went each to his nooning in his own fashion, but in the half light they drew near together.

Since the beginning of the law the antelope had half forgotten his fear of man. He looked upon the shepherd with steadfastness, he smelled the smell of his garments which was the smell of sheep and the unhandled earth, and the smell of wood smoke was in his hair. They had companionship without speech; they conferred favors silently after the manner of those who understand one another. The antelope led to the best feeding-grounds, and Pete kept the sheep from muddying the spring until the buck had drunk. When the coyotes skulked in the scrub by night to deride him, the shepherd mocked them in their own tongue, and promised them the best of his lambs for the killing; but to hear afar off their hunting howl stirred him out of sleep to curse with great heartiness. At such times he thought of the antelope and wished him well.

Beginning with the west gap opposite the Lone Tree Spring about the first of August, Pete would feed all around the broken rim of the crater, up the gullies and down, and clean through the hollow of it in a matter of two months, or if the winter had been a wet one, a little longer, and in seven years the man and the antelope grew to know each other very well. Where the flock fed the buck fed, keeping farthest from the dogs, and at last he came to lie down with it.

That was after a season of scant rains, when the feed was poor and the antelope's flank grew thin; the rabbits had trooped down to the irrigated lands, and the coyotes, made more keen by hunger, pressed him hard. One of those smoky, yawning days when the sky hugged the earth, and all sound fell back from a woolly atmosphere and broke dully in the scrub, about the usual hour of their running between twilight and mid-afternoon, the coyotes drove the tall buck, winded, desperate, and fore-done, to refuge among the silly sheep, where for fear of the dogs and the man the howlers dared not come. He stood at bay there, fronting the shepherd, brought up against a crisis greatly needing the help of speech.

Well—he had nearly as much gift in that matter as Little Pete. Those two silent ones understood each other; some assurance, the warrant of a free-given faith, passed between them. The buck lowered his head and eased the sharp throbbing of his ribs; the dogs drew in the scattered flocks; they moved, keeping a little cleared space nearest the buck; he moved with them; he began to feed. Thereafter the heart of Little Pete warmed humanly toward the antelope, and the coyotes began to be very personal in their abuse. That same night they drew off the shepherd's dogs by a ruse and stole two of his lambs.

The same seasons that made the friendliness of the antelope and Little Pete wore the face of the shepherd into a keener likeness to the weathered hills, and the juniper flourishing greenly by the spring bade fair to outlast them both. The line of ploughed lands stretched out mile by mile from the lower valley, and a solitary homesteader built him a cabin at the foot of the Ceriso.

In seven years a coyote may learn somewhat; those of the Ceriso learned the ways of Little Pete and the antelope. Trust them to have noted, as the years moved, that the buck's flanks were lean and his step less free. Put it that the antelope was old, and that he made truce with the shepherd to hide the failing of his powers; then if he came earlier or stayed later than the flock, it would go hard with him. But as if he knew their mind in the matter, the antelope delayed his coming until the salt pool shrunk to its innermost ring of reeds, and the sun-cured grasses crisped along the slope. It seemed the brute sense waked between him and the man to make each aware of the other's nearness. Often as Little Pete drove in by the west gap he would sight the prongs of the buck rising over the barrier of black rocks at the head of the ravine. Together they passed out of the crater, keeping fellowship as far as the frontier of evergreen oaks. Here Little Pete turned in by the cattle fences to come at La Liebre from the north, and the antelope, avoiding all man-trails, growing daily more remote, passed into the wooded hills on unguessed errands of his own.

Twice the homesteader saw the antelope go up to the Ceriso at that set time of the year. The third summer when he sighted him, a whitish speck moving steadily against the fawn-colored background of the hills, the homesteader took down his rifle and made haste into the crater. At that time his cabin stood on the remotest edge of settlement, and the grip of the law was loosened in so long a reach.

"In the end the coyotes will get him. Better that he fall to me," said the homesteader. But, in fact, he was prompted by the love of mastery, which for the most part moves men into new lands, whose creatures they conceive given over into their hands.

The coyote that kept the watch at the head of the ravine saw him come, and lifted up his voice in the long-drawn dolorous whine that warned the other watchers in their unseen stations in the scrub. The homesteader heard also, and let a curse softly under his breath, for besides that they might scare his quarry, he coveted the howler's ears, in which the law upheld him. Never a tip nor a tail of one showed above the sage when he had come up into the Ceriso.

The afternoon wore on; the homesteader hid in the reeds, and the coyotes had forgotten him. Away to the left in a windless blur of dust the sheep of Little Pete trailed up toward the crater's rim. The leader, watching by the spring, caught a jack-rabbit and was eating it quietly behind the black rock.

In the mean time the last antelope came lightly and securely by the gully, by the black rock and the lone juniper, into the Ceriso. The friendliness of the antelope for Little Pete betrayed him. He came with some sense of home, expecting the flock and protection of man-presence. He strayed witlessly into the open, his ears set to catch the jangle of the bells. What he heard was the snick of the breech-bolt as the homesteader threw up the sight of his rifle, and a small demoniac cry that ran from gutter to gutter of the crater rim, impossible to gauge for numbers or distance.

At that moment Little Pete worried the flock up the outward slope where the ruin of the old lava flows gave sharply back the wrangle of the bells. Three weeks he had won up from the Little Antelope, and three by way of the Sand Flat, where there was great scarcity of water, and in all that time none of his kind had hailed him. His heart warmed toward the juniper-tree and the antelope whose hoof-prints he found in the white dust of the mesa trail. Men had small respect by Little Pete, women he had no time for: the antelope was the noblest thing he had ever loved. The sheep poured through the gap and spread fanwise down the gully; behind them Little Pete twirled his staff, and made merry wordless noises in his throat in anticipation of friendliness. "Ehu!" he cried when he heard the hunting howl, "but they are at their tricks again," and then in English he voiced a volley of broken, inconsequential oaths, for he saw what the howlers were about.

One imputes a sixth sense to that son of a thief misnamed the coyote, to make up for speech—persuasion, concerted movement—in short, the human faculty. How else do they manage the terrible relay races by which they make quarry of the fleetest-footed? It was so they plotted the antelope's last running in the Ceriso: two to start the chase from the black rock toward the red scar of a winter torrent, two to leave the mouth of the wash when the first were winded, one to fend the ravine that led up to the broken ridges, one to start out of the scrub at the base of a smooth upward sweep, and, running parallel to it, keep the buck well into the open; all these when their first spurt was done to cross leisurely to new stations to take up another turn. Round they went in the hollow of the crater, velvet-footed and sly even in full chase, and biding their time. It was a good running, but it was almost done when away by the west gap the buck heard the voice of Little Pete raised in adjuration and the friendly blether of the sheep. Thin spirals of dust flared upward from the moving flocks and signalled truce to chase. He broke for it with wide panting bounds and many a missed step picked up with incredible eagerness, the thin rim of his nostrils oozing blood. The coyotes saw and closed in about him, chopping quick and hard. Sharp ears and sharp muzzles cast up at his throat, and were whelmed in a press of gray flanks. One yelped, one went limping from a kick, and one went past him, returning with a spring upon the heaving shoulder, and the man in the reeds beside the bitter water rose up and fired.

All the luck of that day's hunting went to the homesteader, for he had killed an antelope and a coyote with one shot, and though he had a bad quarter of an hour with a wild and loathly shepherd, who he feared might denounce him to the law, in the end he made off with the last antelope, swung limp and graceless across his shoulder. The coyotes came back to the killing-ground when they had watched him safely down the ravine, and were consoled with what they found. As they pulled the body of the dead leader about before they began upon it, they noticed that the homesteader had taken the ears of that also.

Little Pete lay in the grass and wept simply; the tears made pallid traces in the season's grime. He suffered the torture, the question extraordinary of bereavement. If he had not lingered so long in the meadow of Los Robles, if he had moved faster on the Sand Flat trail—but, in fact, he had come up against the inevitable. He had been breathed upon by that spirit which goes before cities like an exhalation and dries up the gossamer and the dew.

From that day the heart had gone out of the Ceriso. It was a desolate hollow, reddish-hued and dim, with brackish waters, and moreover the feed was poor. His eyes could not forget their trick of roving the valley at all hours; he looked by the rill of the spring for hoof-prints that were not there.

Fronting the west gap there was a spot where he would not feed, where the grass stood up stiff and black with what had dried upon it. He kept the flocks to the ridgy slopes where the limited horizon permitted one to believe the crater was not quite empty. His heart shook in the night to hear the long-drawn hunting howl, and shook again remembering that he had nothing to be fearing for. After three weeks he passed out on the other side and came that way no more. The juniper-tree stood greenly by the spring until the homesteader cut it down for firewood. Nothing taller than the rattling reeds stirs in all the hollow of the Ceriso.

There was a man once who skidded through Lost Borders in an automobile with a balloon silk tent and a folding tin bath-tub, who wrote some cheerful tales about that country, mostly untrue, about rattlesnakes coiling under men's blankets at night, to afford heroic occasions in the morning, of which circumstance seventeen years' residence failed to furnish a single instance; about lost mines rediscovered, which *never* happens, and Indian maidens of such surpassing charm that men married them and went out of the story with intimations of ever-after happiness due to arrive. It is true I did know a man who married his *mahala*, but he was mighty sorry for it, and though it lost him his chance in life the story is not worth telling.

The fact is that only when men struggle with men do you get triumphs and rejoicings. In any conflict with the immutable forces the human is always the under dog, and when the struggle is sharp enough to be dramatic, he wins death mostly; happiest if he gets out of it some dignity for himself and some sweetness for his friends to remember. I was a long time understanding why a great many people cannot abide a story with death in it. To be snatched at the dramatic moment, to be re-absorbed in the vastness of space and the infinitude of silences, to return simply to the native essences—that is nothing to make moan about; but when I had once taken part in a proper Christian funeral, after fifteen years without witnessing one such, I was less surprised at it.

When one has to think of death in connection with strange tiptoeing men felicitating themselves on millinery effects, with the suggestion of what was to be charged for it lurking under the discreetly dropped lids, and all the obvious mechanism of modern burial, one can understand that what happened at Agua Dulce is quite another matter.

VII

AGUA DULCE

THE Los Angeles special got in so late that day that if the driver of the Mojave stage had not, from having once gone to school to me, acquired the habit of minding what I said, I should never have made it. I hailed him from the station, and he swung the four about in the wide street as the wind swept me toward the racked old coach in a blinding whirl of dust.

It wrapped my skirts about the iron gear of the coach as I climbed to the seat beside the driver, and as we dropped the town behind us, lifted my hat and searched out my hairpins. But it was the desert wind, and the smell it carried was the smell of marrow-fat weed and gilias after the sun goes down; so, because I had been very unhappy away from it, and was now drunk with the joy of renewal, and as in my case there would be no time for a toilet proper to the road until we came to the Eighteen-mile house, I was satisfied merely to cling to the pitching front of the coach and let the wind do what it would. The sky was alight and saffron-tinted, the mountains bloomed with violet shadows; as we came whirling by the point of Dead-Man, we saw the wickiups of the Paiutes and the little hearth-fires all awink among the sage. They had a look of home.

"There's some," said the driver to the desert at large, "that thinks Indians ain't properly folks, but just a kind of cattle." Then, as we jolted forward in a chuck, he swore deeply and brought the team about, putting back my instinctive motion to steady the lurching stage with a gesture so sharp and repellant that I sat up suddenly in offence.

"Don't you go for to mind me," he said, only half mindful himself of what he had done, and went on staring after the hearth-fires of the Paiutes. By which I knew there was a story there that had something to do with the twilight fires and the homey look of the little huts. Hours later, when we came out on the mesa above Red Rock, white star-froth flecking the black vault over us, and the road white between the miles of low black sage before, we had got to this point in it.

"It was out there," he said, waving his whip toward the gulf of blackness, "when I was doin' assessment work for McKenna, nigh to the end of nowhere, I . . . took up with an Indian woman." He hurried past this admission with intent to cover it from possible reproach, telling how McKenna had dumped him with three months' grub by a water-hole called Agua Dulce, distant a mile or two from the claims he was expected to work.

"Because," he said, "it was cheaper than packin' water, me bein' alone, and McKenna, for some reason, I never rightly guessed, keen to keep the business on the quiet. McKenna would be visitin' me once a month or so, and I 'lowed I wouldn't lonesome much," he laughed, "and I didn't after I . . . took up with Catameneda.

"Seems like white women can't get to understand why a man takes up with a *mahala*. They think it's just badness, and so they're down on it . . . Maybe it is with some . . . but not when they are like . . . like me . . . and Catameneda. . . . There's something away down in a man that his own women folks never understand . . . an' you spend all your life trying to keep them from understanding . . . though when there's one that does she plays hell with you. . . . It ain't badness. . . . I don't know rightly what, only it ain't all bad . . . but Catameneda . . . she understood . . . and I was glad to have her."

The wind died along the sage, and there was no sound under heaven louder than the grind of the wheels and the clink of the harness chains. Presently he returned upon his track to say that he had been a month at Agua Dulce, going and returning from the mines each day to his little camp kit, laid under a square of canvas with stones upon it to keep it from the wind. He had cached the bulk of his supplies behind the spring, and congratulated himself on it when at the close of one day he found a camp of Indians at Agua Dulce.

Agua Dulce

"You know how it is with these desert tribes," said the stage-driver: "every camp looks as if it might have been there for a hundred years, and when they go there's no more left than a last year's bird-nest. They just scramble up out of nothing and melt away in the sand like a horned toad. But they was friendly . . . sort of . . . when you got to know them . . . and the men talked English considerable. . . . Evenings when a kind of creepy chill comes on, they get around their little fires and crack their jokes . . . good jokes, too . . . there was one old buck real comical, . . . he used to explain them in English afterward. And when they sang their songs . . . when the fires were lit and the voices came out of the dark, and you couldn't see the dirt nor the color of their skins, you would sort of forget they wasn't your own folks.

"And so," he said, after a long silence, "when the camp went on another *pasear* . . . Catameneda . . . she stayed." That was all I was ever to know of that phase of it. "Catameneda stayed." That and the flicker in his voice cast up from the things in him that only the Indian woman could understand, that lit the situation through his scanty speech like the glow of those vanished fires.

"It was a sort of pretty place at Agua Dulce," said he. "The spring came out from the black rock into a basin with a gurgly sound. There was a pink flowering bush behind it, and a smitch of green where it ran over into the sand . . . and the rest was sage-bush, little and low; and crumply, colored hills. There were doves came and built in the flowering shrubs, for they hadn't no fear of man . . . and 'Maneda, she fed them."

He was silent, letting his whip-lash trail outside in the sand, and I had a long time in which to consider how young he was, and how much younger he must have been when he drank sweet water out there at Agua Dulce, before he began again.

"She was mighty lovin'," he said; and suddenly I saw the whole tale as I had constructed it ahead of his halting speech fall apart, and rebuild itself to a larger plan as he went on to say how, when he came from the mine at night and had no caress for her, she would begin to droop and to grieve, to flood with tears and heavy sobbing like a hurt child, which he could still in a moment with a hand upon her hair; and how he would pretend a harshness at times to see her flash and glow with the assurance of tenderness renewed, which he laughed at her for never learning. Sweet water, indeed, at Agua Dulce!

By this I knew the story had come to some uncommon end that lifted it beyond the vulgar adventure of satiety and desertion, for there was no yellowness in the boy that he should blab upon the tenderness of women. There was a good hour yet until we came to Coyote Holes, and I meant to have it all out of him by then. The end had come very quickly. It began in their growing careless through happiness and neglecting the cache. Then one day, when he was at the mine, and Catameneda setting snares for quail in the black rock, a thieving prospector rifled it and left them wofully short of food. Five days of desertness lay between them and any possible base of supplies, and McKenna was not due until the twenty-ninth. They took stock and decided to hold out on short rations until he came. They were very merry about it, being so young, and Catameneda knew the way to piece out their fare with roots and herbs. She promised him he should learn to eat lizards yet, as Indians do. And then suddenly the boy fell sick of a dysentery which he thought might have come from some mistaken economy of Catameneda's in the matter of canned food; and while he was prostrated with that came the sand-storm. The girl had sensed it, Indian fashion, days before it came, but he was loggy with weakness and the want of proper care, and let her warning pass. Then came a night of gusty flaws; the morning showed a wall of yellow cloud advancing from the south.

All that country around Agua Dulce is solid rock and fluctuant sand that moves before the wind with a small, shrill rustle, and no trail can lie in it when the wind blows more than twenty-four hours. On this occasion it blew for three days.

"Time was," said the driver, "I'd lie awake nights to mill it over and over. Times I'd think I could have done better, times again I didn't know as I could. I was too sick to think much, and 'Maneda was mighty uneasy, all for gettin' forward on the trail to meet McKenna, who would be comin' toward us. She calculated he would stop at Beeman's till the storm was past, not knowin' we were short. And the wind would blow three days. I don't know how she knew, but she knew. She kept holding up her fingers to show me how many days, and forgetting what English I had taught her; and between that and me being fair locoed with sickness, I gave in. I don't know if we wouldn't have done better to stick it out at Agua Dulce. And, again, I don't know as we would."

They took the canteen and such food as they had and set out for the next water-hole; by noon the sand-storm overtook them. The push of the wind was steady, and they tacked along the edge of it without too much discomfort. The boy was pitifully weak, and Catameneda laughed as she braced him with her firm, young body. The dark fell early, the wind increased and roared against them; the boy, chilled in the night, grew feverish, and Catameneda was reduced to hiding the canteen to save their scanty drink. By all counts they should have reached the first water-hole that day, but did not until the next noon. And the storm had been before them. The sand lay clean white and drifted smooth over all that place. Come another winter, the spring would work its way to the surface perhaps, but now they could not so much as guess where to dig for it. They walked on and on, Catameneda leading with his hand in hers. This day they faced the wind. The girl's hair blew back, and he held it to his eyes to shield them from the tormenting sting of the sand. The water and food held out better than he expected.

He said that he thought Catameneda must have waked him in the night, when there was a lull in the wind, for he seemed to remember crawling long distances on hands and knees, and other times he leaned upon her body and heard her voice, but did not seem to see her. Always they travelled in a fury of wind and a biting smother of sand.

"I don't know how 'Maneda pulled me through," he said, "but she did. All I remember was the beginning of the basalt wall at the root of Black Mountain, and right away after that the drip of the spring, though it's two mile from where the rock begins. I was long past bein' hungry, but I jest naturally wallowed in that water, and it ain't any great water neither, not like the water at Agua Dulce. But Catameneda she didn't seem to care for none."

He paused so long here that if I had not known his kind very well, I should have thought it all the story he meant to let me have; but at last:

"I reckon I was light-headed," he said, "else I should have sensed what was the matter; but I don't know but it was best as it was. I couldn't have done nothin'. We lay on the sand far spent and sick, the wind was going down, and we could breathe better under the wall. I heard her kind of choke up every little, and by-the-by she was talking quiet like, in her own language, and I made out she wanted her mother . . . she wasn't more than seventeen, I should think. . . . It was cold, too, and I'd lost my blanket somewhere back on the trail, not bein' able to say where. . . . I snuggled her up in my arms, kind of shivery like . . . and by-and-by . . . she knew me, puttin' her hand up to my face, a way she had . . . and sayin' in English, as I had taught her, 'Vera good boy, mucha like.' And it didn't seem no time at all after that when it was broad morning and the wind was down . . . her hair on my face . . . and she was heavy on my arm.

"I sat up and laid her on the sand. . . . It was too much for her . . . all she had been through . . . bein' so young . . . and she had given me all the food and all the water . . . though I hadn't felt to know it before. I knew it as soon as I looked at her . . . I reckon she had a hemorrhage or something . . . there was blood on her face and sleeves like she wiped it from her mouth."

Out in the blackness toward Agua Dulce a coyote howled and night freshened for a sign of morning.

"McKenna came through by noon, and we buried her," he finished, simply, "under a pink flowering bush, because she loved it. I worked on a ranch in the valley for two years after that. . . . I couldn't seem to abide the desert for a spell . . . nor the little fires . . . but I got over that . . . you know how that is."

"Yes, I know how that is."

"But I don't suppose anybody knows," he went on, reflectively, "how it is that.I don't think of her dead any more, nor any of that hard time we had . . . only sometimes when it's spring like this, and I smell sage-brush burning . . . it reminds me . . . of some loving way she had out there . . . at Agua Dulce."

A man's story like that is always so much more satisfactory because he tells you all the story there is, what happened to him, and how he felt about it, supposing his feelings are any part of the facts in the case; but with a woman it is not so. She never knows much about her feelings, unless they are pertinent to the story, and then she leaves them out.

VIII

THE WOMAN AT THE EIGHTEEN-MILE

❦❦❦❦❦

I HAD long wished to write a story of Death Valley that should be its final word. It was to be so chosen from the limited sort of incidents that could occur there, so charged with the still ferocity of its moods that I should at length be quit of its obsession, free to concern myself about other affairs. And from the moment of hearing of the finding of Lang's body at Dead Man's Spring I knew I had struck upon the trail of that story.

It was a teamster who told it, stopping over the night at McGee's, a big, slow man, face and features all of a bluntness, as if he had been dropped before the clay was set. He had a big, blunt voice through which his words rolled, dulled along the edges. The same accident that had flattened the outlines of his nose and chin must have happened to his mind, for he was never able to deliver more than the middle of an idea, without any definiteness as to where it began or ended and what it stood next to. He called the dead man Long, and failed to remember who was supposed to have killed him, and what about.

We had fallen a-talking round the fire of Convict Lake, and the teamster had handed up the incident of Dead Man's Spring as the only thing in his experience that matched with the rooted horror of its name. He had been of the party that recovered the body, and what had stayed with him was the sheer torment of the journey across Death Valley, the aching heat, the steady, sickening glare, the uncertainty as to whether there was a body in the obliterated grave, whether it was Lang's body, and whether they would be able to prove it; and then the exhuming of the dead, like the one real incident in a fever dream. He was very sure of the body, done up in an Indian blanket striped red and black, with a rope around it like a handle, convenient for carrying. But he had forgotten what set the incident in motion, or what became of Lang after that, if it really were Lang in the blanket.

Then I heard of the story again between Red Rock and Coyote Holes, about moon-set, when the stage labored up the long gorge, waking to hear the voices of the passengers run on steadily with the girding of the sand and the rattle of harness-chains, run on and break and eddy around Dead Man's Springs, and back up in turgid pools of comment and speculation, falling in shallows of miner's talk, lost at last in a waste of ledges and contracts and forgotten strikes. Waking and falling asleep again, the story shaped itself of the largeness of the night; and then the two men got down at Coyote Holes an hour before dawn, and I knew no more of them, neither face nor name. But what I had heard of the story confirmed it exactly, the story I had so long sought.

Those who have not lived in a mining country cannot understand how it is possible for whole communities to be so disrupted by the failure of a lode or a fall in the price of silver, that I could live seven years within a day's journey of Dead Man's Spring and not come upon anybody who could give me the whole of that story. I went about asking for it, and got sticks and straws. There was a man who had kept bar in Tio Juan at the time, and had been the first to notice Whitmark's dealing with the Shoshone who was supposed to have stolen the body after it was dug up. There was a Mexican who had been the last to see Lang alive and might have told somewhat, but death got him before I did. Once, at a great dinner in San Francisco, a large, positive man with a square forehead and a face below it that somehow implied he had shaped it so butting his way through life, across the table two places down, caught at some word of mine, leaning forward above the bank of carnations that divided the cloth.

"Queer thing happened up in that country to a friend of mine, Whitmark—" But the toast-master cut *him* off. All this time the story glimmered like a summer island in a mist, through every man's talk about it, grew and allured, caressing the soul. It had warmth and amplitude, like a thing palpable to be stroked. There was a mine in it, a murder and a mystery, great sacrifice, Shoshones, dark and incredibly discreet, and the magnetic will of a man making manifest through all these; there were lonely water-holes, deserted camps where coyotes hunted in the streets, fatigues and dreams and voices of the night. And at the last it appeared there was a woman in it.

Curiously, long before I learned of her connection with the story, I had known and liked her for a certain effect she had of being warmed and nourished from within. There was about her a spark, a nuance that men mistook—never more than once, as the stage-driver told me confidently—a vitality that had nothing, absolutely nothing, but the blank occasionless life of the desert to sustain it. She was one of the very few people I had known able to keep a soul alive and glowing in the wilderness, and I was to find out that she kept it so against the heart of my story. Mine! I called it so by that time; but hers was the right, though she had no more pertinence to the plot than most women have to desert affairs.

She was the Woman of the Eighteen-Mile House. She had the desert mark upon her—lean figure, wasted bosom, the sharp, upright furrow between the eyes, the burned, tawny skin, with the pallid streak of the dropped eyelids, and of course I suppose she knew her husband from among the lean, sidling, vacuous-looking Borderers; but I couldn't have identified him, so like he was to the other feckless men whom the desert sucks dry and keeps dangling like gourds on a string. Twenty-five years they had drifted from up Bodie way, around Panimint, toward Mojave, worse housed and fed than they might have been in the ploughed lands, and without having hit upon the fortune which is primarily the object of every desert adventure. And when people have been as long as that among the Lost Borders there is not the slightest possibility of their coming to anything else. And still the Woman's soul was palpitant and enkindled. At the last, Mayer—that was the husband's name—had settled at the Eighteen-Mile House to care for the stage relays, and I had met the Woman, halting there with the stage or camping nights on some slower passage.

At the time I learned of her connection with the Whitmark affair, the story still wanted some items of motive and understanding, a knowledge of the man himself, some account of his three months' *pasear* into the hills beyond Mesquite, which certainly had to do with the affair of the mine, but of which he would never be persuaded to speak. And I made perfectly sure of getting the rest of it from the Woman at the Eighteen-Mile.

It was full nine o'clock before the Woman's household was all settled and she had come out upon the stoop of the Eighteen-Mile to talk, the moon coming up out of Shoshone land, all the hollow of the desert falling away before us, filled with the glitter of that surpassing wonder, the moon-mirage. Never mind what went before to draw her to the point of talking; it could have come about as simply as my saying, "I mean to print this story as I find it," and she would have had to talk to save it. Consider how still it was. Off to the right the figures of my men under their blankets stretched along the ground. Not a leaf to rustle, not a bough to creak. No grass to whisper in the wind, only stiff, scant shrubs and the sandy hills like shoals at the bottom of a lake of light. I could see the Woman's profile, thin and fine against the moon, and when she put up her hand to drag down the thick, careless coil of her hair, I guessed we were close upon the heart of the story. And for her the heart of the story was the man, Whitmark.

She had been, at the time he came into the country seventeen years before, that which the world knows so little what to do with that it mostly throws away—a good woman with great power and possibilities of passion. Whitmark stood for the best she had known, I should have said from all I learned, just a clean-minded, acute, tolerably cultivated American business man with an obsession for accomplishing results.

He had been sent out to look after a mine to which the title was not clear, and there were counter-machinations to take it away from him. This much may be told without breach, for, as it turned out, I was not to write that story, after all; at least, not in the lifetime of the Woman at the Eighteen-Mile. And the crux of the story to her was one little, so little, moment, that owing to Whitmark's having been taken with pneumonia within a week afterward, was rendered fixed beyond change or tarnish of time.

When all this was going forward the Mayers kept a miner's boarding-house at Tio Juan, where Whitmark was in and out; and the Woman, who from the first had been attracted by the certain stamp of competency and power, began to help him with warnings, intimations of character and local prejudice, afterward with information which got him the reputation of almost supernatural penetration.

The Woman at the Eighteen-Mile

There were reasons why, during his darkest time, Whitmark could find nobody but the Indians and the Woman to trust. Well, he had been wise enough to trust her, and it was plain to see from her account of it that this was the one occasion in life when her soul had stretched itself, observed, judged, wrought, and felt to the full of its power.

She loved him; yes, perhaps—I do not know—if you call love that soul service of a good woman to a man she may not touch. Whitmark had children back East, and a wife whom he had married for all the traditions of niceness and denial and abnegation which men demand of the women they expect to marry, and find savorless so often when they are married to it. He had never known what it meant to have a woman concerned in his work, running neck and neck with it, divining his need, supplementing it not with the merely feminine trick of making him more complacent with himself, but with vital remedies and aids. And once he had struck the note of the West, he kindled to the event and enlarged his spirit. The two must have had great moments at the heart of that tremendous coil of circumstance. All this the Woman conveyed to me by the simplest telling of the story as it happened: "I said . . . and he did . . . the Indian went . . ."

I sat within the shallow shadow of the eaves experiencing the full-throated satisfaction of old prospectors over the feel of pay dirt, rubbing it between the thumb and palm, swearing over it softly below the breath. It was as good as that. And I was never to have it! For one thing the Woman made plain to me in the telling was the guilt of Whitmark. Though there was no evidence by which the court could hold him, though she did not believe it, though the fulness of her conviction intrigued me into believing that it did not matter so much what he was—the only way to write that story successfully was to fix forever against Whitmark's name its damning circumstance. The affair had been a good deal noised about at that time, and through whatever illusion of altered name and detail, was bound to be recognized and made much of in the newspapers. The Woman of the Eighteen-Mile saw that. Suddenly she broke off the telling to show me her poor heart, shrivelling as I knew hearts to warp and shrink in the aching wilderness, this one occasion rendering it serviceable like a hearth-fire in an empty room.

"It was a night like this he went away," said the Woman, stirring to point to the solemn moonlight poured over all the world.

That was after twenty-two months of struggle had left Whitmark in possession of the property. He was on his way then to visit his family, whom he had seen but once in that time, and was to come again to put in operation the mine he had so hardly won. It was, it should have been, an hour ripe with satisfaction.

"He was to take the stage which passed through Bitter Wells at ten that night," said she, "and I rode out with him—he had asked me—from Tio Juan, to bring back the horses. We started at sunset and reached the Wells a quarter of an hour before the time.

"The moon was half high when the sun went down, and I was very happy, because it had all come out so well, and he was to come again in two months. We talked as we rode. I told you he was a cheerful man. All the time when it looked as if he might be tried for his life, the worse it looked the more his spirits rose. He would have laughed if he had heard he was to be hung. But that night there was a trouble upon him. It grew as we rode. His face drew, his breath came sighing. He seemed always on the point of speaking and did not. It was as if he had something to say that must be said, and at the moment of opening his lips it escaped him. In the moonlight I saw his mouth working, and nothing came from it. If I spoke the trouble went out of his face, and when I left off it came again, puzzled wonder and pain. I know now!" said the Woman, shaking forward her thick hair, "that it was a warning, a presentiment. I have heard of such things, and it seems as if I should have felt it too, hovering in the air like that. But I was glad because it had all come out so well and I had had a hand in it. Besides, it was not for me." She turned toward me then for the first time, her hair falling forward to encompass all her face but the eyes, wistful with the desire to have me understand how fine this man was in every worldly point, how far above her, and how honored she was to have been the witness of the intimation of his destiny. I said quickly the thing that was expected of me, which was not the thing I thought, and gave her courage for going on.

"Yet," she said, "I was not entirely out of it, because—because the thing he said at the last, *when* he said it, did not seem the least strange to me, though afterward, of course, when I thought of it, it was the strangest good-bye I had ever heard.

"We had got down and stood between the horses, and the stage was coming in. We heard the sand fret under it, and the moonlight was a cold weight laid upon the world. He took my hand and held it against his breast so—and said— Oh, I am perfectly sure of the words; he said, 'I have *missed* you so.' Just that, not good-bye, and not *shall* miss you, but 'I *have* missed you *so.*'

"Like that," she said, her hands still clasped above her wasted bosom, the quick spirit glowing through it like wine in a turgid glass—"like that," she said. But, no; whatever the phrase implied of the failure of the utterly safe and respectable life to satisfy the inmost hunger of the man, it could never have had in it the pain of her impassioned, lonely years. If it had been the one essential word the Desert strives to say it would have been pronounced like that.

"And it was not until the next day," she went on, "it occurred to me that was a strange thing to say to a woman he had seen two or three times a week for nearly two years. But somehow it seemed to me clearer when I heard a week later that he was dead. He had taken cold on the way home, and died after three days. His wife wrote me; it was a very nice letter; she said he told her I had been kind to him. Kind!" She broke off, and far out under the moon rose the thin howl of coyotes running together in the pack. "And that," said the Woman, "is why I made you promise at the beginning that if I told you all I knew about Whitmark and Lang you would not use it."

I jumped. She had done that, and I had promised light-heartedly. People nearly always exact that sort of an assurance in the beginning of confidences, like a woman wanting to be told she is of nobler courage at the moment of committing an indiscretion, a concession to the sacredness of personal experience which always seems so much less once it is delivered, they can be persuaded to forego the promise of inviolateness. I always promise and afterward persuade. But not the Woman of the Eighteen-Mile. If Whitmark had lived he would have come back and proved his worth, cleared himself by his life and works. As it stood, by the facts against him, he was most utterly given over to ill-repute. The singularity of the incident, the impossibility of its occurring in any place but Death Valley, conspired to fix the ineffaceable stain upon his wife and his children, for, by the story as I should write it, he ought to have been hung. No use to say modestly that the scratchings of my pen would never reach them. If it were not the biggest story of the desert ever written, I had no wish to write it. And there was the Woman. The story was all she had, absolutely all of heart-stretching, of enlargement and sustenance. What she thought about it was that that last elusive moment when she touched the forecast shadow of his destiny was to bind her to save his credit for his children's sake. One must needs be faithful to one's experiences when there are so few of them.

She said something like that, gathering up her hair in both hands, standing before me in the wan revealing light. The mark of the desert was on her. Heart of desolation! But I knew what pinchings of the spirit went to make that mark!

"It was a promise," she said.

"It is a promise."

But I caught myself in the reservation that it should not mean beyond the term of her life.

EVERY NOW AND THEN arises some city-surfeited demand for a great primitive love-story: it is usually a Professor in the English Department or some young man on the Daily News at fifteen per who dreams of writing it. Only those who have learned it at firsthand understand that there is no such thing; that primitive love is the most complaisant, that is to say, the most serviceable to Life of all human passions.

But when we magnify it with bonds it chafes itself to dramatic proportions. Love is Life's own way of reducing the clash of human contacts in order that the pair may turn a more opposing front to the adversary, the Wilderness.

It springs up, oh, it springs up, as Life divinely meant it, wherever, in the press of existence, men and women come together; requires, when the conditions are of a simpleness called primitive, no other inducement. But Life did not invent Society, seems somehow never to be properly aware of it; though it justifies itself of Love, cannot yet square with Respectability, with the Church and Property. Threading through these, Love weaves the fascinating intricacy of story, but here in the Borders, where the warp runs loose and wide, the pattern has not that richness it should show in the close fabric of civilization. If it lived next door to you, you probably wouldn't have anything to do with it.

IX

THE FAKIR

WHENEVER I come up to judgment, and am hard pushed to make good on my own account (as I expect to be), I shall mention the case of Netta Saybrick, for on the face of it, and by all the traditions in which I was bred, I behaved rather handsomely. I say on the face of it, for except in the matter of keeping my mouth shut afterward, I am not so sure I had anything to do with the affair. It was one of those incidents that from some crest of sheer inexplicableness seems about to direct the imagination over vast tracts of human experience, only to fall away into a pit of its own digging, all fouled with weed and sand. But, by keeping memory and attention fixed on its pellucid instant as it mounted against the sun, I can still see the Figure shining through it as I saw it that day at Posada, with the glimmering rails of the P. and S. running out behind it, thin lines of light toward the bar of Heaven.

Up till that time Netta Saybrick had never liked me, though I never laid it to any other account than Netta's being naturally a little fool; afterward she explained to me that it was because she thought I gave myself airs. The Saybricks lived in the third house from mine, around the corner, so that our back doors overlooked each other, and up till the coming of Doctor Challoner there had never been anything in Netta's conduct that the most censorious of the villagers could remark upon. Nor afterward, for that matter. The Saybricks had been married four years, and the baby was about two. He was not an interesting child to anybody but his mother, and even Netta was sometimes thought to be not quite absorbed in him.

Saybrick was a miner, one of the best drillers in our district, and consequently away from home much of the time. Their house was rather larger than their needs, and Netta, to avoid loneliness more than for profit, let out a room or two. That was the way she happened to fall into the hands of the Fakir.

Franklin Challoner had begun by being a brilliant and promising student of medicine. I had known him when his natural gifts prophesied the unusual, but I had known him rather better than most, and I was not surprised to have him turn up five years later at Maverick as a Fakir.

It had begun in his being poor, and having to work his way through the Medical College at the cost of endless pains and mortification to himself. Like most brilliant people, Challoner was sensitive and had an enormous egotism, and, what nearly always goes with it, the faculty of being horribly fascinating to women. It was thought very creditable of him to have put himself through college at his own charge, though in reality it proved a great social waste. I have a notion that the courage, endurance, and steadfastness which should have done Frank Challoner a lifetime was squeezed out of him by the stress of those overworked, starved, mortifying years. His egotism made it important to his happiness to keep the centre of any stage, and this he could do in school by sheer brilliance of scholarship and the distinction of his struggles. But afterward, when he had to establish himself without capital among strangers, he found himself impoverished of manliness. Always there was the compelling need of his temperament to stand well with people, and almost the only means of accomplishing it his poverty allowed was the dreadful facility with which he made himself master of women. I suppose this got his real ability discredited among his professional fellows. Between that and the sharp need of money, and the incredible appetite which people have for being fooled, somewhere in the Plateau of Fatigue between promise and accomplishment, Frank Challoner lost himself. Therefore, I was not surprised when he turned up finally at Maverick, lecturing on phrenology, and from the shape of their craniums advising country people of their proper careers at three dollars a sitting. He advertised to do various things in the way of medical practice that had a dubious sound.

It was court week when he came, and the only possible lodging to be found at Netta Saybrick's. Doctor Challoner took the two front rooms as being best suited to his clients and himself, and I believe he did very well. I was not particularly pleased to see him, on account of having known him before, not wishing to prosecute the acquaintance; and about that time Indian George brought me word that a variety of *redivivus* long sought was blooming that year on a certain clayey tract over toward Waban. It was not supposed to flower oftener than once in seven years, and I was five days finding it. That was why I never knew what went on at Mrs. Saybrick's. Nobody else did, apparently, for I never heard a breath of gossip, and *that* must have been Doctor Challoner's concern, for I am sure Netta would never have known how to avoid it.

Netta was pretty, and Saybrick had been gone five months. Challoner had a thin, romantic face, and eyes—even I had to admit the compelling attraction of his eyes; and his hands were fine and white. Saybrick's hands were cracked, broken-nailed, a driller's hands, and one of them was twisted from the time he was leaded, working on the Lucky Jim. If it came to that, though, Netta's husband might have been anything he pleased, and Challoner would still have had his way with her. He always did with women, as if to make up for not having it with the world. And the life at Maverick was deadly, appallingly dull. The stark houses, the rubbishy streets, the women who went about in them in calico wrappers,the drag-gling speech of the men, the wide, shadowless table-lands, the hard, bright skies, and the days all of one pattern, that went so stilly by that you only knew it was afternoon when you smelled the fried cabbage Mrs. Mulligan was cooking for supper.

At this distance I cannot say that I blamed Netta, am not sure of not being glad that she had her hour of the rose-red glow—*if* she had it. You are to bear in mind that all this time I was camping out in the creosote belt on the slope of Waban, and as to what had really happened neither Netta nor Challoner ever said a word. I keep saying things like this about Netta's being pretty and all, just as if I thought they had anything to do with it; truth is, the man had just a gift of taking souls, and I, even I, judicious and disapproving—but you shall hear.

At that time the stage from Maverick was a local affair going down to Posada, where passengers from the P. and S. booked for the Mojave line, returning after a wait of hours on the same day.

It happened that the morning I came back from Waban, Doctor

Challoner left Maverick. Being saddle weary, I had planned to send on the horses by Indian George, and take the stage where it crossed my trail an hour out from Posada, going home on it in the afternoon. I remember poking the botany-case under the front seat and turning round to be hit straight between the eyes, as it were, by Netta Saybrick and Doctor Challoner. The doctor was wearing his usual air of romantic mystery; wearing it a little awry—or perhaps it was only knowing the man that made me read the perturbation under it. But it was plain to see what Netta was about. Her hat was tilted by the jolting of the stage, while alkali dust lay heavy on the folds of her dress, and she never *would* wear hair-pins enough; but there was that in every turn and posture, in every note of her flat, childish voice, that acknowledged the man beside her. Her excitement was almost febrile. It was part of Netta's unsophistication that she seemed not to know that she gave herself away, and the witness of it was that she had brought the baby.

You would not have believed that any woman would plan to run away with a man like Frank Challoner and take that great, heavy-headed, drooling child. But that is what Netta had done. I am not sure it was maternal instinct, either; she probably did not know what else to do with him. He had pale, protruding eyes and reddish hair, and every time he clawed at the doctor's sleeve I could see the man withhold a shudder.

I suppose it was my being in a manner confounded by this extraordinary situation that made it possible for Doctor Challoner to renew his acquaintance with more warmth than the facts allowed. He fairly pitched himself into an intimacy of reminiscence, and it was partly to pay him for this, I suppose, and partly to gratify a natural curiosity, that made me so abrupt with him afterward. I remember looking around, when we got down, at the little station where I must wait two hours for the return stage, at the seven unpainted pine cabins, at the eating-house, and the store, and the two saloons, in the instant hope of refuge, and then out across the alkali flat fringed with sparse, unwholesome pickle-weed, and deciding that that would not do, and then turning round to take the situation by the throat, as it were. There was Netta, with that great child dragging on her arm and her hat still on one side, with a silly consciousness of Doctor Challoner's movements, and he still trying for the jovial note of old acquaintances met by chance. In a moment more I had him around the corner of the station-house and out with my question.

"Doctor Challoner, are you running away with Netta Saybrick?"

"Well, no," trying to carry it jauntily; "I think she is running away with me." Then, all his pretension suddenly sagging on him like an empty cayaque: "On my soul, I don't know what's got into the woman. I was as surprised as you were when she got on the stage with me"—on my continuing to look steadily at him—"she was a pretty little thing . . . and the life is devilish dull there. . . . I suppose I flirted a little"—blowing himself out, as it were, with an assumption of honesty—"on my word, there was nothing more than that."

Flirted! He called it that; but women do not take their babies and run away from home for the sake of a little flirting. The life was devilish dull—did he need to tell me that! And she was pretty—well, whatever had happened he was bound to tell me that it was nothing, and I was bound to behave as if I believed him.

"She will go back," he began to say, looking bleak and drawn in the searching light. "She must go back! She must!"

"Well, maybe you can persuade her," said I; but I relented after that enough to take care of the baby while he and Netta went for a walk.

The whole mesa and the flat crawled with heat, and the steel rails ran on either side of them like thin fires, as if the slagged track were the appointed way that Netta had chosen to walk. They went out as far as the section-house and back toward the deserted station till I could almost read their faces clear, and turned again, back and forth through the heat-fogged atmosphere like the figures in a dream. I could see this much from their postures, that Challoner was trying to hold to some consistent attitude which he had adopted, and Netta wasn't understanding it. I could see her throw out her hands in a gesture of abandonment, and then I saw her stand as if the Pit yawned under her feet. The baby slept on a station bench, and I kept the flies from him with a branch of pickle-weed. I was out of it, smitten anew with the utter inutility of all the standards which were not bred of experience, but merely came down to me with the family tea-spoons. Seen by the fierce desert light they looked like the spoons, thin and worn at the edges. I should have been ashamed to offer them to Netta

Saybrick. It was this sense of detached helplessness toward the life at
Maverick that Netta afterward explained she and the other women sensed
but misread in me. They couldn't account for it on any grounds except that
I felt myself above them. And all the time I was sick with the strained,
meticulous inadequacy of my own soul. I understood well enough, then,
that the sense of personal virtue comes to most women through an
intervening medium of sedulous social guardianship. It is only when they
love that it reaches directly to the centre of consciousness, as if it were
ultimately nothing more than the instinctive movement of right love to
preserve itself by a voluntary seclusion. It was not her faithlessness to
Saybrick that tormented Netta out there between the burning rails; it was
going back to him that was the intolerable offence. Passion had come upon
her like a flame-burst, heaven-sent; she justified it on the grounds of its
completeness, and lacked the sophistication for any other interpretation.

Challoner was a bad man, but he was not bad enough to reveal to
Netta Saybrick the vulgar cheapness of his own relation to the incident.
Besides, he hadn't time. In two hours the return stage for Maverick left the
station, and he could never in that time get Netta Saybrick to realize the
gulf between his situation and hers.

He came back to the station after a while on some pretext, and said,
with his back to Netta, moving his lips with hardly any sound: "She must
go back on the stage. She must!" Then with a sudden setting of his jaws,
"You've got to help me." He sat down beside me, and began to devote
himself to the baby and the flies.

Netta stood out for a while expecting him, and then came and sat
provisionally on the edge of the station platform, ready at the slightest hint
of an opportunity to carry him away into the glimmering heat out toward
the station-house, and resume the supremacy of her poor charms.

She was resenting my presence as an interference, and I believe
always cherished a thought that but for the accident of my being there the
incident might have turned out differently. I could see that Challoner's
attitude, whatever it was, was beginning to make itself felt. She was
looking years older, and yet somehow pitifully puzzled and young, as if the
self of her had had a wound which her intelligence had failed to grasp. I
could see, too, that Challoner had made up his mind to be quit of her,

quietly if he could, but at any risk of a scene, still to be quit. And it was forty minutes till stage-time.

Challoner sat on the bare station bench with his arm out above the baby protectingly—it was a manner always effective—and began to talk about "goodness," of all things in the world. Don't ask me what he said. It was the sort of talk many women would have called beautiful, and though it was mostly addressed to me, it was every word of it directed to Netta Saybrick's soul. Much of it went high and wide, but I could catch the pale reflection of it in her face like a miner guessing the sort of day it is from the glimmer of it on a puddle at the bottom of a shaft. In it Netta saw a pair of heroic figures renouncing a treasure they had found for the sake of the bitter goodness by which the world is saved. They had had the courage to take it while they could, but were much too exemplary to enjoy it at the cost of pain to any other heart. He started with the assumption that she meant to go back to Maverick, and recurred to it with a skilful and hypnotic insistence, painting upon her mind by large and general inference the picture of himself, helped greatly in his career by her noble renunciation of him. As a matter of fact, Saybrick, if his wife really had gone away with Doctor Challoner, would have followed him up and shot him, I suppose, and no end of vulgar and disagreeable things might have come from the affair; but Challoner managed to keep it on so high a plane that even I never thought of them until long afterward. And right here is where the uncertainty as to the part I really played begins. I can never make up my mind whether Challoner, from long practice in such affairs, had hit upon just the right note of extrication, or whether, cornered, he fell back desperately on the eternal rightness. And what was he, to know rightness at his need?

He was terribly in earnest, holding Netta's eyes with his own; his forehead sweated, hollows showed about his eyes, and the dreadful slackness of the corner of the mouth that comes of the whole mind being drawn away upon the object of attack to the neglect of its defences. He was so bent on getting Netta fixed in the idea that she must go back to Maverick that if she had not been a good deal of a fool she must have seen that he had given away the whole situation into my hands. I believed—I hope—I did the right thing, but I am not sure I could have helped taking the cue which was pressed upon me; he was as bad as they made them, but there I was lending my whole soul to the accomplishment of his purpose, which was, briefly, to get comfortably off from an occasion in which he had behaved very badly.

All this time Challoner kept a conscious attention on the stage stables far at the other end of the shadeless street. The moment he saw the driver come out of it with the horses, the man's soul fairly creaked with the release of tension. It released, too, an accession of that power of personal fascination for which he was remarkable.

Netta sat with her back to the street, and the beautiful solicitude with which he took up the baby at that moment, smoothed its dress and tied on its little cap, had no significance for her. It was not until she heard the rattle of the stage turning into the road that she stood up suddenly, alarmed. Challoner put the baby into my arms.

Did I tell you that all this time between me and this man there ran the inexplicable sense of being bonded together; the same suggestion of a superior and exclusive intimacy which ensnared poor Netta Saybrick no doubt, the absolute call of self and sex by which a man, past all reasonableness and belief, ranges a woman on his side. He was a Fakir, a common quack, a scoundrel if you will, but there was the call. I had answered it. I was under the impression, though not remembering what he said, when he had handed me that great lump of a child, that I had received a command to hold on to it, to get into the stage with it, and not to give it up on any consideration; and without saying anything, I had promised.

I do not know if it was the look that must have passed between us at that, or the squeal of the running-gear that shattered her dream, but I perceived on the instant that Netta had had a glimpse of where she stood. She saw herself for the moment a fallen woman, forsaken, despised. There was the Pit before her which Challoner's desertion and my knowledge of it had digged. She clutched once at her bosom and at her skirts as if already she heard the hiss of crawling shame. Then it was that Challoner turned toward her with the Look.

It rose in his face and streamed to her from his eyes as though it were the one thing in the world of a completeness equal to the anguish in her breast, as though, before it rested there, it had been through all the troubled intricacies of sin, and come upon the root of a superior fineness that every soul feels piteously to lie at the back of all its own affronting vagaries, brooding over it in a large, gentle way. It was the forgiveness—nay, the obliteration of offence—and the most Challoner could have known of forgiveness was his own great need of it. Out of that Look I could see the woman's soul rising rehabilitated, astonished, and on the instant, out there beyond the man and the woman, between the thin fiery lines of the rails, leading back to the horizon, the tall, robed Figure writing in the sand.

Oh, it was a hallucination, if you like, of the hour, the place, the perturbed mind, the dazzling glimmer of the alkali flat, of the incident of a sinful woman and a common fakir, faking an absolution that he might the more easily avoid an inconvenience, and I the tool made to see incredibly by some trick of suggestion how impossible it should be that any but the chief of sinners should understand forgiveness. But the Look continued to hold the moment in solution, while the woman climbed out of the Pit. I saw her put out her hand with the instinctive gesture of the sinking, and Challoner take it with the formality of farewell; and as the dust of the arriving stage billowed up between them, the Figure turned, fading, dissolving . . . but with the Look, consoling, obliterating. . . . He too . . . !

"It was very good of you, Mrs. Saybrick, to give me so much of a good-bye . . ." Challoner was saying as he put Netta into the stage; and then to me, "You must take good care of her . . . good-bye."

"Good-bye, Frank"—I had never called Doctor Challoner by his name before. I did not like him well enough to call him by it at any time, but there was the Look; it had reached out and enwrapped me in a kind of rarefied intimacy of extenuation and understanding. He stood on the station platform staring steadily after us, and as long as we had sight of him in the thick, bitter dust, the Look held.

IF THIS WERE a story merely, or a story of Franklin Challoner, it would end there. He never thought of us again, you may depend, except to thank his stars for getting so lightly off, and to go on in the security of his success to other episodes from which he returned as scatheless.

But I found out in a very few days that whether it was to take rank as an incident or an event in Netta Saybrick's life depended on whether or not I said anything about it. Nobody had taken any notice of her day's ride to

Posada. Saybrick came home in about ten days, and Netta seemed uncommonly glad to see him, as if in the preoccupation of his presence she found a solace for her fears.

But from the day of our return she had evinced an extraordinary liking for my company. She would be running in and out of the house at all hours, offering to help me with my sewing or to stir up a cake, kindly offices that had to be paid in kind; and if I slipped into the neighbors' on an errand, there a moment after would come Netta. Very soon it became clear to me that she was afraid of what I might tell. So long as she had me under her immediate eye she could be sure I was not taking away her character, but when I was not, she must have suffered horribly. I might have told, too, by the woman's code; she was really not respectable, and we made a great deal of that in Maverick. I might refuse to have anything to do with her and justified myself explaining why.

But Netta was not sure how much I knew, and could not risk betrayal by a plea. She had, too, the natural reticence of the villager, and though she must have been aching for news of Doctor Challoner, touch of him, the very sound of his name, she rarely ever mentioned it, but grew strained and thinner; watching, watching.

If that incident was known, Netta would have been ostracized and Saybrick might have divorced her. And I was going dumb with amazement to discover that nothing had come of it, nothing *could* come of it so long as I kept still. It was a deadly sin, as I had been taught, as I believed—of damnable potentiality; and as long as nobody told it was as if it had never been, as if that look of Challoner's had really the power as it had the seeming of absolving her from all soil and stain.

I cannot now remember if I was ever tempted to tell on Netta Saybrick, but I know with the obsession of that look upon my soul I never did. And in the mean time, from being so much in each other's company, Netta and I became very good friends. That was why, a little more than a year afterward, she chose to have me with her when her second child was born. In Maverick we did things for one another that in more sophisticated communities go to the service of paid attendants. That was the time when the suspicion that had lain at the bottom of Netta's shallow eyes whenever she looked at me went out of them forever.

It was along about midnight and the worst yet to come. I sat holding

The Fakir

Netta's hands, and beyond in the room where the lamp was, the doctor lifted Saybrick through his stressful hour with cribbage and toddy. I could see the gleam of the light on Saybrick's red, hairy hands, a driller's hands, and whenever a sound came from the inner room, the uneasy lift of his shoulders and the twitching of his lip; then the doctor pushed the whiskey over toward him and jovially dealt the cards anew.

Netta, tossing on her pillow, came into range with Saybrick's blunt profile outlined against the cheaply papered wall, and I suppose her husband's distress was good to her to see. She looked at him a long time quietly.

"Henry's a good man," she said at last.

"Yes," I said; and then she turned to me narrowly with the expiring spark of anxious cunning in her eyes.

"And I've been a good wife to him," said she. It was half a challenge. And I, trapped by the hour, became a fakir in my turn, called instantly on all my soul and answered—with the Look—"Everybody knows that, Netta"—held on steadily until the spark went out. However I had done it I could not tell, but I saw the trouble go out of the woman's soul as the lids drooped, and with it out of my own heart the last of the virtuous resentment of the untempted. I had really forgiven her; how then was it possible for the sin to rise up and trouble her more? Mind you, I grew up in a church that makes a great deal of the forgiveness of sins and signifies it by a tremendous particularity about behavior, and the most I had learned of the efficient exercise of forgiveness was from the worst man I had ever known.

About an hour before dawn, when a wind began to stir, and out on the mesa the coyotes howled returning from the hunt, stooping to tuck the baby in her arms, I felt Netta's lips brush against my hand.

"You've been mighty good to me," she said. Well—if I were pushed for it, I should think it worth mentioning—but I am not so sure.

WHEN TENNESSEE, after about sixty years of prospecting, grub-staking, and days' wages, had made a little strike, he declared himself done with desertness, and of a mind to go down to the city to some recently developed connections and heirs, to be properly taken care of for the rest of his years. That was along in the beginning of winter, when interest narrowed to watching the snow-line approach and recede along the flank of the Sierras, and the undertaking was accounted to him for wisdom. And about two months later, when I was out looking mesaward for the pale tinge of the freshening sage that, however fast you may seek toward it, is no more to be come up with than the mirage, suddenly across my prospect bulked the large, lumbering figure of Tennessee. What he said was that in the city he could never step out of the door but there was a house right bung up against his eyes.

"A man," said Tennessee, "don't have no chance to stretch his vision."

But when the Rev. William Calvin Gains came down fresh from his seminary somewhere about Oakland to awaken, in the best imitation of a popular city preacher he could manage, our interest in spiritual things, he made just the opposite mistake of not understanding that here the vision stretches beyond the boundary of sense and things. Though the desert has had a reputation in times past for the making of religious leaders, it is no field for converts. Judge how a conventional, pew-fed religion would flourish in the presence of what I am about to relate to you.

X

THE POCKET-HUNTER'S STORY

THE CRUX OF this story for the Pocket-Hunter was that he had known the two men, Mac and Creelman, before they came into it; known them, in fact, in the beginning of that mutual distrust which grew out of an earlier friendliness into one of those expansive enmities which in the spined and warted humanity of the camps have as ready an acceptance as the devoted partnerships of which Wells Bassit furnished the pre-eminent example. It was, he believed, in some such relationship their acquaintance had begun, and from which they now drew the sustenance of those separate devils of hate that, nesting in corrosive hollows of their hosts, rose to froth and rage, each at the mere intimation of a merit in the other.

No one knew what the turn of the screw had been that set them gnashing, but it was supposed, on no better evidence, perhaps, than that such trouble is at the bottom of most quarrels in the camps, to have been about a mine. The final crisis, the very memory of which seemed to hold for him a moment of recurrent, hair-lifting horror, was known by the Pocket-Hunter, and by some of the others, to have been brought on by an Indian woman down Parrimint-way.

She was Mac's woman; though, except as being his, he was not thought to set particular store by her. He used to leave her in his cabin while he was off in the Hills for a three weeks' *pasear;* but the tacit admission of an Indian woman as no fit subject for white men to fight over forbade his being put to the ordinary provocation on account of her.

Therefore, when Creelman projected his offence, which was to excite in his enemy the desire for killing without providing him with a sufficient excuse, there was a vague notion moving in the heavy fibre of his mind that there was a species of humor in what he was about to do. But he would probably not have gone on to Tres Piños and told of it, if he had known how soon it was to come to Mac's ears.

This, you understand, was long after their grudge had climbed by inconsiderable occasions to the point where Mac had several times offered to kill Creelman on no motion but the pleasure of being rid of his company.

Mac was a sickly man, and by that, and his having had the worst of it in their earlier encounters, his rage so much the more possessed him that, when he had come back to his cabin and the Indian woman had told him her story, he was able by that mere spur of a possession trifled with to take the short leap from intent to performance at a bound. There was no such bodily leap possible, of course; he had to trudge the whole of one day on foot to Tres Piños, an old weakness battling with his rage. He was one of those illy-furnished souls whom the wilderness despoils most completely—hair, beard, and skin of him burned to one sandy sallowness, the eyelashes of no color, the voice of no timbre, more or less stiffened at the joints by the poison of leaded ores, his very name shorn of its distinguishing syllable; no more of him left, in fact, than would serve as a vehicle for hating Creelman. When he came to Tres Piños and learned that the other had gone on from there, nobody would tell him where, the rage of bafflement threw him into some kind of a fit, and blood gushed from his nose and mouth.

All this the Pocket-Hunter was possessed of when he set out shortly after with his pack and burros, prospecting toward the Dry Creek district, where in due time he crossed the trail of Shorty Wells and Long Tom Bassit. There was no particular reason why Wells should have been called Shorty, except that Long Tom was of a stature to give to any average man in his vicinity a title to that adjective. Further than that he gave no other warrant to the virtues, aptitudes, propensities with which Shorty credited him, than the negative one of not denying them. In camps where they were known the opinion gained ground that there was very little to Long Tom but his size and his amiability, which was remarked upon, but that Shorty, having discovered this creditable baggage in his own pack, had laid it to

Bassit, not being able to say else how he came by it; but there they were, as inveterate a pair of partners as the camps ever bred, owning to no greater satisfaction than just to be abroad in the hills together following the Golden Hope; and there on a day between Dry Creek and Denman's the Pocket-Hunter found them.

The way he came to tell me about it was this. I had laid by for a nooning under the quaking-asp by Peterscreek on the trail from Tunawai, and found him before me with his head under one of those woven shelters of living boughs which the sheep-herders leave in that country, and he moved out to make room for me in its hand's-breadth of shade.

Understand, there *was* no more shade to be got there. Straight before us went the meagre sands; to every yard or so of space its foot-high, sapless shrub. Somewhere at the back of us lifted, out of a bank of pinkish-violet mist, sierras white and airy. Eastward where the earth sagged on its axis, in some dreary, beggared sleep, pale, wispish clouds went up. Now and then to no wind the quaking-asps clattered their dry bones of leaves.

We had been talking, the Pocket-Hunter and I, of that curious obsession of travel by which the mind, pressing on in the long, open trail ahead of the dragging desert pace, seems often to develop a capacity for going on alone in it, so that it becomes involved in one sliding picture, as it were, of what is ahead and what at hand, until, when the body stops for necessary rest and food, it is impossible to say if it is here where it halted, or there where the mind possessed. I had said that this accounted to me not only for the extraordinary feats of endurance in desert travel, but for the great difficulty prospectors have in relocating places they have marked, so mazed they are by that mixed aspect of strangeness and familiarity that every district wears, which, long before it has been entered by the body, has been appraised by the eye of the mind.

"But suppose," said the Pocket-Hunter, "it really does go on by itself?"

"And where," I wished to know, "would be the witness to that, unless it brought back a credible report of what it had seen?"

"Or done," suggested the Pocket-Hunter, "what it set out to do. That would clinch it, I fancy."

"But the mind can only take notice," I protested. "It can't *do* anything without its body."

"Or another one," suggested the Pocket-Hunter.

"Ah," said I, "tell me the story."

IT WAS, went on the Pocket-Hunter, after he had told me all that I have set down about the four men who made the story, about nine of the morning when he came to Dry Creek on the way to Jawbone Cañon, and the day was beginning to curl up and smoke along the edges with the heat, rocking with the motion of it, and water of mirage rolling like quicksilver in the hollows. What the Pocket-Hunter said exactly was that it was a morning in May, but it comes to the same thing. He had just come out of the wash by Cactus Flat when he was aware of a man chasing about in the heat fog, and making out to want something more than common. Even as early as that in the incident the Pocket-Hunter thought he had encountered some faint, floating films from that coil of inexplicable dreadfulness in which he was so soon to find himself involved, and yet he was not sure that it might not have been chiefly in the extraordinary manner of the man's approach, seeing him caught up in the mirage, drawn out and dwarfed again, "like some kind of human accordion," said the Pocket-Hunter, and now rolled toward him with limbs grotesquely multiplied in a river of mist.

Presently, however, he got the man between him and the sun, in such a way that he was able to make out it was himself who was wanted, and when he had slewed the burros round to come up to him, he could see plainly who it was, and it was Wells. It was altogether so unusual a circumstance to find Shorty Wells anywhere out of eyeshot of Tom Bassit that it was not reassuring, and Shorty himself was so sensible of it that almost before any greeting passed, he had let out with certain swallowings of the throat that Tom was dead.

It appeared the two of them had come over Tinpah two days before, and Bassit, who had a weakness of the heart that made high places a menace to him, had accomplished the Pass apparently in good order. But when they had taken the immense drop that carries one from the crest of Tinpah to Dry Creek like a bucket in a shaft, something had gone suddenly, irretrievably wrong. There had been a half collapse at the foot of the trail, and a complete one a few miles back on the trail to Denman's, toward which they had turned in extremity. Tom had suffered agonizingly, so that if there had been any place nearer from which help might conceivably have come, Shorty could not have left him to go and fetch it; and along about the hour which the Indians call, all in one word, the bluish-light-of-dawn, Tom had died.

All the way back to camp, after he had met the Pocket-Hunter, Shorty kept arguing with himself as to whether, if he had done the one thing or had not done the other, it would have been better for poor Tom, and the Pocket-Hunter assuring him for his comfort that it would not, keeping back, by some native stroke of sympathy, what he had lately heard at Tres Piños—that Creelman had a cabin in the Jawbone, and was living in it what time Mac was camping on his trail. It was no farther from the foot of Tinpah than they had come toward Denman's, but in the opposite direction, and from their not turning there it seemed likely they had not heard of it—kinder if Shorty might never come to know, seeing he had not known it in time to be of use to Tom. And this was a point the Pocket-Hunter was presently to make sure of, that neither Shorty nor Long Tom was acquainted with the location of the cabin, nor with Mac nor Creelman by sight.

As it was, he made the most of comforting Shorty for having stayed by his partner to the last.

"I never left him till he croaked," Shorty told him. "It was along toward morning he went quiet, and just as I was goin' for to cover him with the blanket, he croaked—and I come away."

There was that touch of dread in him which ever the figure of death excites in simple minds, which, perhaps as much as the wish to bring help to the burial, had turned him from the body of the friend who was, and now kept his eyes fixed persistently upon the ground as they came back to it across the flat, which here, made smooth in shining, leprous patches of alkali, presented no screen to the disordered camp higher than the sickly pickle-weed about its borders. The Pocket-Hunter, therefore, as they came on toward the place where from two crossed sticks of Shorty's fire a thin point of flame wavered upward, had time for wondering greatly at what he saw, which was so little what he had been led to expect there that he had not found yet any warrant for mentioning it, when Shorty, gathering himself toward what he had to face, lifting up his eyes, let out a kind of howl and ran.

The Pocket-Hunter said he did not know how soon Shorty grasped the fact, which he himself perceived with his eyes some time before his intelligence took hold of it, that the body lying doubled on the sand some yards from the empty bed was not the same that Shorty had left stiffening under the blanket. He thought they must have both taken account of it at the same time, and been stricken dumb by the sheer horror of it, for he could not remember a word spoken by either of them, between Shorty's sharp yell of astonishment and the time when they took it by the shoulders and turned it to the sun.

The limbs were still lax enough with recent like to settle slowly as they stirred the body; there were no wounds upon it, but blood had gushed freely from the nose and mouth. It was a smallish man of no particular color or complexion, with that slight distortion of the joints common in a country of leaded ores. By these marks, as they discovered themselves in the sharp light, the Pocket-Hunter was able to identify him as a man Shorty had never seen, last heard of at Tres Piños, where he had fallen by rage into some such seizure as had apparently overtaken him upon the trail. That he should be here at all, and in such a case as this, was sufficiently horrifying, but it was nothing to the appalling wonder as to what had become of Tom.

There was the impress of his body upon the bed, and the blanket, shed in loose folds across the foot, now lifted a little and buoyed by the wind, and in all the wide day nothing to hide a man, except where, miles behind, the sheer bulk of Tinpah was split by shadowy gulfs of cañons. Shorty was, for the time, fairly tottering in his mind. He would pry foolishly about the camp, getting back by quick turns and pounces to the stretched body on the sand, as though in the interim it might have recovered from its extraordinary illusion and become the body of his friend again. By degrees the Pocket-Hunter constrained him to piece out the probable circumstance.

They had to begin, of course, with Tom's not being dead, and to go on from that to the previous fact of Mac working his poor body over the long stretches between Tres Piños and the Jawbone, where he must have learned that Creelman was hiding. Well, he *had* a poor body, and it must have given out under him just as he arrived in camp, very shortly after Shorty had left it, and, over-ridden by his errand, had persuaded Long

Tom, then recovering from his trance or swoon, to rise and go on with it.

"To kill Creelman! Tom?"

Shorty's imagination flagged visibly in the eye of Tom's huge amiability, but the Pocket-Hunter came around triumphantly.

"Well, he went!"

"But he couldn't have," Shorty put forward, hopefully, as if any bar to his partner's leaving the camp might somehow result in proving him still there. "He hadn't stood on his feet for twenty-four hours, and suffered something awful. Besides, he didn't know there was a cabin; if he had, I'd have gone there yesterday."

"Mac would have told him, of course."

Shorty drooped dejectedly before a supposition that, however large the hope it entailed of finding his partner still in the flesh, afforded no relief to the incontrovertible persistence of evidence in his own mind. "But he croaked, I tell you—they're dead when they croak, ain't they?"

Whatever was said to that was said by the zt-z-z-t of desert flies punctuating the heavy heat. At the sound of it little beads of sweat broke out on Shorty's face.

"Look a-here," he brought out, finally, "if this other fellow, Mac here, was as bad off as you say, why didn't Tom go to him; kind of ease him off like? What for did he go off and leave him crumpled up like that?

"He wouldn't have died until after Tom left, Mac wouldn't," the Pocket-Hunter reminded him. "What makes you so sure?"

"Tom never walked none after we struck camp." Shorty was secure of his ground here. "And there's no tracks of him except where he came in alongside of me—and goin' out—*there!*" The print of Tom's large feet had turned toward the Jawbone. "Besides," he returned to it with anxiety, "what would he go to Creelman's for?"

This was a point, and the Pocket-Hunter took as much time as was necessary to shroud the dead man in Tom's blanket to consider it. He found this at last:

"Tom," he said, "was a peaceable man?"

"None peaceabler," admitted Tom's partner.

"Well, then, when he found this little—" (the adjective checked out of respect to the object of it being as he was) "Mac here so set on killing, he thought it no more than right to get on ahead and give Creelman a hint of what was coming to him."

This being so much what might have been expected of Tom, it appeared insensibly to give greater plausibility to the whole occasion. It left them for the moment free to set out on Tom's trail with almost a movement of naturalness. It lasted, however, only long enough to see them into the steady, flowing stride of desert travel; the recurrence of that motion, perhaps, set up again in Shorty's mind the consciousness of loss in which it had some two hours earlier begun, and the consideration of mere practical details, such as the distance from the camp to Creelman's, swept back to the full the conviction of unreality.

Looking ahead at the long trudge between them and the mouth of the cañon, where in that clear light, on that level mesa, no man could have moved unespied by them, where, in fact, no man at that moment was moving, he broke out in a kind of exasperated wail:

"But he couldn't have, I tell you; he couldn't have walked it. . . . He was dead, I tell you. . . . He croaked and I covered him up. . . ."

It became momentarily clearer to the Pocket-Hunter that unless they came soon, behind some screening weed, in some unguessed hollow, upon Long Tom's huddled body, collapsed in the recurrent weakness of his disorder, so to restore the event to reasonableness, he must find himself swamped again in the horror of the inexplicable, out of which they had been speciously pulled by the Pocket-Hunter's argument.

It was not until they came to the loose shale and sand at the mouth of the cañon that Shorty reverted again to the form of his amazement.

"Did you notice," said he, "anything queer about Tom's tracks?"

"Queer, how?"

"Well—different?"

"Like he thought he had a game leg?" suggested the Pocket-Hunter.

"Well, he hadn't . . . but the other man . . . back yonder . . . he had a game leg."

"Shorty! Shorty!" the Pocket-Hunter fairly begged. "You ain't . . . you mustn't . . . let your mind run on them things!"

"Well, he had," persisted Wells. His voice clicked with dryness, trailed off whispering. It seemed to the Pocket-Hunter, suddenly, that the twenty steps or so between the man so certainly dead in his tracks on one side the fire back there, and the supposedly dead arising in his on the other, had swelled to immeasurable space. It was then there came into his mind the remainder of that singular obsession of the trail in the notice of which our conversation had begun. He saw on the instant Mac inching out from Tres Piños on his unmatched poor legs, his hate riding far before him, blown forward by some devil's blast, tugging at him like a kite at its ballast, lifting him past incredible stretches of hot sand and cutting stone, until it dropped him there. He wrenched his mind away from that by an effort, and fixed it on the pale pine-colored square of Creelman's cabin, where it began to show in the shadowy gulf of the cañon.

The door was open and the curtains of the two small windows on either side half drawn against a glare which would have been gone from that side of the cañon more than an hour ago. Here, as they halted to take notice of it, some expiring gasps of bluish smoke from Creelman's breakfast fire went up from the tin chimney against the basalt wall. As they came near they observed a large flaccid hand hanging out over the sill. What they made out further was Creelman's body, extended face downward, barring the door. A small lizard tic-tacked on the unpainted boards across the hand that did not start at it, and disappeared into the shadow of the room, where, as if this intrusion gave them leave to look, they perceived among the broken plates and disordered furniture a broken pack-stick, Creelman's knife, open and blooded—the figure of Long Tom, half propped against the footboard of the bunk, dropping weakly from a wound. It *was* Tom, though over his face as it leered up at them was spread a strange new expressiveness, such a superficial and furtive change as frivolous passers-by will add sometimes to the face of a poster with pencil touches, provoking to half-startled laughter; plain enough to have shocked them back, even as against the witness of clothes and hair and features, from the instant's recognition, to produce in them an amazement, momentary, yet long enough for the dying man to take note of them unfriendly, and to have addressed himself to the Pocket-Hunter.

"Came to see the fight, did you? It's damned well over . . . but I did for him . . . the ———, ———, ———!" His body sank visibly with the stream of curses.

But the faith of Shorty was proof even against this. He had cleared the body of Creelman at a stride, and was on his knees beside his partner, crying very simply.

"Oh, Tom, Tom," he begged, "you never done it? Say you never done it, pardner, say you never!"

"Aw, who the hell are you?" The lewd eyes rolled up at him, he gave two or three long gasps which ended in a short choking gurgle, the body started slightly, and dropped.

"Come away, Shorty, he's croaked," said the Pocket-Hunter not unkindly; but Shorty knelt on there, crying quietly as he watched the dead man's features settle and stiffen to the likeness of his friend.

XI

THE READJUSTMENT

EMMA JEFFRIES had been dead and buried three days. The sister who had come to the funeral had taken Emma's child away with her, and the house was swept and aired; then, when it seemed there was least occasion for it, Emma came back. The neighbor woman who had nursed her was the first to know it. It was about seven of the evening in a mellow gloom: the neighbor woman was sitting on her own stoop with her arms wrapped in her apron, and all at once she found herself going along the street under an urgent sense that Emma needed her. She was half-way down the block before she recollected that this was impossible, for Mrs. Jeffries was dead and buried; but as soon as she came opposite the house she was aware of what had happened. It was all open to the summer air; except that it was a little neater, not otherwise than the rest of the street. It was quite dark; but the presence of Emma Jeffries streamed from it and betrayed it more than a candle. It streamed out steadily across the garden, and even as it reached her, mixed with the smell of the damp mignonette, the neighbor woman owned to herself that she had always known Emma would come back.

"A sight stranger if she wouldn't," thought the woman who had nursed her. "She wasn't ever one to throw off things easily."

Emma Jeffries had taken death as she had taken everything in life, hard. She had met it with the same bright, surface competency that she had presented to the squalor of the encompassing desertness, to the insuperable commonness of Sim Jeffries, to the affliction of her crippled child; and the intensity of her wordless struggle against it had caught the attention of the townspeople and held it in a shocked curious awe. She was so long a-dying, lying there in that little low house, hearing the abhorred footsteps going about her rooms and the vulgar procedure of the community encroach upon her like the advances of the sand wastes on an unwatered field. For Emma had always wanted things different, wanted them with a fury of intentness that implied offensiveness in things as they were. And the townspeople had taken offence, the more so because she was not to be surprised in any inaptitude for their own kind of success. Do what you could, you could never catch Emma Jeffries in a wrapper after three o'clock in the afternoon. And she would never talk about the child—in a country where so little ever happened that even trouble was a godsend if it gave you something to talk about. It was reported that she did not even talk to Sim. But there the common resentment got back at her. If she had thought to effect anything with Sim Jeffries against the benumbing spirit of the place, the evasive hopefulness, the large sense of leisure that ungirt the loins, if she still hoped somehow to get away with him to some place for which by her dress, by her manner, she seemed forever and unassailably fit, it was foregone that nothing would come of it. They knew Sim Jeffries better than that. Yet so vivid had been the force of her wordless dissatisfaction that when the fever took her and she went down like a pasteboard figure in the damp, the wonder was that nothing toppled with her. And, as if she too had felt herself indispensable, Emma Jeffries had come back.

The neighbor woman crossed the street, and as she passed the far corner of the garden, Jeffries spoke to her. He had been standing, she did not know how long a time, behind the syringa-bush, and moved even with her along the fence until they came to the gate. She could see in the dusk that before speaking he wet his lips with his tongue.

"She's in there," he said, at last.

"Emma?"

He nodded. "I been sleeping at the store since—but I thought I'd be more comfortable—as soon as I opened the door there she was."

"Did you see her?"

"No."

"How do you know, then?"

"Don't you know?"

The neighbor felt there was nothing to say to that.

"Come in," he whispered, huskily. They slipped by the rose-tree and the wistaria, and sat down on the porch at the side. A door swung inward behind them. They felt the Presence in the dusk beating like a pulse.

"What do you think she wants?" said Jeffries. "Do you reckon it's the boy?"

"Like enough."

"He's better off with his aunt. There was no one here to take care of him like his mother wanted." He raised his voice unconsciously with a note of justification, addressing the room behind.

"I am sending fifty dollars a month," he said; "he can go with the best of them."

He went on at length to explain all the advantage that was to come to the boy from living at Pasadena, and the neighbor woman bore him out in it.

"He was glad to do," urged Jeffries to the room. "He said it was what his mother would have wanted."

They were silent then a long time, while the Presence seemed to swell upon them and encroached upon the garden.

Finally, "I gave Ziegler the order for the monument yesterday," Jeffries threw out, appeasingly. "It's to cost three hundred and fifty."

The Presence stirred. The neighbor thought she could fairly see the controlled tolerance with which Emma Jeffries endured the evidence of Sim's ineptitudes.

They sat on helplessly without talking after that until the woman's husband came to the fence and called her.

"Don't go," begged Sim.

"Hush," she said. "Do you want all the town to know? You had naught but good from Emma living, and no call to expect harm from her now. It's natural she should come back—if—if she was lonesome like—in—the place where she's gone to."

"Emma wouldn't come back to this place," Jeffries protested, "without she wanted something."

"Well, then, you've got to find out," said the neighbor woman.

All the next day she saw, whenever she passed the house, that Emma was still there. It was shut and barred, but the Presence lurked behind the folded blinds and fumbled at the doors. When it was night and the moths began in the columbine under the windows, it went out and walked in the garden.

Jeffries was waiting at the gate when the neighbor woman came. He sweated with helplessness in the warm dusk, and the Presence brooded upon them like an apprehension that grows by being entertained.

"She wants something," he appealed, "but I can't make out what. Emma knows she is welcome to everything I've got. Everybody knows I've been a good provider."

The neighbor woman remembered suddenly the only time she had ever drawn close to Emma Jeffries touching the boy. They had sat up with it together all one night in some childish ailment, and she had ventured a question. "What does his father think?" And Emma had turned her a white, hard face of surpassing dreariness.

"I don't know," she admitted, "he never says."

"There's more than providing," suggested the neighbor woman.

"Yes. There's feeling . . . but she had enough to do to put up with me. I had no call to be troubling her with such." He left off to mop his forehead, and began again.

"Feelings!" he said, "there's times a man gets so wore out with feelings he doesn't have them any more."

He talked, and presently it grew clear to the woman that he was voiding all the stuff of his life, as if he had sickened on it and was now done. It was a little soul knowing itself and not good to see. What was singular was that the Presence left off walking in the garden, came and caught like a gossamer on the ivy-tree, swayed by the breath of his broken sentences. He talked, and the neighbor woman saw him for once as he saw himself and Emma, snared and floundering in an inexplicable unhappiness. He had been disappointed, too. She had never relished the man he was, and it made him ashamed. That was why he had never gone away, lest he should make her ashamed among her own kind. He was her husband, he could not help that though he was sorry for it. But he could keep the offence where least was made of it. And there was a child—she had wanted a child; but even then he had blundered—begotten a cripple upon her. He blamed himself utterly, searched out the roots of his youth for the answer to that, until the neighbor woman flinched to hear him. But the Presence stayed.

He had never talked to his wife about the child. How should he? There was the fact—the advertisement of his incompetence. And she had never talked to him. That was the one blessed and unassailable memory; that she had spread silence like a balm over his hurt. In return for it he had never gone away. He had resisted her that he might save her from showing among her own kind how poor a man he was. With every word of this ran the fact of his love for her—as he had loved her, with all the stripes of clean and uncleanness. He bared himself as a child without knowing; and the Presence stayed. The talk trailed off at last to the commonplaces of consolation between the retchings of his spirit. The Presence lessened and streamed toward them on the wind of the garden. When it touched them like the warm air of noon that lies sometimes in hollow places after nightfall, the neighbor woman rose and went away.

The next night she did not wait for him. When a rod outside the town—it was a very little one—the burrowing owls *whoo-whooed,* she hung up her apron and went to talk with Emma Jeffries. The Presence was there, drawn in, lying close. She found the key between the wistaria and the first pillar of the porch, but as soon as she opened the door she felt the chill that might be expected by one intruding on Emma Jeffries in her own house.

"'The Lord is my shepherd,'" said the neighbor woman; it was the first religious phrase that occurred to her; then she said the whole of the psalm and after that a hymn. She had come in through the door and stood with her back to it and her hand upon the knob. Everything was just as Mrs. Jeffries had left it, with the waiting air of a room kept for company.

"Em," she said, boldly, when the chill had abated a little before the sacred words. "Em Jeffries, I've got something to say to you. And you've got to hear," she added with firmness, as the white curtains stirred duskily at the window. "You wouldn't be talked to about your troubles when . . . you were here before; and we humored you. But now there is Sim to be thought of. I guess you heard what you came for last night, and got good of it. Maybe it would have been better if Sim had said things all along instead of hoarding them in his heart, but any way he has said them now. And what I want to say is, if you was staying on with the hope of hearing it again, you'd be making a mistake. You was an uncommon woman, Emma Jeffries, and there didn't none of us understand you very well, nor do you justice maybe; but Sim is only a common man, and I understand him because I'm that way myself. And if you think he'll be opening his heart to you every night, or be any different from what he's always been on account of what's happened, that's a mistake too . . . and in a little while, if you stay, it will be as bad as it always was . . . Men are like that. . . . You'd better go now while there's understanding between you." She stood staring into the darkling room that seemed suddenly full of turbulence and denial. It seemed to beat upon her and take her breath, but she held on.

"You've got to go . . . Em . . . and I'm going to stay until you do." She said this with finality, and then began again.

"'The Lord is nigh unto them that are of a broken heart,'" and repeated the passage to the end. Then as the Presence sank before it. "You better go, Emma," persuasively, and again after an interval:

"'He shall deliver thee in six troubles, yea, in seven shall no evil touch thee.'"

. . . The Presence gathered itself and was still. She could make out that it stood over against the opposite corner by the gilt easel with the crayon portrait of the child.

. . . "'For thou shalt forget thy misery. Thou shalt remember it as waters that are past,'" concluded the neighbor woman, as she heard Jeffries on the gravel outside. What the Presence had wrought upon him in the night was visible in his altered mien. He looked more than anything else to be in need of sleep. He had eaten his sorrow, and that was the end of it—as it is with men.

"I came to see if there was anything I could do for you," said the woman, neighborly, with her hand upon the door.

"I don't know as there is," said he; "I'm much obliged, but I don't know as there is."

"You see," whispered the woman over her shoulder, "not even to me." She felt the tug of her heart as the Presence swept past her.

The neighbor went out after that and walked in the ragged street, past the school-house, across the creek below the town, out by the fields, over the headgate, and back by the town again. It was full nine of the clock when she passed the Jeffries house. It looked, except for being a little neater, not other than the rest of the street. The door was open and the lamp was lit; she saw Jeffries, black against it. He sat reading in a book, like a man at ease in his own house.

XII

BITTERNESS OF WOMEN

LOUIS CHABOT was sitting under the fig-tree in her father's garden at Tres Piños when he told Marguerita Dupré that he could not love her. This sort of thing happened so often to Louis that he did it very well and rather enjoyed it, for he was one of those before whom women bloomed instinctively and preened themselves; and that Marguerita loved him very much was known not only to Louis but to all Tres Piños.

It was bright mid-afternoon, and there was no sound in Dupré's garden louder than the dropping of ripe figs and the drip of the hydrant under the Castilian roses. A mile out of town Chabot's flock dozed on their feet, with their heads under one another's bellies, and his herders dozed on the ground, with their heads under the plaited tops of the sage. Old Dupré sat out in front of his own front yard with a handkerchief over his face, and slept very soundly. Chabot finished his claret to the last drop (it was excellent claret, this of Dupré's), turned the tumbler upside down, sat back in his chair, and explained to Marguerita point by point why he did not love her.

Marguerita leaned her fat arms on the table, wrapped in her blue reboza; it was light blue, and she was too dark for it; but it was such a pretty color. She leaned forward, looking steadily and quietly at Louis, because she was afraid if she so much as let her lids droop the tears would come, and if she smiled her lips would quiver. Marguerita felt that she had not invited this, neither had she known how to avoid it. She would have given anything to have told Louis to his face that he need not concern himself so much on her account, as she was not the least interested in him; she had called on all her pride to that end, but nothing came.

She was a good girl, Louis told her, such as, if she had pleased him, he would gladly have married. She was a very good girl, and she understood about sheep. *Tres-bien!* Old Dupré had taught her that; but she lacked a trifle—a nuance—but everything where love is concerned, *l'art d'être désiré*, explained the little Frenchman; for though he was only a sheep-herder of Lost Borders, if he had been a boulevardier he could not have been more of a Frenchman nor less of a cad. He leaned back in his chair with the air of having delivered himself very well.

"Salty Bill loves me," ventured Marguerita.

"Eh, Bill!" Louis looked hurt, for though he frequently disposed of his ladies in this negligent fashion, he did not care to have them snapped up so quickly. Marguerita felt convicted of *lèse-majesté* by the look, and hastened to reassure him that she cared nothing whatever for Salty Bill. It was a false move, and she knew it as soon as it was done; but she could not bear to have Louis look at her like that, and Marguerita had never in her life learned the good of pretending. Chabot poured him another glass of claret, and returned to his point.

There was Suzon Moynier, he explained. Such an eye as Suzon had! there was a spark for you! And an ankle! more lovers than few had been won by an ankle. Marguerita, under cover of the table, drew her feet together beneath her skirts. Her ankles were thick, and there was no disguising it.

"So it is Suzon you love?"

"Eh," said the herder, "that is as may be. I have loved many women." Then perhaps because the particular woman did not matter so much as that there should be womanhood, and perhaps because he could no more help it than she could help being wondrously flooded by it, he threw her a look from the tail of his eye and such a smile as drew all the blood from her heart, bent above her, brushing her hair with his lips in such a lingering tenderness of farewell, that though he had just told her she was not to be loved, the poor girl was not sure but he was beginning to love her. Women suffered things like that from Louis Chabot, each being perfectly sure she was the only one, and perhaps, like Marguerita, finding it worth while to be made to suffer if it could be done so exquisitely.

Marguerita was only half French herself, old Dupré having married her mother, Señorita Carrasco, who was only half a señorita, since, in fact, most people in Tres Piños were a little this or that, with no chance for name-calling. Dupré had been a herder of sheep, risen to an owner whom the Desert had bitten. The natural consequence was that when he was old, instead of returning to France, he had married Marguerita's mother, and settled down in Tres Piños to live on the interest of his money.

It was a fact that his daughter had at heart all the fire and tenderness that promised in Suzon's glance; but of what use to Louis Chabot that she had a soul warm and alight if no glow of it suffused her cheek and no spark of it drew him in her eye. She was swarthy and heavy of face; she had no figure, which means she had a great deal too much of it, and there was a light shadow, like a finger-smudge, on her upper lip. Not that the girl did not have her good points. She could cook, that was the French strain in her father; she could dance, that was Castilian from her mother; and such as she was Salty Bill wanted her. Bill drove an eighteen-mule team for the borax works and was seven times a better man than Chabot, but she would have no more of him than Louis would have of her. She continued to say her prayers regularly, and told Tia Juana, who reproached her with losing a good marriage, that she believed yet the saints would give her the desire of her heart, whereat Tia Juana pitied her.

Chabot brought his sheep up from the spring shearing at Bakersfield each year, and made three loops about Tres Piños, so that it brought him to the town about once in three months to replenish his supplies, and the only reason there was not a new object of his attentions each time was that there were not girls enough, for Chabot's taste required them young, pretty, and possessed of the difficult art of being desired. Therefore, he had time to keep hope alive in Marguerita with the glint of his flattering eyes and the trick of his flattering lips, which was such very common coin with him that he did not quite know himself how free he was with it. And after old Dupré died and his daughter inherited his house and the interest on his money, she was enough of a figure in Tres Piños to make a little attention worth while, even though she had a smudge of black on her upper lip and no art but that of being faithful. She lived in the house under the fig-tree with old Tia Juana for a companion, and was much respected. She was said to have more clothes than anybody, though they never became her.

Marguerita kept a candle burning before the saints and another in her heart for the handsome little herder who went on making love to ladies and being loved by them for three years. Then the saints took a hand in his affairs, though, of course, it did not look that way to Louis.

He was sleeping out on Black Mountain in the spring of the year with his flock. The herder whose business it was to have done that was at Tres Piños on a two days' leave, confessing himself, and getting a nice, jolly little claret drunk. Somewhere up in the blown lava-holes of Black Mountain there was a bear with two cubs, who had said to them, bear fashion: "Come down to the flock with me tonight, and I will show you how killing is done. There will be dogs there and men; but do not be afraid, I will see to it that they do not hurt you."

Along about the time Orion's sword sloped down the west, Chabot heard their gruntled noises and the scurry of the flock. Chabot was not a coward; perhaps because he knew that in general bears are; he got up and laid about him with his staff. This he never would have done if he had known about the cubs; he trod on the foot of one in the dark, and the bear mother heard it. She came lumbering up in the soft blackness and took Chabot in her arms.

Toward four of the next afternoon, the herder coming back, still very merry and very comfortable in his mind, found a maimed, bleeding thing by the water-hole that moaned and babbled. One of its arms was gone to the elbow, its face was laid open, and long, red gashes lay along its sides an down one thigh. After a while, when he had washed away the blood and dust, he discovered that this thing was Chabot. The herder laid it as tenderly as he could on the camp burro and took it in to Tres Piños. If there was any question of the propriety of the care of Chabot falling to Marguerita Dupré, it counted for nothing against the fact that nobody was found willing to do it in her stead, and Marguerita was very discreet. Tia Juana was put in charge of the sick-room, and Marguerita gave her whole soul to the cooking.

And if any question had arisen later when Chabot began to hobble about with a crutch under his good arm, and his sleeve pinned up where the other had been, he put an end to it by marrying her. He was thought to have done very well in this, since he could get no more good of himself; and since Marguerita wanted him it was a handsome way of paying her, but there had something gone before that. Tia Juana had been careful there should be no scrap of a mirror about when Chabot began to slip his bandages, and perhaps he had not had the courage to ask for it; certainly there had been no change in Marguerita's face for any change she saw in him. And the day that he knew the thing he was, he asked her to marry him. He had slipped out into the street for the first time, wearying a little of the solicitations of the two women, and, to say truth, wholly misinterpreting Marguerita's reasons for screening him so much from the public gaze, for she, poor girl, when he asked her, could only tell him that he was quite as handsome as ever in her eyes. He felt the pleasant tingle of the air and the sun and the smell of grapes and dropping leafage from the little arbors of Tres Piños, and at the turn of the street in old Moynier's garden the flirt of skirts and the graceful reach of young round arms. Louis straightened himself on his crutches; he felt the stir and excitement of the game . . . he was divided between his old swagger and the pathetic droop of weakness . . . he swung slowly past the garden, and sudden Suzon looked up . . . looked dully at first . . . with dawning recognition. Then she threw her apron over her face and shrieked, and fled into the house. There was something more than coquetry in the way she ran.

Louis turned into the lane and sat down under the black sage, he was not so strong as he had thought, and tried to be quite clear in his mind what this should mean. In a little while he was quite clear. Some children playing in the dust of the roadway at his approach had scuttled away like quail, and now he heard behind him the rustle of the sage, the intimation of hunched shoulders and fingers held over giggles of irrepressible excitement as they dared one another to come and peek at a fearsome thing.

It was that afternoon, when she came in with his soup and claret, that he asked Marguerita. The poor girl put down the bowl, and came and knelt by him very humble and gentle.

"Are you quite sure, Louis?" she asked, with her cheek upon his hand.

"I am sure of nothing," said he, "except that I cannot live without you."

It was very curious that no sooner had he said that than he began to discover it would be very hard to live with her; for to lose an ear and an eye and to have one's mouth drawn twisty by a scar does not make a kiss relish better if it falls not in with the natural desire.

Marguerita did not grow any prettier after she was married, but showed a tendency to take on fat, and she did not dress quite so well because she could not afford it, though there are times, as, for instance, when he has gone out in company and seen the young married women hustled out of sight of his scars, that her plain face looks almost good to him. Marguerita insists on their going out a great deal, to cock-fights and to *bailes,* where he sits in the corner with his good side carefully disposed toward the guests, and his wife has given up dancing, though she is very fond of it, to sit beside him and keep him company; though, to tell the truth, Chabot could bear very well to do without that if only he could find himself surrounded by the lightness, the laughter, the half-revealing draperies, the delicious disputed moves of the game he loves—as he will not any more, for he knows now that such as these are not given save when there is something to be got by them, and though he is only thirty-four, poor Louis is no longer possessed of *l'art être désiré.*

For the rest of his life he will have to make the best of knowing that his wife carries his name with credit, and does not cost him anything. They are not without their comfortable hours. Marguerita takes excellent care of him, and she understands about sheep; if she sees the dust of a flock arising can tuck up her skirts and away to the edge of the town, getting back as much news of where they go, whence they come, and the conditions of the weather as Chabot could have brought himself, and not even her husband knows the extent of her devices for keeping him surrounded with the sense and stir of life. For it was not long after his marriage that Chabot made the discovery that all the quick desire of him toward lovely women warms in his wife's spirit toward the maimed and twisted thing that he is, and thwarted of the subtle play of lip and limb and eye, spends itself in offices of homely comfort.

And this is the bitterness of women which has come to him: that it matters not so much that they should have passion as the power to provoke it, and lacking the spark of a glance, the turn of an ankle, the treasures of tenderness in them wither unfulfilled. Shut behind his wife's fat, commonplace exterior lies the pulse of music, the delight of motion, the swimming sense, the quick, white burning fenced within his scars. Times like this he remembers what has passed between him and many women, and finds his complacency sicken and die in him. Knowing what he does of the state of her heart, and not being quite a cad, he does not make her an altogether bad husband, and if sometimes, looking at her with abhorring eyes—the skaking bosom, the arms enormous, the shade of her upper lip no longer to be mistaken for a smudge—resenting her lack of power to move him, he gives her a bad quarter of an hour, even there she has the best of him. For however unhappy he makes her, with one kiss of his crooked mouth he can set it all right again. But for Louis, the lift, the exultation, the exquisite, unmatched wonder of the world will not happen any more; never any more.

XIII

THE HOUSE OF OFFENCE

🦂🦂🦂🦂🦂

IT BEGAN TO BE called the House when it was the only frame building in the camp, and wore its offence upon its front—long and low, little rooms, each with its own door opening upon the shallow veranda. Such a house in a mining country is the dial finger of prosperity. All the ores thereabout were argent, and as the lords of far market-places made silver to go up a few points, you were aware of it in the silken rustle and the heel-click of satin slippers in the House. When the Jews got their heads together and whispered in the Bourse, the gay skirts would flit and the lights go out in the little rooms behind the two cottonwood-trees that should have screened their entrances, but clacking their leaves as if forever fluttered and aghast at what went on in them, betrayed it all the more.

Inmates came and went; sometimes they had names and personalities, but mostly they were simply the women of the House. It was always spoken of in that way, as if but to pass the door-sill were to be seized of its full inheritance of turbulence and shame; and as the town poised and hung upon the turn of the appointed fortune of mining-camps, the House passed from being an outburst, an excess, to a backwater pool of enticement, wherein men swam or sunk themselves, and at last, as the quality of its attractions fell off with the grade of ores, it became merely the overt sign of an admitted and ineradicable baseness.

Always it served to keep alive in the camp the consciousness of style and the allurement of finery; for when the House was at its best, the conditions in desert camps, the price freight was, scrub-water to be bought by the gallon, the prohibitive cost of service, ground terribly the faces of good women. But they could always tell what kind of sleeves were being worn in San Francisco by watching the House. They all watched it; women whose lean breasts sagged from the lips of many children, virtuous slattern in calico, petted wives secure in a traditional honor; and their comment kept a stir about it like the pattering trail of the wind in the cottonwoods. In time, as the spring of mining interest drew away from that district to flash and rise again in some unguessed other side of the world, even that fell off before the dead weight of stable interests and a respectability too stale to be curious; the ground about it was parcelled off; all the accustomed activities of small towns went on around it screened from its contamination by no more than a high board fence, from which in time the palings rotted away. Good women exercised themselves no more against it than to prevent their children from playing under the shade of the two cottonwoods that broadened before it, like the shadow of professional impropriety, behind which the House had shrunk, and, in its condition of unregarded sordidness, pointed the last turn of the dial.

About this time it came into the sole possession of Hard Mag, who was handsome enough to have done much better by herself, and concerning whom nothing worth recording might have transpired had it not been for Mrs. Henby.

The Henbys had taken the place which faced the adjacent street and abutted on the back yard of the House. Henby was blast foreman at the Eclipse, and came home every other Sunday; and his wife, who was very fond of him, found a consolation for the lack of his company in the ordered life of the town. To wash on Monday, iron on Tuesday, bake on Wednesday, and keep the front room always looking as if nobody lived in it, gave Mrs. Henby a virtuous sense of well-being that she had not known in twenty years of scrambled existence at the mines. The trouble with Mrs. Henby was that she had no children. If there had been small footsteps going about the rooms and small finger-clutchings at her dress she would have been perfectly happy, and consequently had no time to trouble about the doing of the House. There had been hopes—but at forty, though her cheeks were smooth and bright, her hair still black, and her figure looking as if it had been melted and poured into her neat print wrapper, Mrs. Henby did not hope any more. She made a silk crazy-quilt for the bed-lounge in the parlor, and began to take an interest in Hard Mag and the draggled birds of passage that preened themselves occasionally in the dismantled rooms of the House, though being the most virtuous of women she would never have admitted the faintest distraction in the affairs of "such like."

It began by Mrs. Henby discovering, through the cracks of the fence, that Mag, in the intervals of sinning, was largely occupied with the tasks of widowed and neglected women. Mrs. Henby cut kindlings for herself sometimes if Henby was detained at the mine beyond his week-end visits, but to see Mag of the hard, red lips, the bright, unglinting hair, and the burnt-out blackness of her eyes under the pale, long lids, so employed made it of an amazing opprobriousness. For, as Mrs. Henby understood it, the root of sin lay in self-indulgence, and might be fostered by such small matters as sitting too much in rocking-chairs and wearing too becoming hats; she saw it now as the sign of an essential incompetency in the offices of creditable living. Mag, she perceived, did not even know how to pin up her skirts properly when she swept the back stoop. To see her thus fumbling at the mechanism of existence was to put her forever beyond the reach of resentment into the region of pitiable humanness. In time it grew upon Mrs. Henby that the poor creatures, who took the air of late afternoons in the yard behind the House, might have possibilities even of being interested in the crazy-quilt and the garden, and being prevented by some mysterious law of their profession from doing so. She went so far upon this supposition as to offer Mag a bunch of radishes out of her minute vegetable plot, which Mag, to her relief, refused. Mrs. Henby could no more refrain from neighborliness than she could help being large at the waist, but she really would not like to be seen handing things through the fence to the inmates of the House. She came to that in time, though.

Some wretched consort of Mag's fell sick at the House of the lead poisoning common in the mines when the doctor was away at Maverick, and nobody in the neighborhood so skilled in the remedies proper to the occasion as Mrs. Henby. This led to several conferences, and the passage between the palings of sundry preparations of hot milk and soups and custards. Mrs. Henby would hand them out after nightfall, and find the dishes on her side of the fence in the morning. She was so ashamed of it that she never told even her husband, and the man having gone away to his own place and died there, Mag had nobody to tell it to in any case. But Mrs. Henby always entertained a subconscious sureness that something unpleasant was likely to come of her condonings of iniquity, and one morning, when she came out of the kitchen door to find Mag furtively waiting at the fence, she roughed forward all the quills of her respectability at once. Mag leaned her breast upon the point of a broken paling, as though the sharpness of it stayed her. She had no right to the desultory courtesies of back-fence neighborliness, and did not attempt them.

"I've had a letter," she said, abruptly, showing it clinched against her side; the knuckles of her hand were strained and white.

"A letter?"

"From Kansas. My daughter's coming." She lowered her voice and looked back cautiously at the shut House, as if the thing could overhear.

So she had a daughter—this painted piece; and God-fearing women might long and long! Twenty years' resentment began to burn in Mrs. Henby's cushiony bosom.

"What are you doin' with a daughter?" she said.

"Oh," cried Mag, impatiently, "I had her years ago—ten—eleven years! She has been living with my aunt in Kansas: and now my aunt is dead, and they are sending her."

"Who is sending her?"

"I don't know—the neighbors. I've nobody belonging to me back there. They have to do something with her, so they are sending her to me. Here!" She struck upon the paling wickedly with her hand.

"Where's her father?" Mrs. Henby's interest rose superior to her resentment.

"How should I know? I tell you it was a long time ago. I came away when she was a little, little baby. My aunt was religious and couldn't have anything to do with me, but she took care of—her! I sent money."

Mrs. Henby recalled herself to the aloofness of entire respectability. "If your aunt wouldn't have you, I don't see how she could feel to abide your money?"

"I told her I was married," said Mag, "and respectable." She leaned upon the paling and laughed a hard, sharp laugh.

Mrs. Henby gathered up her apron full of kindlings.

"Well, you've made your bed," she said. "I guess you will lie in it."

But she sat down trembling as soon as she had shut the door. A daughter—to that woman—and she— Mrs. Henby went about shaking her head and talking to herself with indignation. All day the House remained shut and slumbering, its patched and unwashed windows staring blankly on the yard; but if ever Mrs. Henby came out of her kitchen door, as if she were the cuckoo on the striking of the hour, Mag appeared from the House. It was evident she had ordered a clear field for herself, for no one came out in draggled finery to take the air that day. It was dusk before Mrs. Henby's humanness got the better of her. She went out to the woodpile and whispered to the stirring of Mag's dress:

"When's she coming?"

"Wednesday. She will be started before I can get a letter to her."

"Well, I reckon you'll have to take her," said Mrs. Henby, unconsolingly. A flash of Mag's insuperable hardness broke from her.

"She'll spoil trade," she said.

Mrs. Henby looked up the dusky bulk of the House beyond her, lines of light at the windows like the red lids of distempered eyes. All at once, and, as she said afterward, without for the moment any consciousness relativity, she recalled the quagmires of unwarned water-holes where cattle sink and flounder, and the choking call of warning that sounds to the last above the stifling slime. When Mag said that about the child and her way of making a living, Mrs. Henby jumped. She thought she heard the smothering suck of the mire. Somebody in the House laughed and cried out coarsely, and then she heard Mag's voice going on hurriedly behind the palings:

"Mrs. Henby! Mrs. Henby! you've got to help me— I must find some place for her to board— She has been well brought up, I tell you. My aunt is religious— She would be a comfort to some good person."

"Meaning me, I suppose," sniffed Mrs. Henby. Mag had not meant anybody in particular, but she swept it up urgently.

"Oh, if you would—she'd be a comfort to you! She's real sweet-looking—they sent me her picture once." She felt for phrases to touch the other woman, but they rang insincerely. "You'd be the saving of her—if you would."

"Well, I won't!" snapped Mrs. Henby; and as soon as she was inside she locked the door against even the suggestion. "Me to take anything off that painted piece!" she quivered, angrily.

It was five days until Wednesday, and Mag struck to her trail insistently.

"You been thinking of what I said last night?" she questioned in the morning interval at the woodpile.

Mrs. Henby denied it, but she had. She had thought of what Henby would say to it, and wondered if Mag's daughter had hard eyes, and bright, unglinting, canary-colored hair. She thought of what explanation she might make to the neighbors in case she decided suddenly to adopt the daughter of—of an old friend in Kansas; then she thought of the faces of the women who went in and out of the House, and resolved not to think any more.

She kept away from the woodpile as much as possible during Saturday and Sunday, but Monday evening she heard Mag calling her from the back of the yard. This was the worst yet, for there was no telling who might overhear.

"Mrs. Henby," demanded the painted piece, "are you going to see that innocent child brought to this place and never lift a hand to it?"

"I don't know as I got any call to interfere," said Mrs. Henby.

"And you with a good home, and calling yourself Christian, and all," went on the hard one. "Besides, I'd pay you."

"I don't feel to need any of your money," thrust in Mrs. Henby, resentfully. "I guess I could take care of one child without—but I ain't going to." She broke off, and moved rapidly toward the house.

"Mrs. Henby, listen to me!" cried Mag, shaking at the palings as though they had been the bars of a cage and she trapped in it. "For Gods' sake, Mrs. Henby, you must! Mrs. Henby, if you won't listen to me here, I shall come to your house."

Mrs. Henby heard the crack of the rotten palings as she shut the door.

"Mrs. Henby! Mrs. Henby!" threatened the voice, "I'm coming in!"

Then the crash of splintering wood, and Mag's hand on the knob. The vehemence of her mood, her tragic movements, the bright vividness of her lips and hair seemed to force Mrs. Henby into the attitude of the offender. She sat limply in a chair twisting her hands in her fat lap while the other assailed her. Behind her on the wall Mag's shadow shook and threatened like the shape of an uncouth destiny.

"I know what you are thinking, Mrs. Henby. You think there's bad blood, and she will turn out like me maybe, but I tell you it's no such thing. Look here—if it's any satisfaction to you to know—I was good when I had her, and her father was good—only we were young and didn't know any better—we hadn't any feelings except what we'd have had if we had been married—only we didn't happen to— It's the truth, Mrs. Henby, if I die for it. Bad blood!" she said, hardness augmenting upon her." "How many a man comes to the House and goes away to raise a family, and not a word said about bad blood! You don't reckon—"

But Mrs. Henby had her apron over her face, and was crying into it. Mag floundered back to the other woman's point of view.

"If it is a question what she'll come to, you know well enough if I have to take her with me. *Me!*" she said. She threw round herself an indescribable air of lascivious deviltry, as though she had been blown upon by the blast of an unseen furnace, and the shadow upon the wall shook and confirmed it. "That's what she will come to unless you save her from it. It's up to you, Mrs. Henby."

"I—I don't know what Henby will say," whimpered Mrs. Henby, afresh.

"Say?" urged Mag, with the scorn of her kind for the well-regulated husband. "He'll say anything he thinks you want him to say. He'll be as fond as anything of her—and you can bring her up to be a comfort to him." The poverty of Mag's experience furnished her with no phrases to express what a child might become.

"A nice time I'd have," burst out the other woman, in a last throb of resentment, "bringing her up to be a comfort to anybody, with her own mother living a sinful life right under her eyes."

"Oh," said Mag, with enlightenment, "so that's what is troubling you! Well—if you say the word—I'll clear out. The girls will kick—but they have to do what I say. Look here, then! If you'll take the kid—I'll go."

"And never come back—nor let her know?"

"Cross my heart to die," said Mag.

"Well, then"—Mrs. Henby let her apron fall tremulously—"I'll take her."

"For keeps?"

"For keeps," vowed Mrs. Henby, solemnly.

They were silent, regarding each other for a time, neither knowing how to terminate the interview without offence.

"What's her name?" asked Mrs. Henby, timidly, at last.

"Marietta."

Mag searched her scant remembrances and brought up this: "She's got dark hair."

Mrs. Henby was visibly comforted.

Mrs. Henby found, after all, that she was not put to any great strain of inventiveness to account for the little girl she had decided to adopt, the event being overshadowed, in the estimation of the townspeople, by the more memorable one which occurred on the very night of Marietta's arrival. This was no less than the departure of Hard Mag and the women of the House. They went out of it as they came, with scant warning, helped by coarse laughter of the creatures they had preyed upon, and with so much of careless haste that about two hours after their flitting—caught, it was supposed, from their neglected fires—the whole shell of the House burst into flame. It made a red flare in the windows in the middle of the night, but, as none of the townspeople had any interest in it and no property was endangered, it was allowed to burn quite out, which it did as quickly as the passions it had thrived upon, to an inconsiderable heap of cinders. The next year the Henbys took over the place where it had stood for a garden, and Henby made a swing under the cottonwood-trees for his adopted daughter.

XIV

THE WALKING WOMAN

THE FIRST TIME of my hearing of her was at Temblor. We had come all one day between blunt, whitish bluffs rising from mirage water, with a thick, pale wake of dust billowing from the wheels, all the dead wall of the foothills sliding and shimmering with heat, to learn that the Walking Woman had passed us somewhere in the dizzying dimness, going down to the Tulares on her own feet. We heard of her again in the Carrisal, and again at Adobe Station, where she had passed a week before the shearing, and at last I had a glimpse of her at the Eighteen-Mile House as I went hurriedly northward on the Mojave stage; and afterward sheepherders at whose camps she slept, and cowboys at rodeos, told me as much of her way of life as they could understand. Like enough they told her as much of mine. That was very little. She was the Walking Woman, and no one knew her name, but because she was a sort of whom men speak respectfully, they called her to her face Mrs. Walker, an she answered to it if she was so inclined. She came and went about our western world on no discoverable errand, and whether she had some place of refuge where she lay by in the interim, or whether between her seldom, unaccountable appearances in our quarter she went on steadily walking, was never learned. She came and went, oftenest in a kind of muse of travel which the untrammelled space begets, or at rare intervals flooding wondrously with talk, never of herself, but of things she had known and seen. She must have seen some rare happenings, too—by report. She was at Maverick the time of the Big

255

Snow, and at Tres Piños when they brought home the body of Morena; and if anybody could have told whether De Borba killed Mariana for spite or defence, it would have been she, only she could not be found when most wanted. She was at Tunawai at the time of the cloud-burst, and if she had cared for it could have known most desirable things of the ways of trail-making, burrow-habiting small things.

All of which should have made her worth meeting, though it was not, in fact, for such things I was wishful to meet her; and as it turned out, it was not of these things we talked when at last we came together. For one thing, she was a woman, not old, who had gone about alone in a country where the number of women is as one in fifteen. She had eaten and slept at the herder's camps, and laid by for days at one-man stations whose masters had no other touch of human kind than the passing of chance prospectors, or the halting of the tri-weekly stage. She had been set on her way by teamsters who lifted her out of white, hot desertness and put her down at the crossing of unnamed ways, days distant from anywhere. And through all this she passed unarmed and unoffended. I had the best testimony to this, the witness of the men themselves. I think they talked of it because they were so much surprised at it. It was not, on the whole, what they expected of themselves.

Well I understand that nature which wastes its borders with too eager burning, beyond which rim of desolation it flares forever quick and white, and have had some inkling of the isolating calm of a desire too high to stoop to satisfaction. But you could not think of these things pertaining to the Walking Woman; and if there were ever any truth in the exemption from offence residing in a frame of behavior called ladylike, it should have been inoperative here. What this really means is that you get no affront so long as your behavior in the estimate of the particular audience invites none. In the estimate of the immediate audience—conduct which affords protection in Mayfair gets you no consideration in Maverick. And by no canon could it be considered ladylike to go about on your own feet, with a blanket and a black bag and almost no money in your purse, in and about the haunts of rude and solitary men.

There were other things that pointed the wish for a personal encounter with the Walking Woman. One of them was the contradiction of reports of her—as to whether she was comely, for example. Report said yes, and again, plain to the point of deformity. She had a twist to her face, some said; a hitch to one shoulder; they averred she limped as she walked. But by the distance she covered she should have been straight and young. As to sanity, equal incertitude. On the mere evidence of her way of life she was cracked; not quite broken, but unserviceable. Yet in her talk there was both wisdom and information, and the word she brought about trails and water-holes was as reliable as an Indian's.

By her own account she had begun by walking off an illness. There had been an invalid to be taken care of for years, leaving her at last broken in body, and with no recourse but her own feet to carry her out of that predicament. It seemed there had been, besides the death of her invalid, some other worrying affairs, upon which, and the nature of her illness, she was never quite clear, so that it might very well have been an unsoundness of mind which drove her to the open, sobered and healed at last by the large soundness of nature. It must have been about that time that she lost her name. I am convinced that she never told it because she did not know it herself. She was the Walking Woman, and the country people called her Mrs. Walker. At the time I knew her, though she wore short hair and a man's boots, and had a fine down over all her face from exposure to the weather, she was perfectly sweet and sane.

I had met her occasionally at ranch-houses and road-stations, and had got as much acquaintance as the place allowed; but for the things I wished to know there wanted a time of leisure and isolation. And when the occasion came we talked altogether of other things.

It was at Warm Spring in the Little Antelope I came upon her in the heart of a clear forenoon. The spring lies off a mile from the main trail, and has the only trees about it known in that country. First you come upon a pool of waste full of weeds of a poisonous dark green, every reed ringed about the water-level with a muddy white incrustation. Then the three oaks appear staggering on the slope, and the spring sobs and blubbers below them in ashy-colored mud. All the hills of that country have the down plunge toward the desert and back abruptly toward the Sierra. The grass is thick and brittle and bleached straw-color toward the end of the season. As I rode up the swale of the spring I saw the Walking Woman sitting where the grass was deepest, with her black bag and blanket, which she carried on a stick, beside her. It was one of those days when the genius of talk flows as smoothly as the rivers of mirage through the blue hot desert morning.

You are not to suppose that in my report of a Borderer I give you the words only, but the full meaning of the speech. Very often the words are merely the punctuation of thought; rather, the crests of the long waves of inter-communicative silences. Yet the speech of the Walking Woman was fuller than most.

The best of our talk that day began in some dropped word of hers from which I inferred that she had had a child. I was surprised at that, and then wondered why I should have been surprised, for it is the most natural of all experiences to have children. I said something of that purport, and also that it was one of the perquisites of living I should be least willing to do without. And that led to the Walking Woman saying that there were three things which if you had known you could cut out all the rest, and they were good any way you got them, but best if, as in her case, they were related to and grew each one out of the others. It was while she talked that I decided that she really did have a twist to her face, a sort of natural warp or skew into which it fell when it was worn merely as a countenance, but which disappeared the moment it became the vehicle of thought or feeling.

The first of the experiences the Walking Woman had found most worth while had come to her in a sand-storm on the south slope of Tehachapi in a dateless spring. I judged it should have been about the time she began to find herself, after the period of worry and loss in which her wandering began. She had come, in a day pricked full of intimations of a storm, to the camp of Filon Geraud, whose companion shepherd had gone a three days' *pasear* to Mojave for supplies. Geraud was of great hardihood, red-blooded, of a full laughing eye, and an indubitable spark for women. It was the season of the year when there is a soft bloom on the days, but the nights are cowering cold and the lambs tender, not yet flockwise. At such times a sand-storm works incalculable disaster. The lift of the wind is so great that the whole surface of the ground appears to travel upon it slantwise, thinning out miles high in air. In the intolerable smother the lambs are lost from the ewes; neither dogs nor man make headway against it.

The morning flared through a horizon of yellow smudge, and by mid-forenoon the flock broke.

"There were but the two of us to deal with the trouble," said the Walking Woman. "Until that time I had not known how strong I was, nor how good it is to run when running is worth while. The flock travelled down the wind, the sand bit our faces; we called, and after a time heard the words broken and beaten small by the wind. But after a little we had not to call. All the time of our running in the yellow dusk of day and the black dark of night, I knew where Filon was. A flock-length away, I knew him. Feel? What should I feel? I knew. I ran with the flock and turned it this way and that as Filon would have.

"Such was the force of the wind that when we came together we held by one another and talked a little between pantings. We snatched and ate what we could as we ran. All that day and night until the next afternoon the camp kit was not out of the cayaques. But we held the flock. We herded them under a butte when the wind fell off a little, and the lambs sucked; when the storm rose they broke, but we kept upon their track and brought them together again. At night the wind quieted, and we slept by turns; at least Filon slept. I lay on the ground when my turn was and beat with the storm. I was no more tired than the earth was. The sand filled in the creases of the blanket, and where I turned, dripped back upon the ground. But we saved the sheep. Some ewes there were that would not give down their milk because of the worry of the storm, and the lambs died. But we kept the flock together. And I was not tired."

The Walking Woman stretched out her arms and clasped herself, rocking in them as if she would have hugged the recollection to her breast.

"For you see," said she, "I worked with a man, without excusing, without any burden on me of looking or seeming. Not fiddling or fumbling as women work, and hoping it will all turn out for the best. It was not for Filon to ask, Can you, or Will you. He said, Do, and I did. And my work was good. We held the flock. And that," said the Walking Woman, the twist coming in her face again, "is one of the things that make you able to do without the others."

"Yes," I said; and then, "What others?"

"Oh," she said, as if it pricked her, "the looking and the seeming."

And I had not thought until that time that one who had the courage to be the Walking Woman would have cared! We sat and looked at the pattern of the thick crushed grass on the slope, wavering in the fierce noon like the waterings in the coat of a tranquil beast; the ache of a world-old bitterness sobbed and whispered in the spring. At last—

"It is by the looking and the seeming," said I, "that the opportunity finds you out."

"Filon found out," said the Walking Woman. She smiled; and went on from that to tell me how, when the wind went down about four o'clock and left the afternoon clear and tender, the flock began to feed, and they had out the kit from the cayaques, and cooked a meal. When it was over, and Filon had his pipe between his teeth, he came over from his side of the fire, of his own notion, and stretched himself on the ground beside her. Of his own notion. There was that in the way she said it that made it seem as if nothing of the sort had happened before to the Walking Woman, and for a moment I thought she was about to tell me one of the things I wished to know; but she went on to say what Filon had said to her of her work with the flock. Obvious, kindly things, such as any man in sheer decency would have said, so that there must have something more gone with the words to make them so treasured of the Walking Woman.

"We were very comfortable," said she, "and not so tired as we expected to be. Filon leaned up on his elbow. I had not noticed until then how broad he was in the shoulders, and how strong in the arms. And we had saved the flock together. We felt that. There was something that said together, in the slope of his shoulders toward me. It was around his mouth and on the cheek high up under the shine of his eyes. And under the shine the look—the look that said, 'We are of one sort and one mind'— his eyes that were the color of the flat water in the toulares—do you know the look?"

"I know it."

"The wind was stopped and all the earth smelled of dust, and Filon understood very well that what I had done with him I could not have done so well with another. And the look—the look in the eyes—"

"Ah-ah—!"

I have always said, I will say again, I do not know why at this point the Walking Woman touched me. If it were merely a response to my unconscious throb of sympathy, or the unpremeditated way of her heart to declare that this, after all, was the best of all indispensable experiences; or if in some flash of forward vision, encompassing the unimpassioned years, the stir, the movement of tenderness were for *me*—but no; as often as I have thought of it, I have thought of a different reason, but no conclusive one, why the Walking Woman should have put out her hand and laid it on my arm.

"To work together, to love together," said the Walking Woman, withdrawing her hand again; "there you have two of the things; the other you know."

"The mouth at the breast," said I.

"The lips and the hands," said the Walking Woman. "The little, pushing hands and the small cry." There ensued a pause of fullest understanding, while the land before us swam in the noon, and a dove in the oaks behind the spring began to call. A little red fox came out of the hills and lapped delicately at the pool.

"I stayed with Filon until the fall," said she. "All that summer in the Sierras, until it was time to turn south on the trail. It was a good time, and longer than he could be expected to have loved one like me. And besides, I was no longer able to keep the trail. My baby was born in October."

Whatever more there was to say to this, the Walking Woman's hand said it, straying with remembering gesture to her breast. There are so many ways of loving and working, but only one way of the first-born. She added after an interval, that she did not know if she would have given up her walking to keep at home and tend him, or whether the thought of her son's small feet running beside her in the trails would have driven her to the open again. The baby had not stayed long enough for that. "And whenever the wind blows in the night," said the Walking Woman, "I wake and wonder if he is well covered."

She took up her black bag and her blanket; there was the ranch-house of Dos Palos to be made before night, and she went as outliers do, without a hope expressed of another meeting and no word of good-bye. She was the Walking Woman. That was it. She had walked off all sense of society-made values, and, knowing the best when the best came to her, was able to take it. Work—as I believed; love—as the Walking Woman had proved it; a child—as you subscribe to it. But look you: it was the naked thing the Walking Woman grasped, not dressed and tricked out, for instance, by prejudices in favor of certain occupations; and love, man love, taken as it came, not picked over and rejected if it carried no obligation of permanency; and a child; *any* way you get it, a child is good to have, say nature and the Walking Woman; to have it and not to wait upon a proper concurrence of so many decorations that the event may not come at all.

At least one of us is wrong. To work and to love and to bear children. *That* sounds easy enough. But the way we live establishes so many things of much more importance.

Far down the dim, hot valley I could see the Walking Woman with her blanket and black bag over her shoulder. She had a queer, sidelong gait, as if in fact she had a twist all through her.

Recollecting suddenly that people called her lame, I ran down to the open place below the spring where she had passed. There in the bare, hot sand the track of her two feet bore evenly and white.

The Walking Woman

Let's have done with stranger faces, let's be quit of staring eyes,
Let's go back across Mohave where the hills of Inyo rise.
There's a word we've lost between us we shall never hear again
In the mindless clang of engines where they bray the hearts of men.
Let's go seek it east of Kearsarge where the seven-mile shadows run,
From the great gray bulk of Williamson heaved up against the sun.

Let's go look for Hassayampa, with your arm across my shoulders,
Through the cañons of lost rivers by the bone-white bleaching bowlders,
Through the scented glooming hollows where the gray wolf shadows flee—
Where from Sur to Ubhebe only you and I shall be;
And the Word—I cannot name it, but we'll learn its sweetest use
In the moonlit sandy reaches when the desert wind is loose.

"The appendix is that part of a book in which you find the really important things, put there to keep them from interfering with the story." Mary Austin, *The Trail Book*

At the end of *The Basket Woman*, Austin defines some of the Indian names and words she uses. In the glossary that follows, I have placed in quotation marks those definitions that are Austin's own words. Unless otherwise noted, the quotations will be from *The Basket Woman*.

ARRASTRA. (Mex.) "arrastre," mining mill.

BAILES. (Sp.) dances.

CAMPOODIE. "A group of Indian huts, from the Spanish *campo*, a field or prairie. In some localities written 'campody.'"

CAÑADA DE LOS UVAS. (Sp.) grapevine ravine.

CERISO. "The Ceriso is not properly mesa nor valley, but a long-healed crater miles wide, rimmed about with the jagged edge of the old cone. It rises steeply from the tilted mesa, overlooked by Black Mountain, darkly red as the red cattle that graze among the honey-colored hills." ("The Last Antelope," *Lost Borders*)

CHÍA. (Sp.) sagebrush.

CUIDADO. (Sp.) Look out! Take care!

FLOCKWISE. "The earliest important achievement of ovine intelligence is to know whether its own notion or another's is most worthwhile, and if the other's, which one. Individual sheep have certain qualities, instincts, competencies, but in the man-herded flocks these are superseded by something which I shall call the flock-mind, though I cannot say very well what it is, except that it is less than the sum of all their intelligences. . . . Understand that a flock is not the same thing as a number of sheep." (*The Flock*)

HASSAYMPA. "In one dialect 'small rocks,' in another 'sacred bear'; river." (*The Land of Journey's Ending*)

INYO. "The name *Inyo,* given by the Shoshone Indians, meant 'the dwelling place of a great spirit'" (Fink 65).

MAHALA. "An Indian woman, perhaps a corruption from the Spanish *mujer,* woman."

MESQUITE. "A thorny desert shrub, bearing edible pods, like the locust tree, which are ground into meal for food."

METATE. (Mex.) curved stone for grinding maize.

OPPAPAGO. "A mountain peak near Mt. Whitney. The name signifies 'The Weeper,' in reference to the streams that run down from it continually like tears." Also referred to as Lone Pine Peak.

PAIUTES. "The name of a large tribe of Indians inhabiting middle California and Nevada. The name is derived from the Indian word *pah,* water, and is used to distinguish this tribe from the related tribe of Utes, who lived in the desert away from running water."

PASEAR. (Sp.) walk or promenade.

PIÑON. "The Spanish name for the one-leaved, nut pine."

REBOSA. (Sp.) shawl.

SHAMAN. "Shaman is not an Indian word at all, but has been generally adopted as a term of respect to indicate men or women who became wise in the things of the spirit. Sometimes a knowledge of healing herbs was included in the Shaman's education, and often he gave advice on personal matters. But the chief business of the Shaman was to keep man reconciled with the spirit world, to persuade it to be on his side, or to prevent the spirits from doing him harm. A Shaman was not a priest, nor was he elected to office, and in some tribes he did not even go to war, but stayed at home to protect the women and